Downscoping

Downscoping

How to Tame the Diversified Firm

by

Robert E. Hoskisson
and Michael A. Hitt

New York   Oxford
OXFORD UNIVERSITY PRESS
1994

Oxford University Press

Oxford   New York   Toronto
Delhi   Bombay   Calcutta   Madras   Karachi
Kuala Lumpur   Singapore   Hong Kong   Tokyo
Nairobi   Dar es Salaam   Cape Town
Melbourne   Auckland   Madrid

and associated companies in
Berlin   Ibadan

Copyright © 1994 by Oxford University Press, Inc.

Published by Oxford University Press, Inc.
200 Madison Avenue, New York, New York 10016

Oxford is a registered trademark of Oxford University Press

Library of Congress Cataloging-in-Publication Data
Hoskisson, Robert E.
Downscoping : how to tame the diversified firm /
by Robert E. Hoskisson and Michael A. Hitt.
p. cm.   Includes index.
ISBN 0-19-507843-8
1. Diversification in industry.   2. Industrial concentration.
3. Industries, Size of.   4. Corporate reorganizations.
5. Competition.   I. Hitt, Michael A.   II. Title.
HD2756.H67   1994
658.1′6—dc20   93-21408

1 3 5 7 9 9 8 6 4 2

Printed in the United States of America
on acid-free paper

Preface

Achieving global competitiveness continues to present major problems for large domestic and multinational firms in the United States, although some companies have improved their competitive posture through corporate restructuring, defined as rebuilding the strength of a firm by changing its asset structure and its resource allocation patterns. This book addresses how inadequate or inappropriate corporate governance and strategy have contributed to the lack of competitiveness and describes alternative ways to revitalize firms. It offers an informed analysis, based on careful research, of the antecedents and the consequences of the difficulties being encountered by U.S. companies forced to compete globally and describes what we believe are the most effective strategies for restructuring and refocusing firms to meet this challenge. The success of these strategic refocusing efforts will largely determine the competitiveness of firms into the twenty-first century.

Corporate restructuring efforts may take one of two basic approaches, expansion (e.g., offensive acquisitions) and contraction (e.g., defensive sell-offs), or they may employ a mixed strategy that combines both approaches. We believe that a systematic and comprehensive examination of the antecedents and the consequences of each of these restructuring approaches is necessary. In this book we emphasize the importance of downscoping (reducing firm diversification and strategically refocusing on the core business or businesses). We also address the ways in which expansion strategies have contributed to the competitiveness problem and emphasize how contraction has been used to restructure firms. The intended contribution, therefore, is a comprehensive and thorough evaluation of corporate restructuring efforts and their effects on global firm competitiveness.

The first part of this book (comprising chapters 1 through 5), studies how weak governance structures (e.g., boards of directors) and poor corporate strategy formulation have contributed to the competitiveness problem. For example, one misguided strategy, overdiversification, has been found to contribute to managerial risk aversion and, therefore, to a decrease in research and development (R&D) activity. Inadequate attention to managing R&D activity is a significant contributor to competitiveness problems. Our research has shown that a number of firms have been forced to restructure as a result of inadequate strategic control, which led managers to become risk averse. Those firms that took more appropriate risks and employed effective strategic control (that is, largely avoided merger and divestiture activity in the 1980s and early 1990s) achieved higher levels of performance. The book illustrates, with examples, problems that can lead to refocusing efforts. For example, in chapter 2 we review the histories of General Motors and Ford in order to illustrate how corporate strategy and organizational structure can produce inadequate strategic control and loss of competitiveness.

The second section of the book (comprising chapters 6 through 12) reviews and evaluates alternative corporate restructuring approaches to restoring competitiveness. These approaches include: incentive and compensation adjustments for executives, leveraged buyouts and capital structure changes, downscoping and divestment of unrelated businesses to focus on "core skills", portfolio adjustments to realize more value from unrelated diversification, and implementation of global diversification strategies. We also provide recommendations and guidelines for implementing downscoping and compare strategic downscoping to downsizing (layoffs without adjusting diversification strategy). This part of the book examines refocusing alternatives and provides case examples for illustration.

We intend this book to be of use to both academics and practicing managers. Practicing managers will be interested in understanding the consequences of restructuring efforts. Although many firms have experimented with corporate restructuring alternatives, no source has systematically examined the consequences of these efforts. We also examine the antecedent strategies that create the need to restructure, along with corporate weaknesses that may result from pursuing particular restructuring alternatives. Maintaining global competitiveness should be a significant concern to executives. Our intent is to help managers prevent future problems and promote strategic competitiveness.

This book will also be of interest to an academic audience because of its comprehensive review of the research on the antecedents and consequences of restructuring. In addition, it provides a comprehensive summary of our own research, which culminated in a major project supported by the National Science Foundation and the Texas Advanced Research Program.

We would like to acknowledge the excellent assistance of Sandra Garfield, who edited the entire manuscript and provided assistance with the figures. We also owe a debt of gratitude to Wanda Bird for her excellent assistance in typing early drafts of a number of chapters. We would like to thank our colleagues at Texas A&M and at other institutions for their helpful comments and insight, from which we benefited. In particular, we are grateful to Bob Albanese, Jay Barney, Barry Baysinger, Bert Cannella, Don Hellriegel, Rick Johnson (University of Missouri), Rita Kosnik (Trinity University), Abby McWilliams (Arizona State University), Doug Moesel (Lehigh University), Tom Turk (Chapman University), and Asghar Zardkoohi. Although we are responsible for the final product, we benefited from their comments on our work.

College Station, Texas   R. E. H.
January 1994   M. A. H.

Contents

I

Problems of Competitiveness

1

Diversification, Multidivisional Structure, and Restructuring

When J. F. (Jack) Welch, Jr., took over General Electric in 1981, it was a different company from the one we know today. Between 1981 and 1989 Welch divested about $9 billion in assets, while acquiring $12 billion. He also squeezed 350 product lines into 13 large businesses, each in first or second place within its industry, while flattening the GE management hierarchy. In so doing, he moved the corporation from eleventh place ($12 billion) in 1980 to second place ($73 billion) among U.S. corporations in stock market value by the end of 1992.[1] GE provides a prime example of the strategy we call "downscoping," or reducing diversified scope. We will return to the GE example several times throughout this book. The GE approach is not without its problems, however (see chapter 5). GE is undergoing a major cultural change, directed by Welch, in order to overcome its problems and prepare for the twenty-first century. Downscoping thus involves more than scope reduction; it requires better internal controls and cultural adjustments to foster longer-term competitiveness and market value.

Corporate restructuring like that experienced by GE was very common in the 1980s and the early 1990s.[2] Larger diversified firms in many industries shuffled their portfolios of assets, especially through divestiture and spin-off, as well as through acquisition. This was also a period of strong global competition in which many highly diversified U.S. firms, responding to decline, refocused their corporate strategies. The central theme of this book, developed in the first five chapters, is that there is a connection between extensive diversification and a decline in the competitiveness of large firms. For instance, a contributing factor to the competitiveness problem is managerial unwillingness to bear the risks of long-term innovative product and process development. Many large firms sought diversification as a central goal in the 1960s and 1970s; as a result, most Fortune 500 firms are diversified into related or unrelated product areas. However, extensive research has shown research and development (R&D) expenditures to be lower in highly diversified firms than in less diversified firms.[3] Single and dominant business (less diversified) firms invested more in long-term activities than did related and unrelated (more diversified) firms.

In part, these differences can be explained by differences in the kinds of control systems implemented in highly diversified companies compared to those used in less diversified ones.[4] Control systems affect managers' incentives to take risks. For instance, in dominant business firms corporate executives usually do not have large spans of control and thus better understand the nature of the businesses under the corporate umbrella (because most or all are highly related to the core business). With narrower spans of control and better strategic understanding of the company's businesses, corporate executives can effectively evaluate the plans and the intended actions of division managers. Such understanding represents strategic control.

Unfortunately, as the firm diversifies, it becomes increasingly difficult for corporate executives to use strategic controls. Their spans of control increase and the volume of information they received consequently is greater. When limits on their information-processing capabilities are reached as differences among divisions increase, executives increasingly rely on financial-outcome controls. Some have argued that adoption of multidivisional structural controls allows corporate-level executives to reduce the amount of information they must process by delegating daily operational decisions to division managers. In the multidivisional firm a mixture of strategic and financial controls is used to modify division manager behavior.

After higher levels of diversification are reached, however, financial controls may be emphasized over strategic controls. Evaluating managers on the basis of financial outcomes rather than strategic intent reduces information processing for corporate executives. Thus, as diversification increases, corporate executives are less able to ascertain whether poor financial outcomes are the result of ineffective strategy formulation and implementation or of events beyond the control of the division manager. Emphasis on financial controls shifts risk to division managers and they no longer have the confidence that corporate-level executives possess, who fully understand divisional strategy. This shift creates risk aversion by divisional managers and a bias toward short-term efficiency. This condition may result in lower investment in R&D and other long-term activities for highly diversified firms.

Aggressive acquisition has contributed to increased levels of diversified growth for a number of years. In fact, this strategy was so widespread in the 1980s that it was dubbed "merger mania" in the popular press. Thousands of merger and acquisitions were completed annually. In addition to affecting control systems, acquisitions require significant managerial oversight and energy if they are to be completed successfully. Acquisition candidates must be thoroughly reviewed before they are selected. Often, significant preparations and negotiations are necessary to complete the acquisition. Executives must review the data, select acquisition targets, formulate a strategy for completing the acquisition, and conduct the negotiations, all of which requires a considerable amount of time. Furthermore, executives must be intimately involved in integrating the target firm into the acquiring firm after the acquisition is completed if the merger is to result in effective performance. Thus, executives in both the acquiring and the target firms expend considerable amounts of energy in the acquisition process. During this period, the attention of managers is diverted from other important issues. While they must continue to make short-term operational decisions, they may postpone taking on long-term commitments. Similarly, managers in target firms continue daily operations but rarely make long-term commitments during the acquisition process unless they do so to avoid a takeover (e.g., by increasing debt). Some have described it as a period of suspended animation. As a result, acquisition strategies may induce short-term perspectives and increased risk aversion among managers. An acquisitive growth strategy often leads to lower investment in both R&D inputs and outputs (e.g., patents).[5]

A significant contributor to poor global competitiveness has been underinvestment in R&D and low managerial commitment to innovation.[6] There may thus be a need to restructure extensively diversified firms built up through acquisitions because the process of diversified acquisitive growth can result in lower R&D investments and fewer new products and processes (R&D outputs). Restructuring often results in downscoping (and downsizing) through sell-offs of divisions. Downscoping through reduced diversification thus provides an opportunity for refocusing corporate strategy and for gaining better strategic control of the company. Corporate restructuring may tame the diversified firm and improve competitiveness through reductions in diversification and size, although sometimes (as in the GE example) there is actually an increase in size. However, such restructuring has its costs and therefore must be done with care. Restructuring through downscoping may allow a firm to regain strategic control. Furthermore, restructuring and refocusing provide an opportunity to reemphasize important organizational factors such as human capital and corporate culture. To understand the weaknesses in a company's competitive posture and the available restructuring alternatives, it is necessary to understand the history and the management of corporate diversification strategy.

A History of the Multidivisional Structure

After World War II, product diversification of business organizations increased significantly in the United States, in Europe, and throughout much of the industrialized world.[7] In 1950 only 30.1 percent of the Fortune 500 companies generated more than a quarter of their revenue from diversified activities. By 1974 this figure had risen to 63 percent.[8] Lagging behind the trend toward diversification were changes in the structures of large multiproduct organizations, which evolved from variants on the simple functional arrangement, with a president and top functional officers, to multidivisional forms with corporate offices and a full complement of corporate staff personnel and semiautonomous divisions. This evolutionary process is probably the most important organizational change to have occurred in modern economic and organizational history. It has changed both the way resources are allocated for most of the industrial assets associated with large firms throughout the world and the incentive structure that guides general managers at both the corporate and the division levels.

In the early 1950s most organizations were managed by simple functional structures. However, by the end of the 1970s even conservative utility firms and government organizations had switched to the multidivisional structure with decentralized operating divisions.[9] Traditional centralized structures organized around functional departments proved inappropriate for managing diversity; the old structure led to an inability to identify the profit contributions of individual businesses, inadequate coordination among different business activities across functional departments and, consequently, loss of strategic control. These control problems, in turn, limited growth.

The solution to the organizational growth limits encountered by functional organization was the introduction and the diffusion of the multidivisional (M-form) structure. The M-form structure has a corporate headquarters office and staff that evaluate and control semiautonomous business divisions run by division general managers. Between 1949 and 1969 the percentage of Fortune 500 companies operating with product divisional structures increased from 19.8 percent to 75.5 percent. (See figure 1.) Virtually all the Fortune industrial and nonindustrial firms currently use this organizational arrangement or some variant of it.

Alfred Chandler, an influential business historian, traced the development of four prominent U.S. firms: General Motors, Du Pont, Standard Oil of New Jersey (now Exxon), and Sears, Roebuck.[10] He found that while each was initially in a different industry, they all developed similar organizational attributes over time. He specifically chose these firms because they were the innovators in the use of the new multidivisional organization form in their respective industries. He found that as these firms grew larger and more complex (that is, as they diversified their product lines), they reached a point where further development was

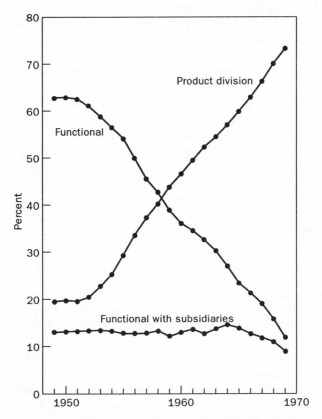

Figure 1. Adoption of the product divisional (M-form) structure among Fortune 500 firms from 1949 to 1969 (*Source:* Rumelt, Richard P. 1974. *Strategy, Structure and Economic Performance.* Boston: Division of Research, Harvard Business School. Copyright © 1974 by the President and Fellows of Harvard College. Reprinted by permission of Harvard Business School Press.)

constrained by their functional structures, motivating them to adopt the M-form structure in order to continue to grow and to diversify.

Expected Benefits of the M-form Structure

From a control perspective, the organizational features of the M-form structure have several beneficial implications for the management of diverse businesses. These benefits accrue primarily to top corporate managers. Formation of distinct business divisions and delegation of operating responsibilities to divisional managers reduce the need for top corporate managers to process day-to-day information regarding operating decisions. Divisional managers are responsible for operating profits that provide objective evaluation criteria for top corporate executives. With divisional managers handling tactical strategic affairs at the business level, top corporate managers are free to focus on overall corporate strategic control and efficient resource allocation. Overall, the M-form increases the information-processing capacity needed to manage a set of diversified businesses.

Oliver Williamson has argued that division managers in M-form companies may set objectives that are more efficient than those in free-standing, functionally organized firms. His "M-form hypothesis" suggests that division managers are more interested in profit maximization than are managers in free-standing firms. The hypothesis requires separate business units (divisions) that are profit-accountable to the corporate office; it also assumes that corporate headquarters will allocate cash according to highest yield uses among divisions. Williamson argues that the corporate office is in effect an "internal capital market" that serves as a governance device, causing division managers to focus on high-yield uses for corporate cash allocations.[11]

Continued Growth and M-form Structural Elaboration

As diversified growth continues, however, managers seek to maintain the efficiency of the M-form. To deal with extensive diversification, a number of control system "add-ons" are implemented. Each control technique has the function of attenuating information-processing costs, thus helping corporate managers to manage extensive diversity. They include the use of "span breakers" such as the creation of strategic business unit (SBU) structures, the application of portfolio planning techniques, the development of a strong corporate culture, the implementation of reward and incentive systems, and the development of sophisticated vertical control devices (e.g., accounting, budget and management information systems). All these mechanisms can be seen as elaborations on the basic M-form structure. They may have the effect of enhancing the ability of corporate managers to lessen the information gap between themselves and divisional managers, thus giving corporate executives the capacity to manage greater amounts of diversity. However, each elaboration has trade-offs associated with its implementation.

Strategic business unit structures

As diversification increases, SBU structures serve to reduce the span of control of top executives and therefore help to reduce executives' information-processing requirements. Divisions in related businesses are grouped together into SBUs, which are then controlled by the corporate office, while SBU general managers control the divisions. Realistically, if this arrangement is to reduce the information-processing demands placed on top executives, critical performance targets for divisions must be negotiated between SBU and divisional executives, while critical performance targets for SBUs are negotiated between the corporate office and SBU executives.[12]

While this arrangement reduces the demands on corporate managers, it also creates problems. The creation of an intervening management tier between corporate and divisional operations distances corporate executives from the businesses in the units. Corporate managers must therefore rely on the reports, knowledge, and interpretations of SBU executives for their own knowledge of divisional operations and outcomes. The distancing of corporate executives from divisional affairs reduces the amount of information available to them and favors SBU executives, enabling SBU managers to negotiate lower performance goals for their units. SBU executives, in turn, can often create organizational slack at the divisional level to serve as a "buffer," allowing the units to meet performance goals even under adverse conditions. As a result, divisional executives are often unwilling to take risks that may deplete the slack. The creation of a three-tier (or more) SBU structure can thus limit incentives for efficiency and risk assumption at the divisional level.

Portfolio planning techniques

Portfolio planning was introduced in the 1970s as a means of managing diversity.[13] Portfolio planning allows use of cash generated by mature businesses to be invested in other growing businesses and markets. However, it creates a knowledge gap between corporate and division managers. Portfolio planning assembles businesses into SBUs, classifies SBUs according to their competitive position and the attractiveness of their product market, designs a strategic mission for each SBU related to its growth and financial objectives, and allocates resources according to these objectives. Thus, it simplifies the management of diverse businesses and in theory helps corporate managers maintain control of resource allocation processes. However, because of the diversity in the firm's businesses and corporate executives' lack of specific product market knowledge, many firms consider each SBU as a portfolio within a portfolio. In other words, SBUs do not necessarily represent a set of homogeneous businesses in which related skills are applied but often comprise a variety of businesses operating in different product market segments. As a result, application of the portfolio concept becomes quite complex in practice, and resource allocation becomes a multilevel decision process reflecting a trade-off between cost efficiency and risk taking. In this way, the potential advantages of SBUs (e.g., encouragement of risk taking) are at least partially offset.

Furthermore, portfolio planning can produce negative outcomes. For example, the portfolio technique suggests managing businesses in weak markets for maximum cash flow. Yet some of these businesses may have opportunities to grow and to increase market share, which would require investment that is not allowed by the portfolio approach. In addition, while portfolio techniques allow corporate managers to make effective divestiture decisions (e.g., to shed poorly performing businesses in weak markets), Richard Hammermesh argues that they are less useful in managing the internal growth and development of existing businesses. The chief executive officers (CEOs) interviewed by Hammermesh indicated that they were having problems generating adequate growth and new business development opportunities after several years of using portfolio techniques. Portfolio planning concepts thus may be useful, but they may also oversimplify the strategic management of businesses. They tend to bias managers in favor of measuring financial cost efficiency (emphasizing financial control over strategic control) and result in sacrificing investment in new business development for financial efficiency.[14]

Corporate culture

Corporate culture is often referred to as a set of values shared by the members of an organization. A strong culture may reduce the need to monitor directly the behavior of divisional managers. Divisional managers who "buy into" the corporate culture maintain their own performance within accepted boundaries, reducing the information-processing requirements placed on corporate management and allowing executives to manage greater diversification. In other words, a strong culture enables corporate managers to "trust" divisional managers to negotiate appropriate critical performance targets. In addition, it may be possible to create a culture that encourages divisional managers to assume risks.[15]

To counter tendencies among managers in diversified M-form companies to prefer risk-averse options, the corporate culture should stress judicious risk taking by divisional executives. A firm may be able to shape its internal culture by the appropriate choice of reward and incentive systems. For example, 3M's culture strongly encourages lower-level managers to champion new product ideas. One way it does this is by approving the so-called 15 percent rule, which allows employees to devote 15 percent of the workweek to developing their own new product ideas as long as the latter have potential benefits for 3M. Employees are not penalized if these ideas fail and are handsomely rewarded for any successes by being given a share in the profits.

Unfortunately, a strong culture is difficult not only to establish but also to maintain in the presence of diversification into unrelated businesses. Although a strong culture may be a source of sustained competitive advantage, a particular culture may not be equally viable in all organizations;[16] what may be appropriate for 3M's adhesives business, for example, may not be appropriate for USX's steel-making operations. That is, different types of business (e.g., different technologies or competitive environments) require different cultures. Even within one corporation, continued diversification may fragment the existing culture into many different subcultures. As a result, in diversified firms, it may be extremely difficult, if not dysfunctional, to attempt to establish a corporatewide culture that stresses trust and risk assumption. This condition is especially applicable where divisions compete for corporate capital allocations. Thus, the ability of corporate culture to attenuate risk-averse behavior in extensively diversified firms is limited.

Reward systems

Reward systems may be used to reinforce or change corporate cultures. One of the most important and potent components of organization is the mechanism by which performance is measured, evaluated, and rewarded. In particular, the system by which rewards are tied to the performance of corporate and divisional executives is critical. Typical compensation arrangements in diversified businesses focus on short-term performance and rely on accounting measures of return rather than on creation of economic value for shareholders. Furthermore, executive compensation may be manipulated by division managers if corporate officers lack strategic control.

However, compensation systems can be designed to reinforce corporate cultures and to promote long-term strategic behavior. For instance, extending evaluation periods, weighting strategic factors, emphasizing developmental investments (as opposed to expenses) through strategic deferrals, and using economic value creation performance measures have been suggested to overcome an emphasis on the short term.[17] However, use of such approaches may be influenced by the degree of diversification. Diversified firms often emphasize simple performance-based reward systems because they aid managers in comparing different businesses. The use of managerial incentives for division managers, such as annual bonuses based on return on investment (ROI), is also common in diversified firms. The use of such incentives has been found to lead to lower R&D investments. Also, the use of long-term incentives offsets the effects of diversification but does not necessarily promote greater risk-taking behavior among managers.[18]

We conclude that although firms may use compensation systems that focus managers on long-term internal development, it is common practice within extensively diversified firms to focus on short-term financial performance. Although this reduces managerial information processing, unless there is adequate executive strategic control, division managers have the opportunity to manipulate resource expenditures to create higher compensation or reduce risk with increased slack.

Vertical control

Another response to the corporate control problems that exist in diversified firms is to increase the capacity of top corporate management to process information effectively. Organizations often develop vertical control devices such as management information systems, strategic planning systems, budgets, standard operating procedures, and decision referral rules in order to maintain control over diversified activities. These devices either reduce the amount of information that must be processed by corporate officers and/or increase the capacity of top officers to process that information. However, they may also be subject to manipulation by division managers. For example, inventory evaluation systems may be manipulated to satisfy managerial subgoals.[19]

Given the preceding discussion of trade-offs, the gains expected from the adoption of the M-form may not materialize, particularly as diversification increases. In fact, the data on performance gains of M-form firms are decidedly mixed, suggesting that the predicted efficiencies may not always be forthcoming. Charles Hill noted that research on Williamson's M-form hypothesis has examined primarily short-term or static efficiency.[20] Although one study found that implementation of the M-form has both immediate and long-run effects on shareholder wealth creation, determined by daily and weekly stock market returns, the sample studied was very small.[21] Therefore, while it is clear that M-form implementation may increase shareholder wealth, there is still some question as to whether the M-form provides long-term efficiency. It may be that the M-form structure generates no more than average long-term returns.

Costs of Implementing the M-form Structure at the Corporate Level

In practice, the M-form may yield high short-term profits — "static efficiency" — at the expense of long-term gains. Samuel Loescher has argued that tight financial controls in the M-form can lead to risk avoidance by divisional managers and that the M-form structure has been a significant contributor to the decrease in the long-term effectiveness of large U.S. firms.[22] Thus, while the functional structure may have offered managers too many opportunities to hide poor performance, the M-form structure can cause a firm to become overly focused on measurable short-term efficiency.

However, boards of directors are starting to get tough with CEOs.[23] For example, CEOs Tom H. Barrett of Goodyear Tire & Rubber Company, Standley H. Hoch of General Public Utilities Corporation, and Fred G. Caney of Greyhound Lines, Inc., were all forced to resign by their firms' boards of directors. CEOs were also forced out at First City Bancorp of Texas, Data General Corporation, Grumman Corporation, Circle K Corporation, Southeast Banking Corporation, and Abbott Laboratories. However, the process is slow and often painful. Most directors lack the time, information, and expertise to confront top management. As a result, they rarely act unless there is intense pressure from shareholders.

The governance system faced by corporate-level executives in M-form firms is similar to that faced by executives in free-standing functional firms. As a result, without adequate additional governance the M-form may not curtail corporate-level decisions that reduce firm value (or do not maximize it). Some critics have argued, for instance, that diversification has been used to reduce corporate managerial employment risk.[24] In short, although the M-form structure may curtail inefficient management at the division level, established governance mechanisms (ownership, boards of directors, and executive compensation) may not adequately restrain corporate executives from enhancing their own positions.[25]

Inadequate governance may allow managers to pursue higher levels of diversification than shareholders would prefer. Diversification often creates large firms that offer higher levels of executive compensation. Furthermore, board oversight may not be effective in controlling strategies implemented by corporate executives.[26] However, if extensive diversification leads to lower relative firm value, participants in the market for corporate control may initiate ownership positions that force corporate restructuring. Alternatively, even the threat of a takeover may cause managers to restructure extensively diversified firms before external ownership positions with the intent to take over the firm are established. Because governance structures at the corporate level have often been quite weak, external capital market pressure may be necessary to keep an extensively diversified M-form firm in line with shareholder objectives. Apparently, the M-form solves one governance problem—that of division manager inefficiency—but may create another in the process—the potential for excessive diversification at the corporate level.[27]

Costs of Implementing the M-form Structure at the Divisional Level

Excessive corporate diversification may also create incentives for division managers to avoid risk. In fact, the M-form may be consistent only with limited or focused diversification.[28] Extensive diversification requires control arrangements that can reduce the efficiency of the M-form. A number of control "add-ons" have been attempted in order to maintain optimal control in extensively diversified M-form firms. All of these mechanisms can be seen as elaborations on the basic M-form structure and may help corporate managers limit the information asymmetry that occurs between them and divisional managers, granting corporate executives the capacity to manage greater diversity. However, each of these control techniques has trade-offs associated with its implementation. For instance, SBU structures represent an intervening management tier between the corporate and divisional level, creating an information gap that favors SBU executives and enables them to buffer their performance in the face of unanticipated adversity. This arrangement lessens the pressure on divisional executives to take risks that may deplete slack and reduces risk taking by division managers (thereby lowering overall M-form efficiency).

The argument so far suggests that continuing diversification ultimately results in loss of control. Although control system elaborations may reduce constraints on effective control, they also have their limits. We conclude that there is a limit to the profitable growth of the diversified M-form firm. Beyond some level of diversity, control loss increases the information gap between corporate and divisional managers and allows divisional managers to reduce critical performance targets. The consequences include missed opportunities (e.g., less new-product development) at the divisional level and declining long-term performance. Furthermore, corporate managers have an incentive to expand diversification because it leads to increased size and therefore to higher compensation.

Overview of This Book

The first five chapters of this book are directed at establishing the link between the strategies implemented by large corporations and the problem of global competition they are experiencing. To establish this link, the evolution of corporate strategy in large firms is described, as well as the resulting general loss of strategic control through extensive diversification. This loss, in turn, leads to lower global competitiveness as a result of a deemphasis on managerial risk taking and innovation.

Chapter 1 has established how diversification and the M-form structure supporting diversification have created problems among large firms competing in global markets.

Chapter 2 offers a resolution of competing claims about the relationship between diversification and managerial risk taking. Economic theory and organization theory research suggest that managerial risk taking and innovation may be enhanced by diversification and decentralization. Other theoretical evidence suggests that diversification creates managerial risk aversion. Both sides of this controversy are reviewed in light of empirical evidence. The former is seen as a historical artifact that was accurate for firms with limited diversification. However, as firms increased their diversification and thereby compromised the multidivisional, or M-form, system, the trade-offs resulted in a loss of strategic control.[29] To demonstrate how these views have affected firms over time, this chapter compares the strategy, structural changes, and performance history of Ford and of General Motors, concluding that the more limited diversification of Ford permitted a balance between strategic control and financial control that optimized managerial risk taking more fully than was the case with General Motors.

Chapter 3 reviews the relationship of corporate governance to diversification and innovation. Corporate governance refers to both internal governance devices (e.g., managerial, or inside, ownership and compensation and boards of directors) as well as to external governance devices (e.g., outside ownership concentration and potential corporate raiders, known more generally as the market for corporate control). These governance devices are used to align potentially divergent objectives of owners (principals) and managers (agents). However, application of specific governance devices may affect managerial risk taking either positively or negatively. In turn, managerial risk taking affects strategic outcomes such as diversification and R&D investment. This chapter emphasizes that corporate governance systems have not been able to curtail extensive diversification and thereby avoid negative results.

There is no question that extensive firm diversification has resulted from the merger and acquisitions wave in the 1960s, the 1970s, and, to a lesser extent, the 1980s. Chapter 4 reviews the theory and evidence concerning the strategy of acquiring other businesses. This evidence is summarized in a model that suggests a trade-off between acquisitive growth and managerial commitment to innovation. Of course, this does not preclude a focused acquisitive growth strategy from being successful (as the example of General Electric in chapter 1 has demonstrated). However, firms participating in acquisitions create value primarily for the shareholders of the firms they purchase, rather than for their current shareholders. The market for buying and selling businesses seems to be quite efficient, so much so that little value is created or lost in transferring assets. As a result, firms participating in such activity usually achieve only average economic returns unless rare or private synergy (or even chance) produces above average returns. However, firms participating in multiple acquisitions without adequate strategic control often become less competitive. Acquisitions may create short-term efficiency at the expense of long-term innovation and performance.

Chapter 5 relates the competitiveness problems of U.S. firms to differences in the economic structure, history, and cultural background of the United States and its overseas rivals, principally Japan. Although these factors affect competitiveness, they no longer explain as much of the variance in competitiveness as they once did. The critical factors affecting the relative competitiveness of firms are now under the control of managers. The most important source of the decline in strategic competitiveness is poor development of new product and process technologies compared to that in other countries. When executed properly, restructuring can help managers regain strategic control, improve their firms' innovativeness, and ultimately increase the competitiveness of their companies.

Chapter 6 introduces the first of several alternative approaches to corporate refocusing. Strategic refocusing refers to the restructuring of the firm's asset base and/or its resource allocation patterns (e.g., capital structure and incentive compensation). For example, restructuring may be directed at reducing the agency problem (i.e., managers who attempt to optimize their own rewards instead of the firm's) by changing incentive compensation for managers. This chapter introduces incentive compensation as a tool for restructuring corporations to meet the competitiveness challenge. Incentive-compensation schemes based on financial performance are designed to reward managers for achieving maximum financial performance in specific businesses. For example, companies can offer financial incentives that provide extra compensation to corporate and division managers who meet financial performance targets. The use of strict financial incentives in highly diversified firms, however, creates shortened time frames and risk avoidance among division managers. Competitive listlessness has been attributed to "management by the numbers" in highly diversified firms. One solution to this problem is to use incentives that focus managers' attention on longer time frames. Although evaluation of financial criteria can be adjusted to longer periods with the intention of reducing the short-term orientation, division managers may remain risk averse. For instance, while corporate managers may be able to lessen their employment risk through diversification, division managers have no way of diversifying their employment risk and thus may choose lower-risk strategies despite longer-term incentives. Furthermore, research suggests that longer-term incentives do not increase R&D investments in extensively diversified firms.[30] Thus, although longer-term incentives may reduce the problem, they do not eliminate managerial risk aversion in extensively diversified firms. Additional restructuring adjustments are needed to gain strategic control beyond changes in the compensation system.

Chapter 7 examines how leveraged buyouts (LBOs) affect capital structure and innovation as a restructuring alternative. Some individuals have argued that privatizing companies by having large investment firms arrange for leveraged financing increases efficiency for the recapitalized firm. These individuals maintain that the recapitalization usually produces a scaled-down firm that becomes more efficient through divestiture of inefficient assets and that the realigned incentive structure puts owners (and debt holders) in greater proximity to the firm and thus improves the monitoring of firm strategy. This, in turn, reduces agency costs (i.e., the costs of managing the differences in objectives between owners and managers). This chapter suggests, however, that increased leverage and domination by debt holders produces strategic costs, and that revelations to external capital markets provide information to competitors. Furthermore, debt holders traditionally are more conservative than equity holders. High debt can lead to low R&D investment. In addition, research suggests that many LBOs are taken public again or sold outright to new owners within five to eight years. Therefore, managers in LBOs may have incentives to maximize short-term returns at the expense of long-term benefits. As a result, this form of restructuring may serve to increase the efficiency only of mature businesses, where conditions are stable and debt holders are likely to prefer investment in businesses that provide appropriate cash flow to service debt. Thus, R&D-intensive firms in strategic industries with rapidly changing technology are less likely to benefit from the kind of financial restructuring that increases leverage.

Chapter 4 proposes that a strategy of acquisitive growth increases both debt and size and creates extensive diversification, which in turn reduces innovation activity. In chapter 8 we suggest that restructuring divestitures may reverse the process if the strategic refocusing results in a reduction in debt, size, and diversification. Furthermore, if the strategic refocusing creates stronger strategic control, an improved emphasis on innovation is likely to follow. R&D investment improves in the postrestructuring period without a trade-off in performance.[31] Thus, strategic refocusing that succeeds in reducing debt, size, and diversification so that appropriate strategic control and incentives can be applied is likely to improve innovation and consequent competitiveness. Downscoping rather than downsizing is preferable because downscoping yields improved strategic control, whereas downsizing can lead to layoffs of key human resources and ceding of market share.

Chapter 9 discusses implementation of unrelated diversification as a restructuring alternative. It suggests that many firms that undertook multiple divestitures as a first step in restructuring remained unrelated diversifiers. The advantages of a multidivisional organization in the allocation of financial resources has been stressed as a reason for unrelated diversification. The multidivisional system of internal controls is particularly well suited to unrelated diversification because businesses are kept separate during the capital allocation process.[32] Many conglomerates are thought to possess the advantage of increasing shareholder value through financial synergy among its businesses.[33] The central challenge for the unrelated diversifier as it restructures is to manage its current businesses according to appropriate control-system operation and to identify acquisition targets with which the appropriate controls can be used. This approach may allow it to capture value while avoiding the pitfalls identified by others. This chapter describes the type of target businesses likely to increase value for an unrelated diversifier, given appropriate control-system characteristics.

Chapter 10 describes international diversification as an offensive strategy to meet the competitiveness challenge and to expand market opportunities. International diversification has been shown to improve a firm's performance more than product diversification. The success of international diversification is at least partially a product of the rationalization of innovation. The costs and risks of innovation in internationally diversified firms can be spread over larger and more diverse markets. Furthermore, innovation may help internationally diversified firms overcome local disadvantages. As a result, internationally diversified firms have incentives to continue to innovate. However, there are limits to the benefits of international diversification. For example, it increases coordination, distribution, and management costs, with the latter resulting from management complexity (e.g., trade barriers, logistical costs, cultural diversity, varied access to resources and skills in different countries). Despite this, firms can develop transnational capabilities that permit them to compete more effectively in international markets, as long as international managers do not become more interested in currency speculation than strategic issues such as product and process innovation.

Chapter 11 addresses the process of downscoping and refocusing. Many firms have restructured in order to become "lean and mean" and consequently more efficient. However, the question then arises as to whether these firms have achieved their goals. Results from a recent survey published in *The Wall Street Journal* found that 89 percent of downsizing firms wanted to reduce expenses, but only 46 percent confirmed that they had achieved that goal. Another 71 percent suggested that their intent was to improve productivity, but only 22 percent of the respondents said they attained this goal. Clearly, downsizing does not necessarily improve corporate fortunes. This suggests that the implementation of restructuring decisions may be critical to achieving a company's goals.[34] This chapter emphasizes the importance of exercising strategic leadership during restructuring. When such core competencies are protected, human capital is developed and an effective organizational culture is nourished. In addition, the creation of a new organizational structure will result in the integration and the development of tacit knowledge and skills.

Chapter 12 summarizes recommendations and conclusions about restructuring alternatives. Managers must be encouraged to take risks. Unfortunately, extensive diversification represents hedging by corporate managers and can lead to incentives for division managers that discourage risk taking. Fortunately, government policy changes (e.g., tax-policy changes and relaxation of antitrust laws); in addition, managerial efforts to avoid excessive diversification have, to some degree encouraged corporate strategies that create more value. Nevertheless, a more concerted effort is required on the part of managers. They must maintain strategic control of the businesses they enter. If financial- rather than strategic-control policies dominate, the most firms may be able to achieve is restructuring in order to keep pace with competition. Such a reactive mode will produce only average or below-average profits. Alternatively, offensive strategy that creates value in unique ways will produce a sustained competitive advantage and above-average profits.

Summary

This chapter has introduced the problem of extensive diversification and controls to manage diversification. It has argued that M-form adoption and extensive diversification has significant tradeoffs for managerial risk taking. The poor competitiveness of diversified firms in global markets has led to the restructuring movement of the 1980s and 1990s. More generally, this book examines the need for restructuring resulting from inadequate corporate governance, which leads to extensive diversification. Also, it discusses acquisition as the central mode to accomplish overdiversification. The next four chapters outline the need to restructure and tame diversified firms. Each of these chapters, as well as subsequent chapters, provides a summary of the issues discussed and highlights implications of concern to practicing managers.

Notes

1. Stewart, T. A. 1991. GE: Keeps those ideas coming. *Fortune*, August 12:41–49.

2. Horowitz, H., & Halliday, D. 1984. The new alchemy: Divestment for profit. *Journal of Business Strategy* 5:112–16; Magnet, M. 1987. Restructuring really works. *Fortune*, March 2:38–46.

3. Baysinger, B., & Hoskisson, R. E. 1989. Diversification strategy and R&D intensity in large multi-product firms. *Academy of Management Journal* 32:310–32; Hoskisson, R. E., & Hitt, M. A. 1988. Strategic control systems and relative R&D investment in large multi-product firms. *Strategic Management Journal* 9:605–21.

4. Hayes, R. H., & Abernathy, W. J.. 1980. Managing our way to economic decline. *Harvard Business Review* 58(4) 67–77; Hill, C. W. L., Hitt, M. A., & Hoskisson, R. E. 1988. Declining U.S. competitiveness: Reflections on a crisis. *Academy of Management Executive* 2:51–60.

5. Hitt, M. A., Hoskisson, R. E., Ireland, R. D., & Harrison J. D. 1991. The effects of acquisitions on R & D inputs and outputs. *Academy of Management Journal* 34:693–706.

6. Franko, L. G. 1989. Global corporate competition: Who's winning, who's losing, and the R&D factor as one reason why. *Strategic Management Journal* 10:449–74.

7. Channon, D. F. 1973. *The Strategy and Structure of British Enterprise*. Boston: Division of Research, Graduate School of Business Administration, Harvard University; Dyas, G. P., & Thanheiser, H. T. 1976. *The Emerging European Enterprise: Strategy and Structure in French and German Firms*. London: Macmillan; Franko, L. G. 1976. *The European Multinationals*. Greenwich, Conn.: Greylock Press; Gort, M. 1962. *Diversification and Integration in American Industry*. Princeton, N.J.: Princeton University Press; Rumelt, R. P. 1974. *Strategy, Structure, and Economic Performance*. Cambridge, Mass.: Harvard University Press.

8. Rumelt, *Strategy*.

9. Russo, M. 1991. The multi-divisional structure as an enabling device: A longitudinal study of discretionary cash as a strategic resource. *Academy of Management Journal* 34:718–33.

10. Chandler, A. 1962. *Strategy and Structure: Chapters in the History of American Industrial Enterprise*. Cambridge, Mass.: MIT Press.

11. Williamson, O. E. 1975. *Markets and Hierarchies: Analysis and Antitrust Implications*. New York: Free Press.

12. Bettis, R. A., & Hall, W. K. 1983. The business portfolio approach: Where it falls down in practice. *Long-Range Planning* 12(2):95–104.

13. Haspeslagh, P. 1982. Portfolio planning: Uses and limits. *Harvard Business Review* 60:58–73.

14. Hammermesh, R. G. 1987. Making planning strategic. *Harvard Business Review* 65:115–20; Haspeslagh, P. 1983. Portfolio Planning Approaches and Stra-

tegic Management Process in Diversified Industrial Companies. Ph.D. diss., Harvard University.

15. Ouchi, W. G. 1980. Markets, bureaucracies and clans. *Administrative Science Quarterly* 25:129–45.

16. Barney, J. B. 1986. Organizational culture: Can it be a source of sustained competitive advantage? *Academy of Management Review* 11:656–65.

17. Galbraith, J., and Kazanjian, R. 1986. *Strategy Implementation: Structure, Systems and Process.* St. Paul, Minn.: West.

18. Hoskisson, R. E., Hitt, M. A., & Hill, C. W. L. 1993. Managerial incentives and investment in R&D in large multi-product firms. *Organization Science* 4:325–41.

19. Dyl, E. A., 1989. Agency, corporate control and accounting methods: The LIFO–FIFO choice. *Managerial and Decision Economics* 10:141–54.

20. Hill, C. W. L. 1985. Oliver Williamson and the M-form firm: A critical review. *Journal of Economic Issues* 19:731–51.

21. Hoskisson, R. E., Harrison, J. S., & Dubofsky, D. A. 1991. Capital market evaluation of M-form implementation and diversification strategy. *Strategic Management Journal* 12:271–80.

22. Loescher, S. M. 1984. Bureaucratic measurement, shuttling stock shares, and shortened time horizons: Implications for economic growth. *Quarterly Review of Economics and Business* 24:1–23.

23. Lublin, J. S. 1991. More chief executives are being forced out by tougher boards. *The Wall Street Journal,* June 6:A–1.

24. Amihud, Y., & Lev, B. 1981. Risk reduction as a managerial motive for conglomerate mergers. *Bell Journal of Economics* 12:605–17.

25. Hoskisson, R. E., & Turk, T. 1990. Corporate restructuring: Governance and control limits of the internal capital market. *Academy of Management Review* 15:459–77.

26. Baysinger, B. D., & Hoskisson, R. E. 1990. Board composition and strategic control: The effect on corporate strategy. *Academy of Management Review* 15:72–87.

27. Hoskisson & Turk, Corporate restructuring.

28. Hoskisson, R. E., Hitt, M. A., & Hill, C. W. L. 1991. Managerial risk taking in diversified firms: An evolutionary perspective. *Organization Science* 2:296–313.

29. Hill, C. W. L., & Hoskisson, R. E. 1987. Strategy and structure in the multiproduct firm. *Academy of Management Review* 12:331–41.

30. Hoskisson, Hitt, & Hill, Managerial incentives.

31. Hoskisson, R. W., & Johnson, R. A. 1992. Corporate restructuring and strategic change: The effect on diversification strategy and R&D intensity. *Strategic Management Journal* 13:625–34.

32. Hill, C. W. L. 1988. Internal capital market controls and financial performance in multidivisional firms. *Journal of Industrial Economics* 37:67–83; Hoskisson, R. E. 1987. Multidivisional structure and performance: The diversification strategy contingency. *Academy of Management Journal* 30:625–44.

33. Leontiades, M. 1989. *Myth Management: An Examination of Corporate Diversification as Fact and Theory.* Oxford, Eng.: Basil Blackwell.

34. Bennett, A. 1991. Downscoping doesn't necessarily bring an upswing in corporate profitability. *The Wall Street Journal,* June 4:B–1, B–4.

2

Strategic Control
and M-form
Implementation

On January 22, 1988, the Eastman Kodak Company agreed to acquire Sterling Drug, Inc., for $5.1 billion. This was the largest nonoil acquisition to that point in U.S. history. While the performance of Sterling had been, at best, stagnant in recent years, Kodak executives felt they could install "Kodak management" and turn around the drug company's performance. Therefore, they attempted to exercise strategic control. Exercise of strategic control represents evaluation of strategic decisions and action, rather than of outcomes (e.g., financial returns). However, the effective exercise of strategic control generally requires extensive knowledge of the firm's operations and of its market. In particular, Kodak management focused on Sterling Drug's R&D operation. However, Sterling's problems became more severe after Kodak installed its management team. The company's new drugs were not testing well; at the same time, its existing product line was facing fierce competition. Kodak managers quietly cut projects that were predicted to generate new products for Sterling Drug. As a result, debt on the acquisition exceeded the firm's operating earnings by $50 million in 1989.[1] Although Kodak executives have a good understanding of the chemicals involved in photography, Sterling Drug represents an unrelated market diversification for Kodak. It was inappropriate for Kodak executives to exercise strategic control because they did not have effective understanding of the drug industry, nor did they know how to manage the internal operations of a drug business. On the other hand, Sterling Drug's performance prior to the acquisition revealed that its managers had not been effective either.

Thus, the best action for Kodak after the acquisition probably would have been to replace key Sterling executives with managers having strong and positive experience in the drug industry and to implement a different control system.

The primary theme of this book is the management of diversification. The focus of this chapter is on implementing and managing limited diversification with a multidivisional structure (M-form). This chapter provides a description of how the use of the M-form within companies with limited diversification provides strategic control advantages over the use of the centralized functional structure. It also describes the loss of strategic control that occurs in the M-form as extensive diversification is implemented. A comparison of the histories of Ford and General Motors provides an example of both the advantages and the disadvantages of diversified growth, M-form implementation, and subsequent continued diversified growth.

Studies of the reasons for changes in organizational structures have been undertaken by scholars from a number of disciplines. Particularly important has been the study of the evolution from the functionally centralized organizational structure to the multidivisional organizational structure. Alfred Chandler offered one of the first explanations for the displacement of the functional by the M-form structure in large companies.[2] Oliver Williamson expanded Chandler's insight that the M-form developed as a response to the difficulties experienced by managers in functional structures in managing diversified growth.[3] The first section of this chapter analyzes why the M-form has displaced the centralized functional structure; the second section analyzes how strategic control becomes ineffective when M-form firms pursue extensive diversification. Finally, the process of change from the functional to the M-form structure and the problems encountered in M-form companies with extensive diversified growth are illustrated by an examination of the strategic and structural histories of Ford and General Motors.

Change from the Functional to the M-form Structure

Oliver Williamson has suggested that M-form structures have advantages over the centralized functional structure for larger diversified firms. He maintains that the M-form structure overcomes problems of information processing and opportunistic behavior on the part of top- and mid-level managers more effectively than does a centralized functional structure. In companies with centralized functional structures, managers' experience reduces their ability to handle increasingly complex operations, and, as a result, they often lose a measure of control over the operations. Although managers intend to act rationally, they are constrained by the normal limitations on human cognitive ability.[4] Merely assuming that managers have information-processing limitations does not imply that they will lose control, however. Only when they are unable to process and manage the information necessary to make effective decisions will they lose control. Executives often experience information overload in firms with centralized functional structures because they must manage daily operational tasks along with entrepreneurial activities such as the development of long-range strategies.

The immediate tendency of managers suffering information overload is to share decision-making authority. This reduces the sheer amount of information each manager must process. Unfortunately, it also gives rise to a second potential problem—opportunism (acting in one's own interest rather than in the interest of the firm) on the part of lower-level managers. Managers acting opportunistically do not necessarily make the best decisions for the organization, even when given complete information. Instead, they may act in their own interest, even employ deception. Once functional department managers become involved in the decision-making process, they sometimes assume a role of advocacy, allowing the interests of their respective departments to take precedence over those of the organization. The result is loss of direction and control and inefficient resource allocation.

It is the coincident appearance of both information-processing problems and opportunism that creates problems in the centralized functional structure. While the centralized functional structure helps top managers combat either one of these problems alone, it has few mechanisms for overcoming the simultaneous loss of control and of direction. The M-form, on the other hand, offers a number of options for maintaining control and direction in the face of cognitive processing limits and opportunistic behavior.

Unlike the centralized functional structure, the M-form separates strategic and operating responsibilities so that top managers can focus on strategic control and direction. Such attention facilitates planning and resource allocation but does not guarantee freedom from problems associated with information processing and opportunism. All M-form firms decompose their organizations into economic units or divisions that are accountable to the central office. These units are autonomous or, at least, functionally self-contained and decide daily operating matters unilaterally. These differences between the centralized functional structure and the M-form structure serve to reduce both the amount of information top executives must process and the potential for self-serving, biased decision making by division managers.

Information processing is simpler in M-form structures primarily because day-to-day problems are eliminated from the top executives' decision-making set. At the same time the need for interdivisional coordination is reduced. Top managers concern themselves almost exclusively with scanning the environment, forecasting threats and opportunities, making strategic decisions, and allocating resources. The M-form structure also is designed to simplify the resource allocation process by allowing the use of objective criteria to evaluate divisional performance.

Resources are allocated among the competing divisions on the basis of measurable performance. Thus, the corporate office operates like an external capital market in allocating resources to the various divisions. Because division auditing is a part of the evaluation process, top management can also fine-tune its control. By aligning division goals, evaluation criteria, and resource allocation, the corporate headquarters can introduce incentives to ensure that each division performs according to an overall plan. Therefore, implementation of an M-form structure can help top management maintain control of the firm.

In addition to increasing profits, use of the M-form structure is intended to help the firm improve its prospects for growth. With the chief executive freed from operational responsibilities and able to monitor and control discrete business units, the limits on growth under the functional structure disappear. In addition, the M-form structure enables top executives to manage a diverse set of businesses efficiently. Companies are no longer restricted to one or even a few lines of business, and further growth is likely.

The M-form structure improves information-processing capacity, allows for increased growth, and facilitates greater diversification. (The increased information-processing capacity in the M-form structure promotes greater diversification according to research.[5]) However, with increased growth come problems associated with managing that growth. The M-form may not be effective in helping manage extensive diversification, especially the problems associated with maintaining strategic control. After the company reaches a certain level of diversified growth, managers begin to emphasize financial control because strategic control requires more information processing, which they lack the time or knowledge to do. Furthermore, the holding company (conglomerate) form does not provide the controls necessary for efficient capital allocation.

According to Oliver Williamson,

> the term M-form is reserved for those divisionalized firms in which the general office is engaged in periodic auditing and decision review and is actively involved in the internal resource allocation process. Cash flows, therefore, are subject to an internal investment competition rather than automatically reinvested at their source, as in most holding company firms. The affirmative assessment of the conglomerate as a miniature capital market presumes that the firm is operated in such a way.[6]

He also suggests, however, that holding company conglomerates often adopt a loosely divisionalized structure in which the controls between the headquarters unit and the separate business units are limited and often unsystematic. The divisions of the holding company conglomerate thus enjoy a high degree of autonomy along with a weak executive structure. This structure, it is argued, is inferior to a mutual fund for investment purposes.[7]

Williamson maintains that replacement of the functional or holding company form with the M-form allows for better internal and strategic control. He sees the M-form firm as an internal capital market that allocates resources and rewards according to the informed judgments of corporate managers. Within the M-form firm, division manager performance is evaluated by corporate managers who have access to information that should be more abundant and of superior quality to that available in the external capital market. Compared to that available to the external capital market, top executives' knowledge of each division operation is "incredibly deep."[8] As a result, division managers' performance is evaluated on the basis of the strategic desirability of their decisions (strategic control), as well as according to more objective performance outcomes (financial control).

Charles Hill has described how the chief financial officer of British Tire and Rubber (BTR), a large conglomerate with more than 500 operating divisions, evaluated divisional performance.[9] The officer examined computerized monthly balance sheets and profit-and-loss reports for individual divisions. These reports compared actual performance against forecasted goals and highlighted the cumulative difference over the year to date. They allowed the corporate office of BTR to practice a system of management by exception, thereby reducing information overload and compensating for top executives' lack of familiarity with division businesses in highly diversified firms.

The approach at BTR, however, also illustrates some of the potential limitations of vertical control devices. Annual performance targets at BTR are set by a process of negotiation among corporate, group (strategic business unit, or SBU), and divisional officers. Despite sophisticated information systems, given the large number of divisions and the extensive diversity of BTR, one may question corporate managers' knowledge of divisional operations. Although there is no specific evidence, the diversity of the company's holdings and the complex organizational structure would seem to favor risk-averse behavior on the part of divisional managers at BTR. Also, because divisional managers may be able to take advantage of information that they possess but corporate officers do not, they may negotiate lower-than-appropriate critical performance targets.

Furthermore, critics claim that the tight financial controls characteristic of the approach used by BTR result in short-run profit maximization and thus do not constitute a solution to control problems.[10] Once financial targets have been set by the corporate office, it may be hard for divisional managers to challenge them. Merit pay and promotional opportunities, however, are frequently contingent on how well divisional executives achieve these very goals. If division managers are having trouble meeting a target, they may resort to less-than-appropriate means to do so, including reducing long-term investments (e.g., R&D), new capital investments, and advertising. Although the immediate effect is to boost returns, the increase is only short-term. The long-term consequences may include declining innovation, productivity growth, and market share, making the company ultimately less competitive (divisional managers may calculate that by the time these effects become apparent, they will hold different positions).

The judicious use of management information systems can allow corporate managers to monitor division manager activities. Improved information systems and auditing technology in large diversified firms facilitate management of large diversified operations.[11] The effectiveness of management information systems must ultimately be judged a function of diversity, however. Strategic control of diversified firms may require more and richer communication than current information technological capabilities allow. For instance, face-to-face lateral relations and committees or other horizontal arrangements between business units are necessary to implement related diversification effectively. As a result, information-processing demands increase geometrically in related diversified firms.[12] The more diverse and/or interconnected a firm's business units, the more difficult it becomes for corporate managers to identify with precision the investments necessary to establish a long-run competitive advantage for individual divisions. This allows divisional executives to focus on the short term as a way of achieving challenging financial targets. Thus, although the M-form extends the ability of corporate officers to manage diversified operations, the potential growth of firms with an M-form structure is not limitless. Extensive diversification creates strategic control problems and affects managerial risk taking and long-term efficiency.

A Comparative History of Strategy and Structural Control at Ford and at General Motors

Competition between GM and Ford can be divided into two periods: an early period from 1925 to 1949 and a late period from 1950 to 1993.[13] These periods represent two distinct phases of competitive history, with the first beginning when GM initiated a marketing strategy and structural innovations in the mid-1920s to which Ford did not at first respond. In the second period, Henry Ford II (Henry Ford I's grandson) sought to duplicate GM's management procedures while maintaining family control of the firm. The intricate will of Henry Ford I allowed the family to hold onto 40 percent of the voting rights once the firm went public after his death. The continuing strong family influence at Ford led to differences in the strategic and the control attributes of the firms, even after Ford tried to duplicate GM's strategy and M-form structure in the second period.

The First Period: Major Differences in Structural Context

For more than a quarter of a century, between 1920 and 1949, Ford and GM operated under CEOs who held opposite beliefs about the ideal strategy and organizational structure for success in the auto industry.

Like many entrepreneurs of the late nineteenth and the early twentieth centuries, Ford organized his company to take advantage of innovations in mass production and mass distribution. He believed that the vertically integrated, centralized functional structure best suited his strategy of low-cost leadership. Alfred Sloan, who became president of GM in 1923, on the other hand, reorganized GM into a multidivisional structure in the early 1920s. The company had endured a crisis of control and had suffered heavy losses in the post–World War I depression. The move from a holding company structure to the M-form was intended to alleviate these problems and to promote an atmosphere in which Sloan's strategies could be pursued successfully. Thus, each CEO chose his firm's structure with certain strategies and control procedures in mind. It was within these two distinct structural contexts—the functional structure at Ford and the multidivisional structure at GM—that the American automobile industry evolved toward maturity.

Ford

In 1908 the Ford Motor Company, under the direction of Henry Ford I, began production of the Model T and initiated a revolution in American transportation. The Model T was the first automobile designed to be produced and sold to the mass market. Not only did Ford emphasize sound engineering and a well-designed product, he bolstered his company's mass production procedures with a nationwide dealer network. To facilitate his high-market-share, low-cost strategy, Ford built fully integrated factories. The facility at River Rouge, Michigan, was the embodiment of this strategy; the factory's generators ran on fuel from Ford-owned mines and even produced its own specialized inputs, such as glass and steel.

This strategy proved successful into the 1920s, as evidenced by Ford's 55.7 percent market share in 1921.[14] Unfortunately, soon thereafter competing manufacturers were able to duplicate Ford's mass production techniques, and its chief rival followed with manufacturing and marketing innovations. Rather than responding to these challenges and adapting to the shifting market, Ford continued to operate as it had for fifteen years. Henry Ford, an engineer and a craftsman, was blind to the subtleties of the market and to the importance of the changes introduced by his competitors. He chose instead to blame the dealers and their supposed lack of enthusiasm in promoting his cars for the firm's lackluster performance in the mid-1920s.

The root of the problem, which Henry Ford never recognized, involved the firm's organizational structure and its single-minded pursuit of his objectives. By keeping power centralized, Ford alienated his most capable lieutenants, many of whom left for other opportunities. Soon authority shifted into the hands of a few men characterized by Alfred Chandler as "tough, unscrupulous, hard-headed, and hard-handed."[15] Two of these men, Ernest G. Liebold, Ford's private secretary, and

Charles Sorenson, the production chief, built their careers on sycophantic relationships with Henry Ford. By supporting Ford, they guaranteed their personal fortunes, even if the company suffered. Ford did not exercise control over their opportunistic behavior. Furthermore, because he refused to share strategic decision-making powers, and because no administrative structure existed to facilitate that process, forecasting, environmental scanning, and product development were practically nonexistent. Henry Ford's effectiveness as a manager deteriorated as the complexities facing him grew, probably because of bounded rationality— the limits on his ability to process information. The company's performance reflected this loss of control. Yet rather than embracing change, Ford clung to the old ways. As late as 1926 he fired Ernest Kanzler, an executive and a relative, for suggesting that the Model T should be replaced.[16]

The next year, however, Ford faced reality. It became apparent that only radical change would rescue the company from its decline. Rather than restructuring the organization, an alternative never considered, Ford reorganized around a new product, the Model A. The company discontinued the Model T, shut down its plants for nine months, and began working on the prototype for the new model in the summer of 1927. The fact that operations had to be temporarily discontinued so that management could turn its attention to the pressing strategic issue of the new product exemplified the bounded rationality problems at Ford.

Ford backed the Model A with all its resources, a move that was essential, considering that the changeover was the greatest retooling task ever undertaken in American industry until that time. The effort seemed worthwhile because it enabled Ford to recapture the premier position in the industry as drivers around the country clamored for the Model A. After a nine-month hiatus, Ford had reestablished its leadership in the automotive market, and Henry Ford expected the Model A to replicate or surpass the success of the Model T. Those expectations were never realized.

The automobile market of the 1930s did not replicate the earlier market; buyers were more sophisticated. Henry Ford refused to make annual model changes similar to those implemented by his competitors, and consequently, five years after its introduction, the Model A was considered obsolete. Ford introduced the V-8 in 1932, but even that was not enough to turn around the company's fortune. Like the Model T and Model A, the V-8 was an excellently engineered automobile, but Ford's marketing techniques had not improved enough to allow it to regain leadership in the industry. In his attempt to run both the strategic and the operational sides of the business simultaneously, Henry Ford grew out of touch with the auto market. Labor problems throughout the decade brought further debilitation. By 1940 Ford's market share had fallen to 18.9 percent. When World War II broke out, the Ford Motor Company limped into battle.

Like so many other firms weakened during the Great Depression of the 1930s, Ford rebounded during the war. The war years provided the opportunity to contribute to the national collective effort and laid the groundwork for a new beginning. Henry Ford I resigned in poor health on September 15, 1945, and his grandson, Henry Ford II, was installed as president. Soon thereafter, the company experienced an influx of capable and eager managers. Ten executives, former Army Air officers who became known as the Whiz Kids, joined the firm in one month (November 1945). The following May the board of directors hired Ernest R. Breech from Bendix Aviation Corporation, a GM affiliate, and he brought with him specialists in finance, engineering, and manufacturing. Ford's efficiency and control problems were tackled almost immediately. Plans were made to reorganize the firm into a decentralized M-form structure. The policy committee approved the plan on September 13, 1946, and the company began to restructure its organization. By 1949 Ford had reorganized to the M-form and had adopted almost all of the management and marketing techniques developed earlier by GM.

General Motors

Henry Ford was not the only one who foresaw America's love affair with the automobile. William C. Durant, president of the Buick Motor Company, was highly optimistic, predicting in 1908 that sales of passenger cars, which had been 63,500 units in that year, would soon be 500,000 annually. To meet the potential demand, he combined a sizable share of Buick's existing assembly and distribution facilities, as well as several parts-and-accessories companies. By the end of 1908, Durant was operating the General Motors Company, a holding company for ten automobile firms, including Buick, Cadillac, and Oldsmobile; three truck-making concerns; and ten parts-and-accessories manufacturers. Whereas Henry Ford had relied on technical and engineering skills to drive his company, Durant's expansion program owed everything to his business and financial acumen. For Durant, expansion was a continuous process, and his strategy included expansion through acquisition and combination. The unforeseen decline in demand in 1910 and the outbreak of World War I slowed him momentarily, but he remained optimistic and continued on.

Durant began the development of a dynasty, but he was not an administrator. While he transformed GM from a holding to an operating firm, the change was in name only. Subsidiaries became divisions but still operated independently, linked only by financial disclosure requirements and by Durant. This structure would have been difficult to manage in most situations, but it became practically impossible after World War I. Although GM was already huge by American industrial standards, Durant embarked on a massive acquisition campaign that was to be the culmination of the expansion program he had begun in 1908. The combination of postwar inflation and the lack of internal controls resulted in cost overruns in almost every GM division. Little attention was paid to administration. As Alfred Sloan described GM during this period, there was "management by crony, with the divisions operating on a horse-trading basis."[17] It was a case of competition among the divisions for available capital and of different preferences at the top." *Opportunistic behavior* was the norm.

Recession enveloped the nation in 1920 and revenues at GM dropped precipitously. This forced the resignation of Durant. Because Du Pont had substantial ownership in GM, Pierre S. Du Pont came out of semiretirement and took over as president in December 1920. Alfred Sloan was drafted to formulate a new organizational plan. Sloan's plan, which was approved by the board of directors, called for the decentralization of operations at the division level and the creation of advisory staffs to administer corporate finance and marketing. After a lean year in 1921 — market share was only 12.7 percent — GM began to show signs of recovery. Implementation of the new structure began soon thereafter. After having begun to restructure the firm, Du Pont retired, and Sloan became president in 1923.

Alfred Sloan understood the maturing automobile industry. He realized that competition, rather than growth, was the key and that marketing should take precedence over production, because production facilities of competitors were equivalent. By 1925 GM had fully recovered from its crisis, and Sloan and his managers were convinced that they had created the ideal structure to take advantage of market opportunities. Furthermore, market planning and divisional control processes were functioning as expected. The results were impressive. By 1927 GM had captured 43.3 percent of the market and had forced Ford to abandon the Model T. The next year the company reported one of the largest profits ever earned by an American firm up to that time — $296,256,203. GM's preeminent position was secure.[18]

GM's innovations reached beyond the automobile industry. Decentralization had been possible under the auspices of the holding company organization, but coordination was sorely lacking. Sloan's plan, which was similar to a holding company structure, allowed operating units to retain full autonomy over their own production, marketing, purchasing, and engineering. The breakthrough was the creation of a general office, consisting of general managers and advisory staffs, to ensure overall coordination, control, and planning. Great care was taken to define divisional activities so that they complemented one another and to ensure that general, staff, and operating executives' roles were reasonable and workable. The plan also stressed hierarchical lines of authority and the necessity of communication channels. The development of financial controls (evaluation of divisional performance on the basis of financial criteria such as return on investment and return on assets) probably had the greatest effect on combating opportunism and reducing executives' information overload. Financial information flowed throughout the organization and provided a clear and continuous picture of the performance of each of the divisions and of the corporation as a whole. Forecasts, based on the data, helped determine costs, prices, production schedules, purchasing, and, of course, resource allocation. The forecasts also established criteria by which the general office could compare division performance. The general office allowed implementation and maintenance of strong strategic and financial controls.

In addition to reshaping GM's administrative organization, Sloan's group focused serious attention on selling automobiles. It was no accident that the restructuring fit with Sloan's marketing strategy. His plan was to offer a coherent product line, with a car for every person's taste and pocketbook. In 1925 GM acquired Pontiac to complete the market segment hierarchy Durant had started. Taken together, Cadillac, Buick, Oakland, Oldsmobile, Pontiac, and Chevrolet, the high-volume competitor to Ford, made up the largest array of products available from one company in the industry. GM allowed Ford to carry the market in product innovation while it focused on the future, basing production on annual market forecasts, adjusting its engineering incrementally, and making annual model updates.

The new organizational structure and process controls served GM well. Even in 1929, the year that Ford launched its Model A, GM recorded higher market share and much higher profits than did Ford. During the Depression GM was able to minimize the effect of market saturation, whereas Ford languished. By the close of the 1930s, GM's share of total car sales reached 47.5 percent. GM had forged ahead while Ford stuck stubbornly to the policies with which it had begun. Clearly, the penalties for inflexibility were as significant as the rewards for innovation.

The Second Period: The Achilles' Heel of the M-form at General Motors

After World War II the strategies and the structures of the two giants in the domestic automobile industry were ostensibly similar. Although Ford went public in 1956, the issuance of two classes of stock allowed the Ford family to retain 40 percent of the voting rights while providing only 12 percent of the capital.[19] Because the dominant family members wished to continue to focus on the auto business, Ford did not drift into the corporate diversification typical of many large corporations in the 1960s, 1970s, and 1980s. Even though both Ford and GM now had M-form structures, the dominant issue during this period was the influence of the ownership structure, which led to the differences between the two firms in the more recent period. Ford, although very large, maintained a high degree of family control, especially through the dominance of a key family member, Henry Ford II. GM, on the other hand, had relatively diffuse ownership, resulting in stronger management domination and control.

During this second period, GM began to overemphasize financial controls, resulting in a loss of market responsiveness compared to Ford. Furthermore, the GM diversification program, whatever the justification, resulted in a dilution of focus on the firm's core business, automobiles. Ford, although subject to many of the same pressures for diversification as GM, maintained its focus, primarily because of the close relationship between ownership and managerial control.

Ford

In early 1946 Henry Ford II recruited Ernest Breech, who at the time was employed by a GM affiliate. Breech helped Ford adapt GM's management practices to his company. Henry Ford II had great admiration for GM because GM (and its management's skills) had set the standards for competing in the car industry since the late 1920s. Breech also helped Ford implement profits centers, allowing Ford to identify which areas of activity within the firm were profitable and to analyze effectively what was wrong with those that were not.

Henry Ford II, even before he took over from his grandfather, realized that, to raise the capital necessary to compete with GM, he would have to take the firm public. It was the Ford Foundation, however, that provided the vehicle to accomplish this task. After the deaths of Henry I and Edsel (son of Henry Ford I), the Ford Foundation was endowed with close to $1 billion of equity in Ford Class A stock. Although family members retained only 12 percent of the equity (5 percent class B—they owned all of this stock—and 7 percent class A stock), they were able to maintain 40 percent of the voting rights. In the event of a tender offer, therefore, they would have to buy only 11 percent to maintain effective control of the company at 51 percent. Even under this arrangement, the stock sold rapidly. By January 17, 1956, two days after the stock went on the market, the price had risen from $64.50 to $70.50 a share.[20] Although family control can be autocratic and capricious, the company retained the firm's focus on its core business.

Ford pursued the strategy set by the family through the leadership of Henry Ford II, and this meant a focus on cars. The strategy would become global, beginning with a special emphasis in Europe. Although Henry Ford II dabbled with minor diversification moves when it became popular to do so in the late 1960s, the dominant strategy remained focused on the car business. (Although GM followed a similar strategy in the early part of this period, by the late 1970s and early 1980s GM had diversified and placed less emphasis on its core business, automobiles.)

Subtle differences between the two auto giants can be seen by examining their failures and successes. For instance, the failure of the Edsel in the mid-1950s was based on Ford's desire to copy GM's strategy and organization too closely, whereas the success of the Ford Mustang grew out of Ford's traditional approach of engineering the right car for the right time.

The Thunderbird, the '49 Ford, the V-8, the Model A, and, most seminally of all, the Model T—these were the triumphs. They were the essence of Ford's history, the combinations of glass and steel and rubber that people liked to drive. What did the general public care about management organization charts or proliferating corporate divisions? Perhaps Lee Iacocca had found the way ahead for Ford: do not let corporate theorizing get in the way of the basic business of car making.[21]

Henry II was delighted in the mid-1960s by the success of the Mustang, developed largely by Lee Iacocca. Although GM had the Monza-Mustang idea first, Ford was the first to develop and market the right recipe. Although Iaccoca became head of the Ford division in 1960, largely because its former president, Robert McNamara, had nominated him before becoming a member of President John F. Kennedy's cabinet, Iaccoca had earned the job by gaining Henry II's confidence.

However, as Iaccoca gained in prominence and continued to aspire to the chairmanship at Ford, Henry Ford II saw him as a threat to family control. As a result, Phillip Caldwell gained Ford's support, and Iaccoca began to lose his grip on operational control of the company. Henry Ford had the support of the finance group in combatting Iaccoca's proposals, which included the production of front-wheel-drive technology. This new technology was more efficient than the existing rear-wheel drive, thereby meeting public demand and satisfying government pressure to produce more fuel-efficient cars.

At Ford, there was no more salient champion for this move than Hal Sperlich. However, Sperlich was perceived as one of Iaccoca's men, and he broke several rules of protocol in seeking to promote the idea of front-wheel-drive cars. Unfortunately, this idea was also associated with small-car production, which was perceived by Henry Ford to produce small profits.

In addition, Henry Ford, who was in poor health, seemed to grow more conservative over time. John Bugas, his longtime friend, was aware of the change.

> When Henry first came to the company, it was teetering on the edge of collapse. What there was of it was virtually beyond preserving; in a sense it had to be completely recreated. In those days Henry Ford had been filled with hope and ambition and enthusiasm. Everything was possible. Nothing daunted him. Now he was older and weary, feeling more mortal and vulnerable, and plagued by doubt and pessimism. For the first time in Bugas's memory Henry Ford was making references to the fact that it was his money they were spending, coming right out of the family's pocket. Optimism had been replaced by extreme wariness. All of this worked against a car that if successful might not make very much money.[22]

Without the support of the Ford finance department and partly because of Henry Ford's opposition to Iaccoca, Sperlich lost the battle for front-wheel-drive products and his job as well. Don Lennox, one of the Whiz

Kids who went into manufacturing, stated that, in rejecting this opportunity, "the vaunted Ford finance department completely blew the most important call of the modern era."[23] Sperlich, along with Iacocca, later helped revive the Chrysler Corporation through the introduction of the innovative K-car front-wheel-drive technology.

Although Henry Ford II had obvious weakness as a corporate leader, he also helped the company develop critical strengths. Married to a European woman, he decided to develop a stronger organization in the European market. He created Ford of Europe and put together the best foreign-car organization in Europe. Because of GM's organizational predisposition, its Vauzhall and Opel subsidiaries continued without coordination and centralized direction until the early 1980s. In contrast, Ford of Europe had coordinated its separate businesses almost painlessly, on the basis of Henry Ford's concerted effort in the late 1960s. "Ford of Europe has helped make Ford far and away the most profitable European manufacturing company of any sort in the post–World War II era—and it also gave Henry II himself an international statesman's stature," one commentator wrote.[24] Ford of Europe turned out to be a crucial part of the corporate identity and a profit crutch for Ford of North America during the oil crises of the 1970s.

Although Ford's organization structure resembled GM's M-form, the top-level control of the organization and the strategy that evolved from it were quite different. Because of its control by one dominant family, Ford maintained a focus on the car business in both strategy and structure, whereas GM's strategy, emphasizing diversification, lacked focus at the top, and its structure evolved to one emphasizing financial control.

General Motors

After gaining market dominance in the late 1920s and 1930s, GM continued to pursue the strategy that had been outlined by Alfred Sloan. Sloan suggested that GM would not be an innovator but would let others pioneer new markets. Afterward GM would imitate the innovation and follow up with new and more aggressive sales efforts.

Sloan's basic organization required a delicate balance between centralized coordination and decentralized operational control. He realized that

> good management rests on a reconciliation of centralization and decentralization, or decentralization with coordinated control. . . . From decentralization we get initiative, responsibility, development of personnel, decisions close to the facts, flexibility—in short, all the qualities necessary for an organization to adapt to new conditions. From co-ordination we get efficiencies and economies. It must be apparent that co-ordinated decentralization is not an easy concept to apply. There is no hard and fast rule for sorting out the various responsibilities and the best way to assign them. The balance which is struck between corporate and divisional responsibility varies according to

what is being decided, the circumstances of the time, past experience, and the temperaments and skills of the executives involved.[25]

Sloan noted, however, that centralized planning was becoming increasingly the rule as he neared retirement. He discussed this in reference to the styling process:

[A]t one time, responsibility for the styling of the cars and other products was vested in the divisions. Since then it has been found desirable to place the responsibility for developing the general style characteristics of all our major products in the Styling Staff. This was suggested partly by the physical economies to be gained by coordinated styling. In addition, we learned from experience that work of higher quality could be obtained by utilizing, corporation-wide, the highly developed talents of these specialists. The adoption of any particular style is now a joint responsibility of the division concerned, the Styling Staff, and the central management.[26]

The balance between division and central office was upset in the late 1950s when Albert P. Bradley retired as GM chairman and was succeeded by Frederic G. Donner. John De Lorean, in his book on GM, claimed that Donner was the first to tip the balance toward stronger centralized financial controls; Donner was the first in a long line of chief executive officers who had not been "well schooled" in the operations side of the car business, and his only work experience was in financial management.[27]

Although performance was strong during Donner's administration, De Lorean claimed that the balance between corporate and divisional responsibility had been disrupted and that the financial controls developed by Donner created short-term profits at the expense of long-term returns:

What was happening was a predictable result, however, when the control of a consumer goods company moves into the hands of purely financial managers. Short-term profits are dramatically improved, but a lack of sensitivity for product, for markets and for customers also sets in, which is usually detrimental to the long-term strength of the corporation. Therefore, those lauding GM's management in the 1960s could not see the organizational fissures developing as they looked at the bright figures appearing on the corporate cash register.[28]

When Ed Cole came to the presidency after Harlow Curtice retired in 1967, the office was stripped of its clout. The chairman and CEO at this time was Roche, who although not strictly finance-oriented by training, was certainly under the influence of the money side of the business. When Roche was absent, Cole was not the top corporate officer; instead, the power passed from Roche to the new position of vice chairman, to be filled by a financial person who also eventually took on responsibility for overseas operations. Thus, in 1967 the power of the GM presidency had reached an all-time low. According to De Lorean, "A weakened presidency had taken from the top the emphasis on sound, broadly viewed operational policy making and intelligent planning in product and organizational areas. . . . In this respect GM is much more centralized. The divisions are more under the operational control of corporate management than at any time in the peacetime history of the corporation."[29]

One result of the centralized focus on financial issues was a reduced emphasis on individual product styling in the divisions. In the late 1970s and early 1980s, many analysts labeled the emphasis on centralized styling "GM generic." Many of the designs began to look quite similar, and this lack of differentiation blurred traditional divisional boundaries.[30] This trend also resulted in the drive to become more cost-efficient in all divisions by building cars around the same or similar chassis.

The centralized focus on the financial aspects of the business, as opposed to operations and manufacturing automobiles, continued at GM. For example, although Robert C. Stempel, had ample car building experience, the chairman, Roger B. Smith, and the vice chairman, Donald J. Atwood, came from the financial and corporate staff ranks and lacked direct car operations experience. The central approach at GM continued to emphasize financial solutions to product problems.

To meet foreign competition, the typical approach at GM has been to buy external innovative ideas and to reduce overhead expenses—an approach typical of companies using financial control. From 1981 to 1986 GM spent more than $40 billion on plant and equipment, buying the most advanced robotics and automation. It also entered into a joint venture with Toyota in hope of acquiring more effective methods of manufacturing small cars. Although this venture seems to be working as of this writing, its success is dependent on management of manufacturing methods rather than on investment in electronic wizardry. Other international joint ventures, such as the one with South Korea's Daewoo Auto Company, have been unprofitable (the one with Daewoo has been dissolved.) In 1984 GM acquired Electronic Data Systems (EDS) from its founder, Ross Perot, in order to increase its use of automated manufacturing and to facilitate communications through modern information system networking. GM acquired the Hughes Aircraft Company in 1985, paying more than $5 billion. For the same reason; it expects that Hughes's space-age knowledge of electronics technology and materials will benefit the design and manufacturing of the automobile of the future.

For the short term, however, these moves represented pure diversification to provide a buffer against the auto industry's periodic downturns, as well as against GM's loss of market share to competitors. Therefore, one goal of the acquisitions was to reduce risk. Roger Smith stated publicly that he wanted to make nonauto operations account for 20 percent of sales by the turn of the century. As Simon Ramo, CEO at (TRW), suggested, GM seemed to be buying technology the hard way: "If expertise is what you want, you could go out and hire the hundred best engineers in the defense industry for far less money."[31] Ultimately, these acquisitions only further entrenched the emphasis on financial controls (as we explain in chapter 5). GM's recent top executives have had no operational expertise in car manufacturing, defense electronics, or aircraft engineering. (Robert Stempel possessed a deep understanding of the car business, but his efforts to salvage the company's fortunes were considered by the board to be inadequate.)

In contrast to GM, Ford was spared many of the pressures to diversify because of dominant family ownership and control, although at times decision making was political and capricious. However, since 1979 and Henry Ford's retirement, and especially with the earnings records established in 1986 and 1987, there has been speculation that the company might move to diversify outside the auto industry. In 1989 Ford bid against GM for control of Jaguar, the British luxury car maker, and won, for a price of $2.5 billion. GM is moving quickly to establish a major presence in eastern Europe, whereas Ford is making some smaller investments in the region; its executives are not projecting a sales volume as great as that expected by GM. With its major operations in England, Ford could move swiftly to compete with GM in eastern Europe if its investments begin to pay large returns.[32]

During the 1980s Ford outperformed GM. Under Donald Peterson's guidance, the firm achieved record profits and stockpiled hordes of cash. However, in the early 1990s its fortunes were stagnant (although GM faded more). Peterson retired, and the Ford family's involvement and influence began to wane. GM's fortunes, in the meantime, continued on the same downward trend experienced throughout the 1980s. During 1990 and 1991 both firms experienced net losses.[33]

In December 1991, after GM's market share slipped below 30 percent—a four-year low—GM's board pushed CEO Robert Stempel to restructure. On December 18, 1991, he announced the closing of 21 plants and the elimination of 74,000 jobs. Furthermore, in February 1992 he announced a reorganization, consolidating three car and truck operations into a single North American Group. Unhappy with Stempel's timetable, the outside directors on the board revolted and promoted John Smith to the head of the North American Group over Lloyd Reuss, Stempel's nominee. Also, John Smale, an outside director and a former chairman of the board at Procter & Gamble, replaced Stempel as chairman of the executive committee of the board. One may ask why the board did not act sooner. The governance system at GM appeared to move too slowly and did not apply pressure until GM was at the brink. Only later was Stempel removed as CEO and replaced with John Smith.[34] As of this writing, Ford's stock price continues to lead that of General Motors.

Summary

GM outperformed Ford on every measure of performance, from profit to market share, in the earlier period of their history. Ford was able to stabilize its situation in the late 1940s through better organization and a focus on its core business. In the late 1980s, as GM's lead faded, Ford was able to produce some of its strongest performances ever.

The historical description provided concrete examples of bounded rationality and opportunism in the centralized functional structure at Ford. The M-form at GM facilitated stronger strategic control that attenuated these problems early and helped GM to outperform Ford in the early period. Later, the weaknesses of the M-form became apparent at GM; the company lost strategic control and emphasized financial control. This approach fostered an emphasis on financial solutions to operational problems, such as a focus on increasing diversification and declining operational oversight by top executives. Ford was able to maintain an operational focus in its M-form structure, although at the price of idiosyncratic family control. However, Ford's performance eclipsed that of GM in recent years, despite GM's greater size. This strong performance can be attributed largely to strong strategic control by key executives at Ford. Strategic control was possible primarily because of Ford's more focused diversification and its concentrated ownership and control.

The information in this chapter suggests the following managerial implications:

- The multidivisional structure (M-form) affords benefits over a centralized functional structure as a firm begins to grow and to diversify its product lines.
- The M-form allows the use of strategic control in addition to financial control because it reduces the amount of information that must be processed by top executives by decentralizing operational decisions to divisions.
- Use of strategic control reduces opportunistic behavior among division managers and encourages a long-term vision.
- Continued diversification produces a loss of strategic control and an overemphasis on financial controls.
- Overemphasis on financial controls stifles innovation and reduces long-term competitiveness.

Notes

1. Hammonds, K. H. 1989. Kodak may wish it never went to the drugstore. *Business Week*, December 4:72–76.

2. Chandler, A. D. 1962. *Strategy and Structure: Chapters in the History of American Industrial Enterprise.* Cambridge, Mass.: MIT Press.

3. Williamson, O. E. 1975. *Markets and Hierarchies: Analysis and Antitrust Implications.* New York: Macmillan.

4. Simon, H. A. 1947. *Administrative Behavior: A Study of Decision-making Processes in Administrative Organizations.* New York: Macmillan.

5. Keats, B. W., & Hitt, M. A. 1988. A causal model of linkages among environmental dimensions, macro organizational characteristics, and performance. *Academy of Management Journal* 31:570–98.

6. Williamson, O. E. 1985. *The Economic Institutions of Capitalism: Firms, Markets, and Relational Contracting.* New York: Free Press, p. 144.

7. Williamson, O. E., *Markets and Hierarchies,* p. 144.

8. Williamson, O. E. 1970. *Corporate Control and Business Behavior.* Englewood Cliffs, N.J.: Prentice-Hall.

9. Hill, C. W. L. 1985. Diversified growth and competition: The experience of twelve large U.K. firms. *Applied Economics* 17:827–47.

10. Hayes, R. H., & Abernathy, W. J. 1980. Managing our way to economic decline. *Harvard Business Review* 58(4):67–77; Hill, C. W. L, Hitt, M. A., & Hoskisson, R. E. 1988. Declining U.S. competitiveness: Innovation, the M-form structure and the capital markets. *Academy of Management Executive* 2:51–60.

11. Leifer, R. 1988. Matching computer-based information systems with organizations. *MIS Quarterly* 72:63–73.

12. Hill, C. W. L., & Hoskisson, R. E. 1987. Strategy and structure in the multiproduct firm. *Academy of Management Review* 12:331–41.

13. Hoskisson, R. E., & Buenger, V. 1986. Effects of structural context on performance: A historical comparison of Ford and General Motors. Paper presented at the Academy of Management Meetings, Chicago.

14. Chandler, A. D. 1964. *Giant Enterprise: Ford, General Motors, and the Automobile Industry.* New York: Harcourt, Brace and World.

15. Ibid., p. 14.

16. Geldman, C. 1981. *Henry Ford: The Wayward Capitalist.* New York: Dial Press, pp. 208, 257–58.

17. Sloan, A. P. 1963. *My Years with General Motors.* Garden City, N.Y.: Anchor Books, pp. 30–31.

18. Chandler, *Giant Enterprise,* p. 14.

19. Lacey, R. 1986. *Ford, the Men and the Machine.* Boston: Little, Brown, p. 475.

20. Ibid., p. 476.

21. Ibid., p. 540.

22. Ibid., p. 531.

23. Ibid., p. 532.

24. Ibid., p. 554.

25. Sloan, *My Years,* p. 505.

26. Ibid., p. 506.

27. De Lorean, J. Z., 1979. *On a Clear Day You Can See General Motors: John Z. DeLorean's Look Inside the Automotive Giant.* Grosse Point, Mich.: Wright Enterprises, p. 227.

28. Ibid., p. 229.

29. Ibid., p. 248–49.

30. Ingrassia, P. 1986. Pontiac revives "sporty" image, setting a marketing example for other GM units. *The Wall Street Journal,* August 15:B–15.

31. Nag, A., & Harris, R. J. 1985. GM's winning offer for Hughes may set heavy-industry trend. *The Wall Street Journal,* June 6:A1, 14.

32. Fuhrman, P. 1990. A tale of two strategies. *Forbes,* August 6:42.

33. Clark, L., and Frame, P. 1990. GM, Ford profits due: Both blame incentives. *Automotive News,* July 30:4.

34. Treece, J. B. 1992. The board revolt: Business as usual won't cut it anymore at a humbled GM. *Business Week,* April 20:30–36.

3

Corporate Governance and Diversification

In chapter 2 we discussed the historical development of General Motors and some of the latest changes in management structure. As a result of the restructuring initiated by Stempel before he was forced to step down, by the year 1994 GM expects to close 21 plants and lay off approximately 74,000 employees. Many of these plant closings and employee layoffs will occur in their domestic U.S. auto operations. However, even with these significant changes, the board of directors became restless because of the continued huge losses of net profit, particularly in the North American operations. As a result, the board of directors, led by the outside board members, removed CEO Stempel from the chair of the executive committee of the board. Consequently, Stempel eventually resigned and was replaced as CEO by John Smith. One institutional owner of GM stock noted that "with the plant closings, they shook up the troops, but with this board action, they shook up the generals."

In this chapter we examine how owners and boards of directors, which govern large firms such as GM, affect the strategies formulated by top executives. As boards become more active, their increased role may have both positive and negative outcomes for firm strategy and control. For example, as discussed in chapter 2, there was concern among the outside directors at General Motors that the company needed to make some major changes in its management and operations in order to become more competitive and to stem the tide of net losses. They were not pleased with former CEO Robert Stempel's slow action and felt that quicker, more radical actions were necessary. Outside directors became concerned when Stempel failed to deliver a visionary long-term plan and instead presented a plan to help the company reach a break-even point. Many observers believe that the board's action in dismissing Stempel and reaching for bolder steps was long overdue. On the other hand, it represented a critical action on the part of corporate boards of directors; some have referred to it as a watershed event and suspect that other boards, following GM's example, will become more proactive.[1]

In chapter 2 we explained that Ford was able to make a comeback against GM because it maintained its focus on the auto business. This unwavering focus was attributed, in part, to the strong ownership position of the Ford family. In contrast, outside director control at GM resulted in changes in management and in corporate direction. This chapter addresses the types of corporate governance, such as ownership, that are intended to direct the firm toward preferred stakeholder objectives. Usually these governance devices are in place to prevent severe problems, rather than to provide strategic direction. However, as the examples of Ford and GM indicate, the application of such governance devices does have an effect on CEOs and on the strategies that they implement.

One instance in which governance devices may have proved inadequate is executive pay. During the 1980s and through 1990 chief-executive pay rose faster than inflation and profits, creating a significant protest that has been regularly chronicled in the media.[2] Because CEO pay at Fortune 500 companies has risen more rapidly than worker or middle manager pay, workers are reported to be demoralized and therefore, perhaps, less loyal to their employers. CEOs, of course, feel that they earn their pay. They also maintain that much of the increase in their pay results from long-term incentives and that therefore their current pay should not be compared to current earnings. However, some critics claim that the problem is the result of ineffective governance by boards of directors. These critics assert that board compensation committees often survey the pay of executives from other firms; when the pay of the CEO at the surveying company falls into the third quartile, the committee may increase it. Shareholders are protesting because this approach is not tied to performance. For instance, the California Public Employee Retirement System voted its 1 percent share of ITT stock against election of key board members because the CEO's 1990 compensation more than doubled while profits rose by only 3.9 percent.

As this example indicates, shareholders, especially institutional investors, are becoming more vigilant and aggressive in taking action against CEOs who receive excessive pay or perks. In addition, the number of outside directors on boards is increasing compared to the number of inside directors, and these outside directors are becoming more vigilant. (The ratio of outside to inside directors of large firms was 3 to 1 in 1990, compared to 2 to 1 in 1980.) According to Lublin, "these [outside] directors now run important board committees and outnumber insiders at 96 of 100 large U.S. companies surveyed by executive recruiters SpencerStuart. That's up from 81 a decade ago. The firm says the number of those boards with a 4-to-1 or greater ratio of outsiders to insiders has doubled to 40 in the past decade."[3] As a result of this aggressive stance, CEOs may be replaced or leave to "pursue other interests" on an involuntary basis.

With this increased action by shareholders and outside directors, what is the likely reaction by CEOs? One CEO was quoted as saying, "It begins to smack of micromanaging the company," which isn't the board's job.[4] Furthermore, managers may become risk averse and implement low-risk strategies (low-risk for the CEO, that is), such as increasing diversification.

Managers generally formulate corporate strategies to foster increased returns to shareholders. However, strategy formulation and allocation of firm resources are examined by a number of stakeholders to ensure that strategy, investment, and wealth distribution (stock price, dividend payments) fulfill stakeholder objectives. This chapter examines the relationship between shareholders and managers, looks at the ways governance devices affect strategy formulation and implementation, and examines how the decisions of two chief stakeholders—owners and managers—affect firm strategy.

Manager Versus Owner Preferences for Product Diversification

The modern public corporation is based on the efficient separation of ownership and managerial control.[5] Owners (shareholders) purchase stock that entitles them to the returns in the firm after obligations have been paid. This privilege, however, requires that they also bear risk, which they seek to manage through investment diversification.[6] Managers contract to oversee decision making in the large open corporation and receive compensation for services rendered. The contractual nature of the publicly held corporation provides specialization of risk bearing for owners and specialization in strategy development and decision making for managers.

Shareholders can diversify their risk by owning shares in several firms. As owners diversify their wealth over a number of firms, the cost of their risk declines (that is, the poor performance or failure of any one firm in which they invest has less overall effect on the owners' wealth).[7] Without specialization of management and risk bearing, the firm's prospects likely would be limited by the managerial abilities of the owner.[8] The separation and specialization of ownership (risk bearing) and managerial control is thus economically efficient.

The separation, however, also creates costs that owners must bear. Delegation of management responsibilities creates the opportunity for conflicts of interest. Managers in pursuit of their own best interests may select strategic alternatives different from those they would have chosen had they pursued exclusively the interests of shareholders. Major deviations from owner expectations are controlled by an active external takeover market (referred to as the market for corporate control). However, control of moderate deviations from decisions appropriate to maximize firm value for shareholders rests with the internal governance, such as the board of directors. For example, product diversification can be beneficial for both shareholders and managers. Managers, however, may prefer more product diversification than do shareholders. To prevent diversifying beyond the level desired by shareholders, strict internal governance may be necessary.

Product diversification provides two benefits to managers that shareholders do not enjoy. First, diversification and firm size are highly correlated, as are firm size and executive compensation.[9] Thus, diversification provides an opportunity for increased managerial compensation. Second, diversification can reduce managerial employment risk. Managerial employment risk is defined as the risk of job loss, loss of compensation, or loss of managerial reputation. These risks are reduced with increased diversification because the firm (and the manager) is less vulnerable to a reduction in demand for one product line. Furthermore, large firms may have free cash flows (slack resources) over which managers have discretion. Free cash flows are those generated after investment in all projects that have positive net present values within the firm's current product lines.[10] These funds may be used by managers to diversify the firm.

Risk-averse managers may desire to invest resources in unrelated diversification beyond the point where the expected rate of return from the new business equals the estimated cost because such diversification reduces their employment risk. Shareholders diversify their risk over a portfolio of investments and generally prefer not to invest in only one firm because portfolio diversification provides a more acceptable overall level of risk.[11] However, managers cannot work for a diverse portfolio of firms in order to diversify their employment risk.

Although a certain amount of product diversification may be good for shareholders, one may ask at what point product diversification becomes a liability to shareholders.[12] Shareholders prefer the amount of diversification that maximizes firm value, but managers want to maximize firm value in addition to increasing their risk-adjusted compensation. To the extent that increasing diversification also increases size and reduces employment risk, managers may prefer more product diversification than do shareholders.

Curve S in figure 2 depicts the optimal diversification positions that might be selected by owners and managers. Owners desire a level of diversification that reduces the risk of total business failure and increases the value of the firm through economies of scope and/or synergy. Curve S locates this position somewhere between the dominant business and the related business categories. (The optimum level of diversification will, of course, vary by firm.)

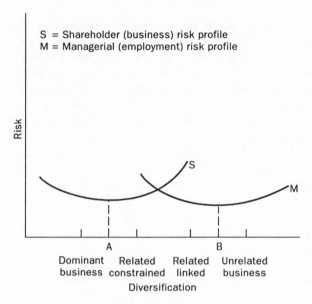

S = Shareholder (business) risk profile
M = Managerial (employment) risk profile

Figure 2. Manager and shareholder risk and diversification

Like shareholders, managers generally do not prefer unlimited diversification. Declining performance increases the probability of a takeover by another firm and can dramatically increase target firm managers' employment risk.[13] Furthermore, a manager's market worth may be determined by the market for managerial talent.[14] Therefore, managers prefer diversification, but not to the point that the firm experiences poor relative performance, which produces higher employment risk and increases managers' difficulty in obtaining new jobs.

Curve M suggests that managers prefer a higher level of diversification than do shareholders (curve S). Shareholders prefer riskier strategies that have more focused diversification, whereas managers prefer broader diversification in order to maximize firm size and compensation and to reduce employment risk.

Given the potential conflict of interests between shareholders and managers over the optimal amount of diversification, the preferences of managers will likely prevail if the internal governance is weak and management is allowed high discretion. If management discretion is properly controlled, firm diversification will approach the shareholders' optimum.

There are a number of factors related to internal governance that may curtail managerial discretion: ownership concentration (large-block ownership, institutional shareholders, and managerial stock ownership), boards of directors, executive compensation, and organizational structure. The next sections detail how emphasizing these means of governance can affect managerial decisions to diversify the firm's product lines.

Ownership Concentration and Diversification

As ownership becomes more dispersed, shareholders' incentive to monitor managerial decisions declines. The shareholder bears the cost of the monitoring but shares the benefit in proportion to percentage of ownership. Owners of large blocks of stock are more interested in monitoring manager decisions, especially if their wealth is not widely diversified in other investments, whereas shareholders with smaller holdings and more diversified portfolios are less interested in monitoring. In general, diffuse ownership produces weak monitoring of managerial decisions and actions. It is likely that the more diffuse the ownership, the higher the level of product diversification in the company. Alternatively, concentrated ownership often is correlated with closer monitoring of managerial decisions, which helps avoid inefficient levels of product diversification and thereby reducing the likelihood of excessive compensation paid to managers. Research has found that concentration of ownership is associated with lower levels of diversification in R&D-intensive firms and with a lower incidence of so-called poison pill devices designed to prevent takeovers.[15]

Monitoring by shareholders is usually accomplished through the board of directors, which is elected by the shareholders to oversee managers and to ensure that the firm is operated in the shareholders' best interests. Obviously, owners with large blocks of stock have more opportunity to elect directors they desire, given that the number of votes given to each shareholder is equal to the proportion of outstanding shares held. With diffuse ownership, shareholders often have less knowledge of particular directors and are less likely to affect the election of such directors. Furthermore, directors are more likely to respond to large-block shareholders than to shareholders who have much lower ownership positions.

An example of such pressure on the board of directors occurred at Digital Equipment Company. Although DEC was formerly one of the industry leaders, in the early 1990s it fell on tough times. One reason for the firm's problems was that it stayed out of the once-lucrative personal computer market. As a result, the board of directors placed pressure on the CEO, Kenneth H. Olsen, to step up restructuring efforts and to bring strong outsiders into senior executive positions, such as the chief financial officer's post. Although Olsen was the only inside executive on the board, many of the outside directors on DEC's board were closely allied with him. These alliances made it difficult for the board to assume a monitoring role. However, the poor performance of the firm increased the pressure on the board to take action. Eventually, the pressure became so great that the board ousted Olson, the firm's founder, and replaced him with Robert B. Palmer, who took a number of restructuring actions to turn around DEC's fortunes.[16]

Recent trends in institutional ownership may affect managerial decisions regarding diversification. Although large-block ownership by individuals has decreased in recent years, concentration of ownership positions by institutional owners has increased. The 1930s classic work by Adolph Berle and Gardiner Means suggested that the "modern" corporation was characterized by a separation of ownership and control.[17] However, this view of diffused ownership has become somewhat outdated. Over the last several decades, major changes in the nature of the capital market have had far-reaching implications for the objectives pursued by corporate managers. One significant trend is the concentration of stock ownership among investment institutions; institutional holdings increased from 34.2 percent of all stocks in 1969 to 43.3 percent of all stocks in 1978.[18] Furthermore, in the early 1990s institutional investors held between $1.5 trillion and $2 trillion in assets and owned one third of the equity in all publicly traded U.S. firms and 50 percent of the equity in large firms.[19]

Institutional investors may attempt to avoid highly diversified firms, concentrating instead on firms whose strategic moves and performance are more visible and easily interpreted. Institutional managers must process large amounts of information on the firms in their portfolio (as well as on potential portfolio firms). As a result, they may attempt to simplify their information processing and invest in firms they can readily understand. Furthermore, because institutional investors desire to diversify their portfolio to control their risk, they may prefer to invest in less diversified firms. In fact, research has found that institutions tend to invest in firms that are R&D-intensive and less diversified.[20] This suggests that institutional investors pursue firms that assume more risk. However, it is likely that the CEOs of these firms seek compensation for the higher risk through increased diversification, higher pay, or contracts that include protection against employment risk, such as golden parachutes and poison pills. For example, one study has shown that institutional ownership is positively related to the adoption of poison pills by boards of directors. This finding suggests that managers attempt to protect themselves against employment risks when there are large institutional shareholders; they likely see institutional shareholders as willing to vote in favor of an acquiring firm and therefore desire takeover protection.[21]

Ownership of firms by CEOs and other top executives often leads to strategies different from those common with institutional ownership. First, it is difficult for a single manager or even a coalition of managers to assemble a significant ownership position in large corporations, even if one manager is a member of a wealthy family. The following institutions hold the greatest bulk of wealth by descending portfolio size: banks, insurance funds, pension funds, and mutual funds.[22] Owner-managers and individual outside owners hold far less wealth. However, institutional owners, except for investment banks, are restricted as to how they may deploy their wealth. These restrictions are designed to keep coalitions of individuals and banks from exercising too much power over industrial firms (and their wealth).

Individual managers who have high levels of ownership control and who also diversify their portfolio of personal investments are more likely to take greater strategic risk in their decisions for the firm. For instance, firms managed by such owner-managers are likely to be more R&D-intensive and less diversified. However, compared to institutional investors, owner-managers who have a great deal of individual wealth invested in the firm and who lack personal portfolio diversification prefer higher levels of firm diversification. Other strategically risky expenditures, such as R&D, are also likely to be lower. Managerial ownership leads to increased risk taking, but no studies to date have examined managers in different ownership categories (those with concentrated and those with diversified individual wealth) to determine if there are systematic differences.[23]

Although institutional investors have remained largely passive, some have become more active in monitoring executive actions. For example, the California Public Employee Retirement System, the nation's largest public fund (approximately $68 billion), first worked for changes at 12 companies in which it owned stock. It later threatened a proxy war on directors at eight of those companies that refused to meet its terms. Similarly, Colorado's employee pension fund hired a proxy consultant and withheld votes for directors (which takes place annually) at American Express, Westinghouse Electric Corporation, and Travelers Corporation. Because the shareholders vote for directors, and not for managers, boards are feeling the increased pressure. On the other hand, the primary targets of shareholders' wrath are firms' top executives.

The Securities and Exchange Commission (SEC) is expected to give shareholders another boost by easing its rule on communications among shareholders. As of this writing, shareholders cannot communicate as a group except through a cumbersome and expensive filing process. However, under the new rules approved by the SEC, shareholders are allowed to meet to discuss the company's direction by giving a simple notification to the SEC. If they agreed, they could also vote as a block. For example, the 20 largest shareholders at Philip Morris Companies own approximately 25 percent of the firm. A 25 percent vote against a management proposal or a director would send a powerful message. Some refer to this block voting as shareholder empowerment. Moreover, there are some who argue that there should be even fewer restrictions on mutual funds and on other institutional owners and managers who wish to sit on boards of directors. Therefore, it is possible that a slumbering giant in the corporate governance arena is beginning to awaken.[24]

Boards of Directors and Diversification

Notwithstanding the increase in concentrated institutional ownership, dispersed ownership remains the most common form of ownership in U.S. firms. This ownership pattern implies limited individual shareholder monitoring of managers. Because of this diffusion, and because large financial institutions that control much wealth are prevented from owning firms directly and their representatives are barred from sitting on boards of directors, there is a need for collective monitoring that is fulfilled through a board of directors.

The general role of the board is to maintain the efficient separation of risk and managerial control, and its primary function is to monitor managerial decisions to protect the interests of owners. A board's ability to perform this function is largely determined by the objectivity, expertise, and motivation of its members.[25] Several scholars have argued that boards are not honoring their primary fiduciary duty; that is, increases in executive compensation are not in line with increases in stockholder wealth, as measured by firm market value.[26] A number of noted researchers believe that managers dominate boards and exploit their personal ties with them.[27] Not surprisingly, those who question the current effectiveness of boards advocate reforms to ensure that independent outside directors represent a significant majority of board members.[28]

Boards also have a secondary function—to protect the contractual relationship between the firm and its managers. However, board reforms have focused on the first role, namely, protecting diffuse owners from powerful managers.[29] These reforms have generally increased the number of outside directors on the board.[30] For example, in 1984 the New York Stock Exchange started requiring that listed firms have board audit committees composed solely of outside directors.[31] Unfortunately, this trend has probably reduced the viability of the secondary role of the board;[32] with fewer inside (management) directors on the board, managers' concerns may not be adequately represented at the very top level, creating a situation with strategic implications.[33]

The central function of outside directors is to safeguard the shareholders' investment in the firm against potential managerial opportunism or incompetence. Outsiders fulfill this obligation by reviewing and approving management initiatives and by monitoring the quality of managerial decision making as these initiatives are implemented. Outside directors, however, do not have contact with the day-to-day operations of the firm. To evaluate strategic initiatives effectively, they often need detailed information about the quality of management and of management decisions. This type of information is best obtained over time through frequent interactions between board and management at board meetings. Inside board members also have access to voluminous information by virtue of their positions. Thus, boards, with a critical mass of insiders can be more fully informed.[34] Without this in-depth information, outsider-dominated boards may emphasize financial, rather than strategic, evaluations; in other words, they may evaluate managers on the basis of financial outcomes rather than strategic actions. This shifts risk to managers, who in turn may seek to reduce their risk by lowering R&D investments, diversifying the product line of the firm, and/or increasing their compensation (to compensate them for the extra risk).[35]

Of course, as at GM, outside board members increasingly are becoming a dominant force. This change is likely to have both positive and potentially negative outcomes. Outside board members at GM (as at any company) are likely to be more objective and less tied to internal political issues. In addition, as representatives of the stockholders and as observers with no other ties to the corporation, they should be able to use their objectivity to affect both strategic actions and outcomes. On the other hand, if our arguments are accurate, GM may become more profitable in the short term but also may emphasize short-term performance over long-term strategic actions. The actions announced by GM in 1992 were mixed in this regard. The choice of John Smith, formerly chief operations officer, as the new CEO suggested a stronger focus on the bottom line, an emphasis for which he was known. His actions as COO and as the new CEO supported this notion. For example, he reorganized the headquarters staff and reduced the number of models from GM's product lines in order to focus on fewer and more profitable models. His reorganization of the headquarters staff is likely to produce significant staff reductions. These actions may be appropriate and needed, but they also suggest a strong emphasis on bottom-line results. On the other hand, GM's overall reorganization plan suggests that the firm is willing to sell off units that are unrelated to its automobile operations, thereby downscoping and reducing diversification. It will be some time before the full impact of these changes at GM is apparent.[36]

The evidence on the effects of board involvement in strategic decisions is mixed. For example, boards are more likely to be involved in strategic decisions in nondiversified firms; in large, diversified firms, boards are less likely to be active. In diversified firms, it is difficult for board members, whether inside or outside, to have the in-depth information necessary to evaluate strategic actions (because of the large number of different businesses that require evaluation). Instead, board members are often limited to evaluating the financial outcomes of these actions.

However, the relationship between board composition and evaluation of managers' decisions may be even more complex. For example, inside members of boards often are less involved in board actions because they also report to the CEO. Although they are likely to have rich information, they may be less willing to share this information with the other board members when it is to be used to evaluate the CEO's actions. That is, inside directors may face a conflict of interest between their roles as managers reporting to the CEO and their positions as inside members on the board of directors who must evaluate top executive actions and performance. On the other hand, when boards become involved in strategic decisions, firms perform better. As a result, while the effect of having insiders on boards is mixed, board involvement in strategic decisions (e.g., evaluation of strategic actions by executives) clearly produces higher performance in the firm over time.[37]

Executive Compensation and Diversification

Another means of governance used to align managers' and owners' interests is the establishment of a link between executive compensation and firm performance.[38] There has been a significant increase in incentive-based top executive compensation in lieu of salary-based compensation during the 1980s and 1990s.

However, incentive compensation is complicated. First, the strategic decisions made by top executives are typically complex and nonroutine. Behavioral controls (e.g., supervision) may be inappropriate when the task is as complex as strategic decision making.[39] In this situation, outcome controls (incentive compensation tied to financial outcomes) become more appropriate. Second, management decisions often affect firm financial outcomes over extended periods of time, making it difficult to assess the effect of current decisions on firm performance.[40] In fact, strategic decisions are more likely to have long-term rather than short-term effects on firm performance. Third, a number of variables intervene between management behavior and firm performance. Unpredictable economic, social, or legal changes can affect the outcomes of what seem to be desirable strategic decisions and may in fact lead to unfavorable outcomes even when the decision appeared to be sound before implementation. Although performance-based compensation may provide incentives to managers to make decisions that will benefit owners, it is imperfect in its ability to produce the desired managerial behavior.

Although incentive compensation plans may increase firm value in line with owner expectations, they are subject to managerial manipulation.[41] Annual bonuses may provide incentives for managers to pursue short-term objectives at the expense of the long-term viability of the firm. For example, bonuses based on annual performance often lead to lower investments in R&D, which may affect adversely the long-term competitiveness of the firm.[42] Although long-term performance-based incentives may reduce the temptation to underinvest in the short term, they increase executive exposure to risks associated with uncontrollable events, such as market fluctuations. The longer the term of the incentive compensation focus, the greater the long-term risks borne by the executive.

One way managers can compensate for this increase in their risk is to propose higher levels of diversification for the firm. For example, incentive compensation may lead to higher diversification.[43] Although diversification is not the only way managers can reduce their risk, it is a common way to do so. The evidence suggests that short-term incentive compensation schemes are related to diversification because they shift risk to managers (in large publicly held firms that have diffused ownership).

One area that has angered stockholders is executive pay, as we noted at the beginning of this chapter. For example, stockholders were quite upset when the 1990 pay package of Rand Araskog, CEO of ITT Corporation, was announced to be $11.4 million. There was a concern that the performance of ITT had not matched Mr. Araskog's compensation. In fact, the United Shareholders Association added ITT to its target list of 50 companies it considers most unfair to shareholders. However, Mr. Araskog negotiated with the United Shareholders and announced a plan to work with ITT's board to link executive pay more closely to firm performance. As a result, the United Shareholders Association removed ITT from its target list. In addition, Mr. Araskog met with members of one of ITT's large institutional shareholders, the California Public Employee Retirement System, and agreed to press the ITT board to amend its bylaws and to require that a majority of the directors be independent.[44]

The case of ITT suggests that boards of directors may not have been as effective as would be desirable in developing and implementing executive incentive compensation plans. The increases in incentive compensation approved by boards are largely responsible for large increases in total executive compensation. Boards may have been overly reliant on this form of governance, and managers may be implementing strategies to take advantage of these incentives.

The M-form as a Governance Device and Diversification

Oliver Williamson, a well-known scholar, has argued that organization structure, particularly the multidivisional (M-form) structure, serves as a governance device. Williamson suggests that the M-form structure overcomes the problems of managerial opportunism in large, functionally organized firms and that division managers are more interested in profit maximization than are managers in functionally organized firms.[45] Although division manager opportunism may be curtailed by the M-form structure, it may not constrain corporate-level managers from pursuing their self-interests. In fact, the governance of corporate-level executives in M-form firms is similar to that in independent functionally organized firms. As a result, the M-form, without additional means of governance, may not adequately control corporate-level managerial decisions. In fact, firms using M-form structures are more likely to continue further diversification because the M-form structure facilitates further diversification,[46] and continued diversification may create internal governance that encourages divisional executives to focus on short-term results. If the firm becomes highly diversified, corporate executives may be forced to change from strategic to financial controls. As noted earlier, overemphasis on financial outcomes to evaluate strategic decisions on the part of managers often focuses their attention on short-term as opposed to long-term investments.

In addition, a "depth-for-breadth trade-off" often occurs in an extensively diversified M-form firm. For instance, if internal controls are limited because of extensive diversification, only external capital and labor markets provide controls on managerial opportunism. However, because external markets lack access to internal information (at low cost), these markets are less efficient than are internal systems for monitoring corporate executive performance.[47] While the market for corporate control (acquisitions/takeovers) may become active, the cost of executing takeovers makes the threat of a takeover feasible only if a firm is significantly undervalued. Therefore, even M-form firms require additional strong governance devices to control corporate managerial opportunism, without which the M-form may facilitate overdiversification and inappropriately high compensation for corporate executives, while causing division managers to focus excessively on short-term performance.

Summary

Under limited governance, corporate managers may control the firm without adequate restraint. Without appropriate governance, higher levels of diversification are likely to be implemented by managers to increase firm size and executive compensation and to reduce executives' employment risk. Increased diversification, however, may negatively affect firm performance and lead to external capital market intervention. If effects on performance are marginal, intervention is less likely to occur. Under this scenario, risk-averse managers may be allowed to invest resources in unrelated acquisitions beyond the point where the expected rate of return from the new business equals the estimated costs.[48] Of course, shareholders prefer that management invest resources in new product and process development or related diversification because these are more likely to yield higher long-term performance. As long as managers perceive personal benefits from managing a diversified portfolio of firms, however, excessive diversification is likely to occur.[49]

Of course, managers do not make diversification decisions in an internal vacuum. Large-block shareholders may scrutinize firms for possible inappropriate managerial actions. Although less assertive because they are one step removed from typical ownership and prevented by law from exercising excessive control, institutional owners are becoming more aggressive and voicing stronger opinions regarding internal governance issues, such as CEO pay. Managerial owners also have incentives to maximize firm value. Unfortunately, if their own personal wealth is not diversified, managerial owners also continue to have incentives to diversify the firm.

Dominance of outside members of the board of directors also appears to be related to higher levels of diversification. In contrast, boards on which inside directors play an important role in the decision control process may reduce the employment risks associated with dominant and related business diversification strategies and hence reduce the need for excessive diversification. Because managers operating under effective strategic evaluation of their actions are rewarded on the basis of the strategic relevance of their decisions, they should not avoid the higher employment risk associated with related or dominant business strategies. This is not to say that outside directors are indifferent to the choice of corporate strategy. However, greater outsider representation on the boards is associated with more diversified scope of business and a lower concentration in related activities.[50]

It is important to emphasize that inside board members may face a conflict in that they are responsible to the CEO for their managerial activities and to the board for the provision of information that may be used to evaluate that same CEO. As a result, it may not be uncommon for some inside board members to withhold information from the board, particularly if it is unfavorable to the CEO.

Shareholders of firms competing in R&D-intensive industries may tacitly accept an emphasis on strategic control because of the high risk of a competitor's gaining a technological advantage, referred to as "technological mugging."[51] On balance, then, strategic controls combined with the presence of insiders on the board are congruent with investment in R&D as a critical success factor.[52] There is less investment in R&D in firms in which outsiders dominate the board control process.[53]

The effects of incentive compensation may be enhanced by strategic control exercised by the board. Without a balance of strategic control, a link between rewards and performance shifts excessive risk to managers, who, in turn, seek to reduce that risk through further diversification or higher compensation. Although the use of the M-form structure with focused diversification may limit division manager opportunism, corporate managers may use the M-form to create more extensive diversification because it reduces their risk and often increases their compensation. As a governance device, the M-form may function properly as long as additional strong internal governance exists; without such additional governance, the M-form may be used as a vehicle to fulfill corporate officers' individual objectives at the expense of shareholders. Furthermore, extensive diversification creates risk aversion and a focus on shorter time horizons for division managers. Thus, the M-form, without adequate additional governance, may lead to lower risk taking and lower long-term performance, over time affecting the competitiveness of the firm compared to foreign competitors.

Top managers' power also plays a critical role in strategic decision making.[54] Obviously, top executives have more power when corporate governance is not strong. On the other hand, even strong governance can lead managers to inappropriate actions. There are other potential ways that managerial actions can be influenced. One of these is through the selection of the successor to a CEO, in which the board of directors plays a critical role. Research has shown that if a firm is performing poorly, there is an increased likelihood that the new CEO will be selected from the outside. However, boards with a large proportion of inside members often select an inside successor, regardless of the performance level of the firm. Of course, the choice of an inside successor when a firm is performing poorly suggests that major changes are less likely and that the poor performance may continue, raising questions about the efficacy of inside board members and the extent to which they will operate independently.[55]

In conclusion, we suggest that internal governance of large diversified firms is often inadequate. In general, even though owners and board members are becoming more vigilant, it does not appear that current governance devices effectively control extensive diversification without the help of external capital market intervention (which creates its own set of problems; see later chapters). Tying executive compensation to firm performance may not provide an effective solution; without strong strategic control, many incentive compensation plans shift excessive risk to managers and provide rewards on the basis of financial outcomes, without regard to the appropriateness of strategic decisions. As a result, managers seek to reduce their risk through further diversification, reduced long-term investments, or other activities that result in higher compensation. The key is to maintain strong strategic control, which is likely to require focused diversification; limited governance has led to a need to restructure many firms because of overdiversification.

Our recommendations for managers are quite similar to those made by a panel charged by the Council on Competitiveness with finding answers to the question as to why U.S. managers have been shortsighted and developing recommendations for increasing U.S. competitiveness.

- Large firms should seek committed long-term investors and give them a voice in the governance of the firm.
- Directors, whether inside managers or outside directors, may be more committed and involved in strategic direction if they are substantial owners.
- Boards of directors should use a balance between strategic controls and financial evaluation. Outside directors need to have strategic information and should not rely solely on financial criteria. Inside directors need to be independent from the CEO. This may necessitate a separation of the position of CEO from that of company president.
- Boards should avoid overreliance on incentive compensation that can reward executives for inappropriate strategic initiatives. All decisions on executive compensation should be informed by strategic evaluation by the board.

- M-form structures that lead to inappropriate unrelated diversification need to be carefully monitored by boards.[56]

Notes

1. Woodruff, D., & Treece, J. B. 1991. GM can't downshift fast enough. *Business Week*, December 30:37; Treece, J. B. 1992. The board revolt: Business as usual won't cut it anymore at a humbled GM. *Business Week*, April 20:30–34, 36.

2. Lublin, J. S. 1991a. Are chief executives paid too much? *The Wall Street Journal*, June 4:B–1.

3. Lublin, J. S. 1991b. More chief executives are being forced out by tougher boards. *The Wall Street Journal*, June 6:A–1, A–10.

4. Ibid.

5. Fama, E. F., & Jensen, M. C. 1983. Separation of ownership and control. *Journal of Law and Economics* 26:301–25.

6. Jensen, M. C., & Meckling, W. H. 1976. Theory of the firm: Managerial behavior, agency cost, and ownership structure. *Journal of Financial Economics* 3:305–60.

7. Ibid.

8. Fama & Jensen, separation.

9. Ciscel, D. H., & Carroll, T. M. 1980. The determinants of executive salaries: An econometric survey. *Review of Economics and Statistics* 62:7–13; Dyl, E. A. 1988. Corporate control and management compensation – Evidence on the agency problem. *Managerial and Decision Economics* 9:21–25; Tosi, H., & Gomez-Mejia, L. 1989. The decoupling of CEO pay and performance: An agency theory perspective. *Administrative Science Quarterly* 34:169–89.

10. Jensen, M. C. 1986. Agency costs of free cash flow, corporate finance, and takeovers. *American Economic Review* 76:323–29.

11. Amihud, Y., & Lev, B. 1981. Risk reduction as a managerial motive for conglomerate mergers. *Bell Journal of Economics* 12:605–17.

12. Penrose, E. 1959. *The theory of the growth of the firm*. Oxford, Eng.: Basil Blackwell; Teece, D. J. 1980. The diffusion of an administrative innovation. *Management Science* 26:464–70.

13. Walsh, J. 1989. Doing a deal: Merger and acquisition negotiations and their impact upon target company top management turnover. *Strategic Management Journal* 10:307–22.

14. Fama, E. F. 1980. Agency problems and the theory of the firm. *Journal of Political Economy* 88:288–307.

15. Hill, C. W. L., & Snell, S. A. 1988. External control, corporate strategy, and firm performance in research intensive industries. *Strategic Management Journal* 9:577–90; Mallette, P., & Fowler, K. L. 1992. Effects of board composition and stock ownership on the adoption of poison pills. *Academy of Management Journal* 35:1010–35.

16. Wilke, J. R. 1992. On the spot: At Digital Equipment Company, Ken Olsen is feeling pressure to produce. *The Wall Street Journal*, May 13:A–1, A–8; McWilliams, G. 1993. DEC's comeback is still a work in progress. *Business Week*, January 18:75–76.

17. Berle, A., & Means, G. 1932. *The Modern Corporation and Private Property*. New York: Macmillan.

18. Farrar, D. E., & Gerton, L. 1982. Institutional investors and the con-

centration of financial power. *Journal of Finance* 32:369–82; Drucker, P. F. 1986. A crisis of capitalism. *The Wall Street Journal*, September 30:30.

19. Drucker, A crisis; Mallette & Fowler, Effects of board composition.

20. Hill, C. W. L., & Hansen, G. S. 1991. A longitudinal study of the cause and consequences of changes in diversification in the U.S. pharmaceutical industry 1977–1986. *Strategic Management Journal* 12:187–99; Baysinger, B. D., Kosnik, R. D., & Turk, T. A. 1991. Effects of board ownership structure on corporate R&D strategy. *Academy of Management Journal* 34:205–14.

21. Mallette & Fowler, Effects of board composition.

22. Roe, M. 1990. Political and legal restraints on ownership and control of public companies. *Journal of Financial Economics* 27:7–41.

23. Hill & Snell, External control.

24. Salwen, K. G., & Lublin, J. S. 1992. Activist holders: Giant investors flex their muscles more at U.S. corporation. *The Wall Street Journal*, April 27:A–1,A–5; Roe, M. J. 1993. Mutual funds in the board room. *Journal of Applied Corporate Finance* 5(4):56–61.

25. Baysinger, B. D., & Hoskisson, R. E. 1990. Board composition and strategic control: The effect on corporate strategy. *Academy of Management Review* 15:72–87.

26. Kerr, J., & Bettis, R. A. 1987. Boards of directors, top management compensation, and shareholder returns. *Academy of Management Journal* 30:645–64.

27. Herman, E. S. 1981. *Corporate Control, Corporate Power*. New York: Cambridge University Press; Jones, T. M., & Goldberg, L. D. 1982. Governing the large corporation: More arguments for public directors. *Academy of Management Review* 7:603–11.

28. Eisenberg, M. 1986. *The Structure of the Corporation*. Boston, Mass.: Little, Brown.

29. Baysinger & Hoskisson, Board composition.

30. Lublin, More chief executives; Patton, A., & Baker, J. C. 1987. Why won't directors rock the boat? *Harvard Business Review* 65(6):10–18.

31. Kesner, I. F. 1988. Director characteristics in committee membership: An investigation of type, occupation, tenure, and gender. *Academy of Management Journal* 31:66–84.

32. Baysinger & Hoskisson, Board composition.

33. Ibid.

34. Ibid.

35. Hill & Snell, External control; Baysinger, B. D., & Zeithaml, C. P. 1985. A contingency approach to diversification and board composition: Theory and empirical evidence. Paper presented at the Academy of Management meetings, San Diego.

36. Treece, The board revolt; Treece, J. B., & Templeman, J. 1992. Jack Smith is already on a tear at GM. *Business Week*, May 11:37.

37. Judge, W. Q., Jr., & Zeithaml, C. P. 1992. Institutional and strategic choice perspectives on board involvement in the strategic decision process. *Academy of Management Journal* 35:766–94.

38. Hoskisson, R. E., Hitt, M. A., Turk, T., & Tyler, B. 1989. Balancing corporate strategy and executive compensation: Agency theory and corporate governance. In G. R. Ferris and K. M. Rowland, eds., *Research in Personnel and Human Resources Management*, vol. 7, 25–57. Greenwich, Conn.: JAI Press; Tosi & Gomez-Mejia, Decoupling.

39. Eisenhardt, K. 1985. Control: Organizational and economic approaches. *Management Science* 31:134–49.

40. Eaton, J., & Rosen, H. 1983. Agency, delayed compensation, and the structure of executive remuneration. *Journal of Finance* 38:1489–1505.

41. Dyl, Corporate control.

42. Hoskisson, R. E., Hitt, M. A., & Hill, C. W. L. 1993. Managerial incentives and investment in R&D in large multiproduct firms. *Organization Science* 4:325–41.

43. Kerr, J. 1985. Diversification strategies and managerial rewards: An empirical study. *Academy of Management Journal* 28:155–79; Kerr, J., & Slocum, J. W., Jr. 1987. Managing corporate culture through reward systems. *Academy of Management Executive* 1:99–107; Napier, N. K., & Smith, M. 1987. Product diversification, performance criteria, and compensation at the corporate manager level. *Strategic Management Journal* 8:195–201.

44. Salwen & Lublin, Activist holders.

45. Williamson, O. E. 1985. *The Economic Institutions of Capitalism: Firms, Markets, and Relational Contracting.* New York: Free Press.

46. Keats, B. W., & Hitt, M. A. 1988. A causal model of linkages among environmental dimensions, macro organizational characteristics, and performance. *Academy of Management Journal* 31:570–98.

47. Williamson, *Economic Institutions.*

48. Amihud & Lev, Risk reduction.

49. Markides, C. C. 1992. Consequences of corporate refocusing: Ex ante evidence. *Academy of Management Journal* 35: 398–412.

50. Hill & Snell, External control.

51. Kay, N. M. 1982. *The Evolving Firm: Strategy and Structure in an Industrial Organization.* New York: St. Martin.

52. Hoskisson, R. E., & Hitt, M. A. 1988. Strategic control systems and relative R&D investment in large multiproduct firms. *Strategic Management Journal* 9:605–21; Ettlie, J. E., Bridges, W. E., & O'Keefe, R. D. 1984. Organization strategy and structural differences for radical versus incremental innovation. *Management Science* 30:682–95.

53. Hill & Snell, External control.

54. Finkelstein, S. 1992. Power in top management teams: Dimensions, measurement, and validation. *Academy of Management Journal* 35:505–38.

55. Boeker, W., & Goodstein, J. 1993. Performance and successor choice: The moderating effects of governance and ownership. *Academy of Management Journal,* 36:172–86.

56. Dobrzynski, J. H. 1992. A sweeping prescription for corporate myopia. *Business Week,* July 6:36–37.

4

Acquisition Strategies and Innovation

In the 1980s Philip Morris focused on acquisitions and increased its debt load, at least in the short run, through the purchase of General Foods and Kraft. Over time, Philip Morris focused more on product line extensions than on new product development.[1] Executives at Philip Morris apparently preferred to let other firms take the risk of intense new product development. Also, CEO Michael A. Miles told *The Wall Street Journal* that he expected the company to continue to grow primarily through acquisitions, because the rate of growth of cigarette sales is decreasing and the food business is not growing as fast as in the past: "If the company expands operating earnings around 15 percent each year, it can still raise per share net income at that magical 20 percent rate by borrowing heavily for acquisitions, then tapping the cash-flow fountain to rapidly pay back debt."[2] Philip Morris continued to generate exceptional cash flows that it used to reduce its debt.

Over the last three decades firm diversification has increased through two waves of mergers and acquisitions, one in the 1960s and the early 1970s and the second in the 1980s.[3] Managers had a relatively free rein in pursuing acquisitions that increased the level of diversification in many firms. As Chapter 3 stressed, the means of governance have not restricted acquisitive growth and diversification. In fact, the relationship between pay and performance has grown smaller, while the association between CEO pay increases and diversification has grown larger. As a result, this chapter critically examines the strategy of acquiring other businesses. Our evaluation suggests that there is a trade-off between growth through acquisition and internal growth, especially growth through internal innovation. In other words, firms that follow an acquisition strategy invest less in the internal development of new products (e.g., R&D). We discuss the reasons for this trade-off in this chapter.

Of course, these trade-offs do not preclude a focused strategy of acquisition from being successful. However, firms that make acquisitions often create value primarily for the shareholders of the firms they purchase, rather than for their own shareholders. The market for buying and selling businesses seems to be quite efficient, neither creating nor losing significant value in transferring assets. As a result, firms participating in such activity usually achieve average returns unless either unique or private synergy (unobtainable by or unknown to companies in the bidding process) or chance provides above-normal returns.[4]

During the period of increased acquisition activity in the 1980s, the decline in global competitiveness among U.S. firms continued.[5] One must ask, therefore, if the increase in merger-and-acquisition activity in the 1980s is associated with the cure or the decline in competitiveness. While this activity in the market for corporate control (the takeover market) has created efficiencies, these efficiencies may occur at the expense of long-term performance. The purpose of this chapter is to create some balance in the arguments by examining both the short-term efficiency gains and the long-term trade-offs associated with an acquisitive growth strategy. In particular, we examine the potential link between competitiveness and acquisition activity.

To illustrate, capital investment in manufacturing in the United States during the 1980s increased at a snail's pace compared to that in previous decades.[6] Although the overall rate of increase was 4.3 percent for the decade, capital investment in manufacturing during the decade of the 1980s decreased by approximately 50 percent compared to the rate for the previous three decades. However, manufacturing productivity increased during the decade; the rate was 4.5 percent between 1982 and 1990 and 3.9 percent for the decade. This compares favorably to the Japanese pace of 5.5 percent between 1979 and 1989 and is considerably better than Germany's 2 percent. The reason for the growth rate has been attributed to U.S. companies learning to "work smarter." One author maintains that "companies closed obsolete plants, pared redundant employees, and overhauled management of the factory floor, leveraging small expenditures on new equipment into big output gains. Many American companies learned they could get higher returns from their human capital before they needed to make heavy investments in physical capital."[7]

However, one must question how effective this restructuring process has been. The process of restructuring was sparked by the binge of mergers and acquisitions, as well as by sell-offs and divestitures. During the 1982–88 period, the average debt-to-equity ratio increased from .48 to .65 among manufacturing firms.[8] This increased debt load is the result of the main approach to restructured growth during the decade—mergers and acquisitions. In order to meet their debt loads, firms pursued either or both of two basic strategies—selling off unproductive assets and laying off employees. Thus, increased productivity may have come at the expense of human capital and of assets that performed poorly for the acquiring company. Is making more acquisitions, increasing debt, and laying off employees the answer?

Of course, restructuring activity can be positive, reducing the number of levels in the traditional hierarchical structure and bringing in new management teams.[9] However, beyond the public relations hype, in many cases restructuring may represent the ceding of market share to more efficient foreign competitors. This explanation seems more in agreement with the huge trade deficits experienced in the 1980s and may be a sign that U.S. firms are losing the competitiveness battle.

The debt leveraging associated with manufacturing may not represent the menace that some have suggested; companies' increased cash flows may be adequate to service the increased debt loads. Most manufacturing debt has been taken on by noncyclical firms that have inelastic demand and strong cash flows.[10] Higher debt loads, for instance, can be handled by firms, such as R.J.R. Nabisco in the food industry, that have relatively steady cash flows even in a recession.

In the process of reducing high debt, however, there are opportunity costs. Free cash flows have been used to diversify firms such as Philip Morris.[11] With increased debt, however, free cash flows must be used to service the higher debt costs. In the process, long-term investments such as capital investment and R&D may be reduced, as evidenced by the lower capital investment during the 1980s.[12]

Acquisitions financed with public debt rather than with internal funds require full disclosure of financial as well as strategic information in capital markets. Financial experts focus on the value of this disclosure to capital markets for the proper valuation of firms.[13] However, information disclosed to markets is also disclosed to competitors. Michael Porter, for example, provides an approach to gleaning competitive information from market signals.[14] Because of the nature of the bidding process for corporate assets, it is rare that acquisitions realize above-average returns. In fact, since federal legislation was first adopted in 1968 and since enhanced—requiring greater disclosure and opportunities for target firm managers to sue hostile would-be acquirers, thereby prolonging takeover battles—acquirers have gained little, while gains to target firms' shareholders have risen sharply.[15] Accordingly, acquisitions funded by public debt are likely to have strategic costs that reduce returns on the target firm to only normal or possibly even below-normal levels. Therefore, although restructuring has increased short-term productivity, increases in long-term values have not generally been realized.

This analysis suggests that, while short-term productivity has improved due to acquisition and restructuring activity, overall long-run competitiveness has not. For example, acquisitions have led to a decreased investment in R&D inputs and outputs (e.g., patents).[16] Furthermore, a strong relationship exists between investments in R&D and competitiveness in many industries. Investment in R&D has been found to be a principal indicator of subsequent sales growth for a five-to-ten-year period; as one observer wrote, "Insofar as many U.S. and U.K. firms have lost global market share relative to Asian and European competitors over the past two decades, a significant contributory factor would appear to have been negligence on the part of many U.S. and U.K. firms of investment in technology as a factor determining strategic, competitive advantage."[17] Lessons from history suggest the importance of being a first mover in the market.[18] Furthermore, because many acquisitions performed poorly, they were divested either voluntarily or through the threat of hostile takeovers.[19] This chapter explores why some acquisitions performed poorly and how acquisitions affect managerial incentives for innovation and improved competitiveness.

The Market for Corporate Control and Innovation

The relationship between acquisitions and innovation is complex. For example, innovations may be incremental (e.g., addition of small amounts of cumulative knowledge regarding current products or processes) or radical (e.g., path-breaking new products or processes). Innovations may also occur in areas unrelated to new products, technologies, and processes linked to marketplace opportunities (e.g., new management practices, new organizational structures). If a company reduces its commitment to innovation, it will likely invest fewer resources in R&D, in obtaining patents, and in transferring innovation to the market, compared to similar firms in which commitment to innovation is higher. Innovation activity, for the most part, requires significant financial resources if it is to yield successful innovative outputs. Similarly, achieving patents requires managerial time to champion innovations with the intent of taking them to the marketplace. Investing both financial resources and time reflects managerial risk taking.

One important element of the relationship between acquisitions and innovation is the amount of managerial energy absorbed in negotiating deals.[20] Managers also may use acquisitions as a substitute for innovation to avoid the risk associated with investments in R&D.[21] In addition, certain firm characteristics tend to change when an acquisition or divestiture is completed; thus, by altering various firm attributes (e.g., level of debt, level of diversification, size, organizational control systems), acquisitions or divestitures also affect innovation. For example, almost by definition, firms pursuing growth through acquisitions become larger, and the range of their operations may become more diversified. In turn, increases in size and diversification affect the type of control systems used within the acquiring firm following an acquisition. The rest of this chapter outlines the relationships suggested in figure 3, except for the relationships arising from downscoping. These relationships are discussed in chapter 8.

Acquisitions as a Substitute for Innovation

Investment in R&D entails high risk because of the high failure rate of innovations.[22] Although innovation is in the best interests of and is preferred by stockholders, managers, rather than stockholders, have to bear most of the consequences of failure. In contrast, although acquisitions involve some risk, their relative certainty is attractive to many managers. Target firms have established products and markets and observable track records. In addition, acquisitions offer either immediate entrance to new markets or a larger share of one or more of the markets currently served by the firm (as in the Philip Morris example). Managers however, are tempted to act in their own self-interest, particularly when an action carries a high degree of uncertainty, because such uncertainty increases employment risk. As a result, managers often prefer making acquisitions to the riskier option of investing in R&D.[23]

Acquisitions represent one of several possible strategic actions for entering new markets. Firms may grow and develop through acquisitions or innovation and may substitute acquisitions for innovation, particularly when resources are inadequate to pursue both strategies. One example of the reduction in innovation is the fate of the David Sarnoff Research Center, which produced many innovations for RCA. among them is the electron gun, used as a receiver for the color system found in most televisions sets in the United States. In 1988 GE acquired the center as part of its acquisition of RCA. GE reduced the center staff by 25 percent by discharging three hundred employees and then transferred ownership of the center to SRI International, an independent nonprofit organization. NBC, a division of RCA, had the largest market share of viewers in 1986, when it was acquired by GE. However, NBC failed to produce any major hit shows in 1989 and 1990. As a result, its ratings fell by 12 percent, and its operating profit was reduced by 27 percent in 1990.

NBC's loss of market share, and consequent loss of profit for its parent, GE, and the virtual giveaway of the acclaimed Sarnoff Research Center show that even good firms like GE sometimes stumble. Furthermore, the example dramatically illustrates the linkage between acquisitions and innovation. Well-known authors and consultants criticized GE for its actions during this period; for example, Michael Porter of Harvard suggested that GE's strategy led managers to focus on size rather than on building competitive advantage, and Tom Peters argued that the strategy also stifled creativity, noting that GE had not created a new business in decades.[24] Arguably, GE's lack of business innovation may have been created by its fascination with and its emphasis on mergers and acquisitions. For example, in 1988, GE reduced total R&D expenditures by $300 million from their 1987 level. (Recognizing this problem,

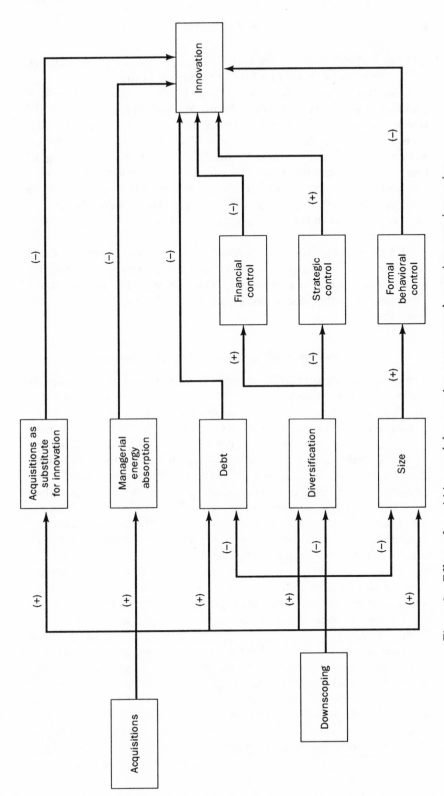

Figure 3. Effects of acquisitions and downscoping on managers' commitment to innovation

CEO Jack Welch began in the early 1990s a process designed to change GE's culture and to prepare it for the twenty-first century.)

One fact is clear: U.S. firms have been highly attracted to acquisitive growth in the last three decades. Dennis Maxwell, vice president of SRI International, has claimed that one result of the frenzied pace of acquisitions has been a reduction in in-house R&D by acquiring companies. Kenneth Flamm, an economist for the Brookings Institution, has argued that acquisitions and other types of restructuring have focused executives on short-term returns, contributing to a reduction in basic research. In 1988 approximately 3 percent of R&D expenditures were allocated to basic research, down from 5.4 percent in 1979. Total R&D expenditures may also have been reduced.

Of course, acquisitions may also be used to support innovation. A company may, for example, buy a firm that has manufacturing capability which complements the commercialization potential of a new innovation. However, often the process represents a potential way for managers to avoid risk.

Acquisitions and Managerial Energy Absorption

The acquisitions process often absorbs significant amounts of managerial energy and time, thereby diverting attention from other important matters. Firms following an active strategy of acquisitions search for viable acquisition candidates, which requires extensive data gathering and analyses. Although top executives generally are not involved in the data gathering and analyses, they must review all data to narrow the list of candidates. Furthermore, they must select the acquisition target(s) and formulate an effective acquisition strategy. Once this is accomplished, negotiations begin. Negotiations alone can consume considerable time, particularly if the acquisition involves an unfriendly takeover. This process, then, demands much attention and energy on the part of executives (from both the acquiring and acquired firms). As a result, managers' attention is often diverted from other internal matters and in particular from important long-term issues such as allocating R&D investments and selecting and championing new products to take to the market.

Operations in firms that are being pursued vigorously for acquisition frequently resemble a state of "suspended animation." Daily operations continue, but decisions requiring long-term commitments often are postponed pending outcome of the merger. In fact, target firm managers generally are reluctant to make long-term commitments of resources (e.g., R&D expenditures) unless for defensive purposes (e.g., to reduce the firm's cash position, thus making the firm less attractive for acquisition). The process of acquisition therefore creates a short-term perspective and heightens risk aversion among top managers of both the acquiring and the target firms. Time and energy spent on acquisitions are traded for time and energy that could have been spent on operational and long-term strategic decisions.

Two examples of this diversion of energy are illustrated in the acquisition of Kraft and of R.J.R. Nabisco's leveraged buyout. Basing their views on Philip Morris's actions following its acquisition of General Foods, experts predicted that the conglomerate's acquisition of Kraft would mean more retreads of current products in multiple varieties (e.g., "new and improved" versions). Product-line extensions were the least risky way for Philip Morris to pursue its markets; profits were increased at the possible expense of future growth through new product development. While Philip Morris focused on product-line extensions in its General Foods and Kraft businesses, Nestlé, in contrast, invested in and developed innovations in nutrition, health foods, and elaborate freshly prepared chilled (refrigerated, not frozen) entrees.[25]

After R.J.R. Nabisco's leveraged buyout by Kohlberg, Kravis, Roberts & Company, Nabisco's business grew by 40 percent and RJR's operating income increased by 31 percent. However, Nabisco also aggressively reduced costs by firing high-paid research engineers and reducing marketing expenditures. Thus, much of its innovative potential was reduced after the buyout.[26]

Debt and Innovation

The effects of debt after an acquisition may be demonstrated by looking at the Eastman Kodak $5.1 billion acquisition of Sterling Drug. Kodak executives felt they could install "Kodak management" and turn around the drug company's performance. In particular, Kodak management focused on Sterling's R&D operation. However, Sterling's problems became more severe after Kodak's acquisition and the installation of Kodak's management team. Its new drugs did not test well, while at the same time its existing product line faced fierce competition. Nonetheless, Kodak managers quietly cut projects that were predicted to generate new products for Sterling. As a result, debt costs on the Sterling acquisition exceeded the firm's operating earnings by $50 million in 1989. Critics argued that Kodak had paid too much for a business that it lacked the expertise to manage. In reality, Kodak management was not doing a good job managing even its own business. The company's earnings in 1991 and 1992 were lackluster and termed unsatisfactory by its chairman, Kay R. Whitmore. In fact, Kodak management came under significant criticism; the chief financial officer admitted that Kodak needed to reduce its $10 billion debt.[27] For these reasons, the board replaced Whitmore.

The use of debt as a source of capital has increased since Modigliani and Miller did their classic work.[28] Often, there is a need for substantial resources to complete acquisitions, and firms have commonly used leverage as one source of such capital. Firms following an acquisition strategy (especially those acquiring unrelated businesses) often employ more leverage than do other types of firms.[29] These firms may increase diversification to reduce their business risk (although greater amounts of leverage increases financial risk). In turn, these firms often reduce costs to decrease their financial risk, thereby using potential increased returns to pay debt costs and reduce overall debt.

Moreover, high levels of debt may create greater managerial risk aversion because of the increased power of debt holders, who tend to be more risk averse than stockholders (equity holders).[30] As debt holders gain power, they may force the firm to avoid risky projects. Lack of capital and an avoidance of risk form major barriers to innovation, as we have seen in the Kodak example.[31] A lack of internal capital and/or a lack of access to increased equity capital forces firms to employ additional leverage. Furthermore, debt is more costly for risky projects in which the assets are not usable for other purposes (not valuable to external parties), such as the creation of innovation through R&D.[32]

It is unlikely that R&D will be financed through debt. Assets from acquisitions are perceived to be more valuable to other parties (more easily sold to other parties if necessary) and thus are more likely to be financed through debt. For example, existing assets associated with acquisition are easier to collateralize, whereas R&D is not acceptable as collateral. This line of reasoning is supported by the empirical work showing a negative relationship between R&D intensity and long-term debt.[33] Increasing levels of debt may produce managerial risk aversion and, in turn, a lower level of innovation.

Moreover, economic gains to acquiring firms stem from private and valuable information of the acquirer, unique synergies between the target and the acquirer, or luck.[34] For highly leveraged firms, internal funds may be insufficient to finance large acquisitions. Therefore, highly leveraged firms generally must finance large acquisitions with external capital, thereby signaling to competitors their acquisition strategy. If the gains from the acquisition result from unique synergies, the information leaked during the process of raising external capital will dissipate the gains from the acquisition, or the need to finance the acquisition externally may leak information to other potential acquirers, putting the anticipated gain to the acquirer from the acquisition at risk during a bidding war. In short, the benefits of acquirers are substantially reduced by disclosure of debt and equity markets.

Diversification, Size, and Innovation

Acquisitions produce larger firms and often result in an additional degree of diversification. Because managers naturally wish to increase their own compensation, they may find acquisition a popular strategy. As chapter 3 suggested, top executives search for means to exert or maintain organizational control. As diversification increases, especially through acquisitive growth, top-level managers find it increasingly difficult to process effectively the volume of information they receive.[35] As corporate executives struggle to cope with their growing spans of control, they increasingly emphasize financial controls (e.g., ROI goals) over strategic controls (evaluation of strategic actions).[36] The use of short-run performance controls, as indicated in chapter 1, may lead to less innovation and ultimately to depressed market values for diversified firms.

Larger organizations promote more structural complexity, formalization, and decentralization, all of which are negatively related to new product introductions. Furthermore, larger firms tend to adopt centralized and cumbersome review procedures for evaluating investments in new projects. In general, these formal bureaucratic or behavioral controls (actions that formalize authority and reporting relationships, resulting in standardized procedures and predictable behaviors) often result in lower levels of innovation.[37]

Bureaucratic controls may involve planning, budgeting, and auditing procedures that structure managerial actions so that predictable outcomes are achieved. Although bureaucratic controls are more applicable if interdependence exists between business units, at lower levels these controls result in formalization of role behaviors. As bureaucratic controls result in more rigid and standardized behavior, they in turn contribute to organizational inertia and thereby reduce innovation. As a result, innovation is likely to decrease as formalized controls are increased.

In summary, acquisitions may lead to an emphasis on both financial and bureaucratic controls that have negative effects on innovation. This is especially true when top managers' understanding of business unit operations is insufficient, and strategic control is therefore weak. Financial controls are often emphasized primarily because of the firm's larger size and diversification.

Empirical Research Findings

We conducted a study in which the effects of acquisitions on R&D intensity (R&D divided by firm sales) and patent intensity (the number of patents obtained divided by firm sales) were examined.[38] Data were collected on 191 acquisitions that were completed between 1970 and 1986 and that involved 29 different industries. The design examined combined acquiring and target firm data for three years prior to the merger and for three years after merger completion. The results indicate that R&D intensity increased slightly in the postmerger period. However, the increases resulted primarily from overall growth in R&D expenditures in the acquiring and the target firms' industries. In fact, when adjusted for average industry R&D intensity, acquiring firms invest less (compared to the industry as a whole) in R&D after acquisitions.

Some have argued that R&D spending should decrease after acquisitions because of economies of scale or scope.[39] Schumpeter's classic work in economics suggests that larger firms (e.g., those created by mergers) enjoy scale economies and therefore operate more efficiently. Thus, larger firms are thought to use R&D inputs more efficiently. We not only examined R&D inputs but also measured R&D outputs (measured by patent intensity, which can be thought of as a measure of R&D input efficiency). Our results showed that acquisitions also have a negative effect on patent intensity. The average annual change in new patents for firms prior to acquisition was positive ($+1.69$) but was negative (-1.88) after acquisition. Clearly, these results do not support the notion that firms derive efficiencies in R&D through acquisitions. Rather, the results suggest a negative effect of acquisitions on innovation, as measured by both R&D inputs and outputs.

Others have found that R&D intensity is negatively related to high levels of diversification in firms using the M-form structure.[40] Low levels of diversification within M-form firms may be positively related to R&D investment. Advocates of the market for corporate control suggest that the takeovers in the 1980s were focused on poorly performing firms. The purpose was to gain control of underperforming (undervalued) firms, replace poor managers, and increase the efficiency of those firms. However, a recent study of the takeover attempts of the top eight corporate raiders in the 1980s showed that more than 50 percent of their takeover attempts were focused on firms that were outperforming their industries.[41] This suggests that the market for corporate control may not be as efficient as once thought. Also, takeover attempts aimed at high-performing firms may have forced these firms to take actions (e.g., assume greater debt, make acquisitions to use up available cash) in order to reduce their attractiveness and that produce lower performance over time. Therefore, the takeover market may have produced poorer performance in both the short and the long term for many firms.

The diversification activities of the 1960s and 1970s were not very successful. David Ravenscraft and Frederic Scherer have estimated that one third of the purchased in the 1960s and 1970s were sold off and that these sell-offs were precipitated by poor managerial control leading to poor relative performance. The arguments presented herein suggest that cumulative loss of control is the result, at least in part, of higher levels of diversification. Restructuring divestitures likely reduces the level of diversification so that better strategic control may be established.

Summary

Based on our arguments and our review of empirical evidence, it can be concluded that merged firms as a rule invest less in innovation than do their industry counterparts. It appears that managers are able to acquire technology and/or products that may be new to the firm but not necessarily new to the market.[42] Therefore, acquisitions may be utilized by managers as a substitute for innovation. However, the fact that relative

R&D expenditures and resulting outputs (e.g., patents) are reduced following acquisitions suggests that, over time, acquired firms become less innovative. It may be, for instance, that patents within target firms are not pursued as a result of the loss of innovation champions within the firm. This loss may occur because target firms experience high turnover among their managers.[43] Furthermore, the reduction in the relative number of patents obtained following acquisitions suggests that relatively young technologies are not being acquired, or that acquired technologies are not being fully exploited by the merged firm.

Increases in leverage are usually accompanied by decreases in relative R&D investment after acquisition. Many firms increase debt in order to finance acquisitions. As a result, more revenues must be used to service debt costs and to reduce debt. To accomplish this, other expenditures may have to be reduced, with long-term investments such as R&D likely targets. Increased leverage also may be strategically costly because of information disclosures to competitors leaked through capital markets.

Executives in nondiversified firms can more readily emphasize strategic controls in managing related businesses. They have smaller spans of control and fewer information-processing demands as they evaluate the performance of divisions. However, as firms diversify, corporate executives have greater spans of control and higher information-processing demands, leading them to emphasize financial controls. These controls focus divisional managers on short-term results and increase managerial risk aversion. Furthermore, incentive compensation schemes for divisional managers often are tied to financial performance criteria, providing incentives for managers to reduce investments in long-term projects (e.g., R&D) and to maximize short-term financial performance.[44] We have suggested that acquisitive growth firms are becoming more diversified and have lower R&D investments than do their less diversified competitors.

We also found that postmerger increases in size are also accompanied by corresponding reductions in R&D investments. Because merged firms are larger, many may have moved beyond the point where the positive effects of size on innovation (e.g., economies of scale, increasing specialization, quality colleagues, and ability to exploit opportunities) level off. Commitments to existing technology therefore become stronger and bureaucratic controls are applied, producing inertia. Bureaucratic controls and commitment to the status quo have increasingly negative effects on managers' commitment to innovation. As a result, managers may invest fewer resources in R&D.

The evidence reviewed has significant implications for executives. Acquisitive growth became increasingly popular in the 1980s and is likely to continue, possibly at a reduced rate in the U.S. but at an increased rate in Europe, in the 1990s. While the short-term effects of reduced investments in R&D may appear negligible, the long-term effects on a firm's competitiveness may be far more significant. The reduced competitiveness of U.S. and European firms in international markets may be partly the result of acquisitive growth strategies. While some argue that mergers improve acquired firms' shareholder value, the evidence reviewed in this chapter suggests that caution is necessary in predicting the long-range effects of acquisitions on acquiring firms' shareholder value.

The examples offered in this chapter suggest that managers, especially in R&D-intensive industries, should approach acquisitions carefully and with caution, because past acquisition activity appears to have contributed substantially to the need to reduce overdiversification through restructuring. However, managers may consider the following suggestions:

- Approach acquisitions cautiously, and seek acquisitions with highly complementary assets where positive synergy can be created.
- Avoid too much diversification.
- Maintain the debt/equity at reasonable levels.
- Manage growth so that it occurs neither too fast nor allows the firm to grow too large.
- Attempt to balance financial and strategic controls, and emphasize evaluation of divisional managers' strategic actions/performance.

Notes

1. Freedman, A. M. 1988. Philip Morris's bid for Kraft could limit product innovation. *The Wall Street Journal*, October 20:A–1.

2. Sellers, P. 1992. Can he keep Philip Morris growing? *Fortune*, April 6:92.

3. Ravenscraft, D. J., & Scherer, F. M. 1987. *Mergers, Sell-offs and Economic Efficiency*. Washington, D.C.: The Brookings Institution.

4. Barney, J. 1988. Returns to bidding firms in mergers and acquisitions: Reconsidering the relatedness hypothesis. *Strategic Management Journal* 9:71–78.

5. Hitt, M. A., Hoskisson, R. E., & Harrison, J. S. 1991. Strategic competitiveness in the 1990's: Challenges and opportunities for U.S. executives. *Academy of Management Executive* 5(2):7–22.

6. Spiers, J. 1991. A coming surge in capital spending. *Fortune*, April 22:113–19.

7. Ibid., p. 114.

8. Roach, S. S. 1989. Living with corporate debt. *Journal of Applied Corporate Finance* 2(1):19–30.

9. Dumaine, B. 1991. The bureaucracy busters. *Fortune*, June 17:36–50.

10. Fisher, A. B. 1991. Don't be afraid of the big bad debt. *Fortune*, April 22:121–28.

11. Jensen, M. C. 1986. Agency costs of free cash flow, corporate finance takeovers. *American Economic Review* 76:323–29.

12. Hall, B. H. 1990. The impact of corporate restructuring on industrial research and development. *Brookings Papers on Economic Activity* 3:85–135.

13. Bettis, R. A. 1983. Modern financial theory, corporate strategy and public policy: Three conundrums. *Academy of Management Review* 8:406–15.

14. Porter, M. E. 1980. *Competitive Strategy: Techniques for Analyzing Industries and Competitors.* New York: Free Press.

15. Jarrell, G. A., & Bradley, M. 1980. The economic effects of federal and state regulations of cash tender offers. *Journal of Law and Economics* 23:371–407.

16. Hitt, M. A., Hoskisson, R. E., Ireland, R. D., & Harrison, J. S. 1991. The effect of acquisitions on R&D inputs and outputs. *Academy of Management Journal* 34:693–706.

17. Franko, L. G. 1989. Global corporate competition: Who's winning, who's losing, and the R&D factor as one reason why. *Strategic Management Journal* 10:449.

18. Chandler, A. 1990. *Scale and Scope: The Dynamics of Industrial Capitalism.* Cambridge, Mass.: Belknap Press.

19. Porter, M. E. 1987. From competitive advantage to corporate strategy. *Harvard Business Review* 65(3):43–59; Williams, J. R., Paez, B. L., & Sanders, L. 1988. Conglomerates revisited. *Strategy Management Journal* 9:403–14.

20. Walsh, J. P. 1989. Doing a deal: Merger and acquisition negotiations and their impact upon target company top management turnover. *Strategic Management Journal* 10:307–22.

21. Hitt, M. A., Hoskisson, R. E., & Ireland, R. D. 1990. Acquisitive growth and commitment to innovation in M-form firms. *Strategic Management Journal* (Special Issue) 11:29–47.

22. Biggadike, R. 1979. The risky business of diversification. *Harvard Business Review* 57:103–11.

23. Constable, J. 1986. Diversification as a factor in U.K. industrial strategy. *Long Range Planning* 19:52–60.

24. Taylor, J. H. 1991. General Electric: Whither NBC's peacock? *Business Week*, March 4:40–41.

25. Browning, E. S. 1992. Nestle looks to realms beyond food for the future: Swiss company maps takeovers, including skin care, pharmaceuticals. *The Wall Street Journal*, May 12:B–40.

26. Waldman, P. 1989. After RJR's buy-out: Successes, worries, operating profits soar, but questions remain. *The Wall Street Journal*, October 27:B–10.

27. Hammonds, K. H. 1989. Kodak may wish it never went to the drugstore. *Business Week*, December 4:72, 76. Maremont, M., & Lesly, E. 1993. Getting the picture: Kodak finally heeds the shareholders. *Business Week*, February 1:24–26.

28. Modigliani, F., & Miller, M. H. 1958. The cost of capital, corporation finance and the theory of investment. *American Economic Review* 48:261–97.

29. Michel, A., & Shaked, I. 1985. Evaluating merger performance. *California Management Review* 27:109–18.

30. Smith C. L., & Warner, J. B. 1979. Bankruptcy, secured debt, and optimal capital structure: A comment. *Journal of Finance* 34:247–51.

31. Myers, R. L. 1984. Lowering barriers to innovation. *Journal of Business Strategy* 5:80–82.

32. Williamson, O. E. 1988. Corporate finance and corporate governance. *Journal of Finance* 48:567–91.

33. Baysinger, B. D., & Hoskisson, R. E. 1989. Diversification strategy and R&D intensity in large multiproduct firms. *Academy of Management Journal* 32:310–32.

34. Barney, J. B., Returns to bidding firms.

35. Hill, C. W. L., & Hoskisson, R. E. 1987. Strategy and structure in the multiproduct firm. *Academy of Management Review* 12:331–41.

36. Hoskisson, R. E., & Hitt, M. A. 1988. Strategic control systems and relative R&D investment in large multiproduct firms. *Strategic Management Journal* 9:605–21.

37. Hlavcek, J. D., & Thompson, V. A. 1978. Bureaucracy and venture failures. *Academy of Management Review* 3:242–48.

38. Hitt et al., The effect of acquisitions.

39. Morbey, G. K., & Reithner, R. M. 1990. How R&D affects sales growth, productivity and profitability. *Research-Technology Management* May–June:11–14.

40. Baysinger, B. D., & Hoskisson, R. E., Diversification strategy; Hill, C. W. L., & Snell, S. A. 1988. External control, corporate strategy and firm performance in research intensive industry. *Strategic Management Journal* 9:577–90; Hill, C. W. L., & Snell, S. A. 1989. Effects of ownership structure and control on corporate productivity. *Academy of Management Journal* 23:25–46; Hoskisson & Hitt, Strategic control systems.

41. Walsh, J. P., & Kosnik, R. 1993. Corporate raiders and their disciplinary role in the market for corporate control. *Academy of Management Journal* 36:671–700.

42. Clarke, K., Ford, D., & Saren, M. 1989. Company technology strategy. *R&D Management* 19:215–29.

43. Walsh, J. P. 1988. Top management turnover following mergers and acquisitions. *Strategic Management Journal* 9:173–83.

44. Hoskisson, R. E., Hitt, M. A., & Hill, C. W. L. 1993. Managerial incentives and investment in R&D in large multiproduct firms. *Organization Science* 4:325–41.

5

Corporate Refocusing and Global Strategic Competitiveness

In a 1987 survey of 4,000 executives, 92 percent agreed that U.S. competitiveness was declining. A concurrent survey of opinion leaders (e.g., economists, political leaders, small business owners, labor leaders, CEOs of large corporations) revealed a similar conclusion.[1] While the decline of U.S. competitiveness against Japanese firms has been widely publicized, America's competitiveness problems are not limited to its trade deficit with Japan. According to a report by the Council on Competitiveness, the United States has not fared well in comparison to Canada, France, Italy, the United Kingdom, or West Germany either. While the United States still ranks first in productivity, each of these six countries have outperformed the United States in gains in standard of living, trade, productivity and investment since 1974.[2] Another key study traced the world market share of firms in fifteen major industries over 20 years. The United States held over two-thirds of the world market in ten of these industries in 1960; in 1970 it still dominated nine industries. In 1980, however, U.S. domination was limited to only three industries (aerospace, paper, and computers and office equipment).[3] While some U.S. firms always remained competitive (e.g., Merck) and others have regained competitive strength, particularly in special market niches (e.g., Chrysler), U.S. industry continues to have significant problems. In fact, Michael Porter of Harvard suggests that one of the main reasons for the competitiveness problems experienced by U.S. firms in the early 1990s is an ineffective system of allocating investment capital within and across firms.[4]

Although there is much disagreement over the cause of decline, it is imperative that U.S. firms remain competitive in technology to stay in the race over the long term. This chapter describes the general state of U.S. competitiveness and explains why there is a need for restructuring (refocusing strategy) to improve competitiveness.

The competitiveness problems are perhaps best exemplified by the loss of market share experienced by General Motors. In 1978 GM had 48 percent of the domestic automobile market. In 1993 it held only a 33 percent share, reflecting a 15 percent decline in 15 years.[5] Much of GM's reduction in share of the domestic automobile market was due to Japanese competition—along with Ford's improvement in competitiveness at GM's expense. (Other reasons for GM's decline were given in chapter 2.)

Although the United States is among the leading countries in technology and innovation, that leadership is eroding. For instance, the United States remains the leader in central processing computer chips, but the Japanese have overtaken the United States in memory chips. While the central processing chips are the main brain of the computer, the memory chips represent the bulk of sales.

The reasons for this competitiveness erosion are complex. Some have argued that U.S. firms have not been effective in their research and development efforts. Evidence of this fact is shown in the declining number of patents issued to large U.S. firms.[6] U.S. firms have tended to reduce R&D expenditures and to focus on short-term gains. U.S. executives seem unwilling to accept the long-term risks of innovation because of the uncertainty of commercial success. These problems are exacerbated by the fact that the overwhelming majority of U.S. R&D investment is concentrated in large firms; more than 85 percent of R&D expenditures are made in firms with greater than 10,000 employees.[7] However, small firms in the United States are more effective at producing innovative products, whereas large firms are more effective at the mass production and distribution of those products. (Large firms spend almost twice as much on R&D per patent as do small firms.) In addition, small firms utilize a greater proportion of their patents than do large firms, suggesting that large firms may not effectively exploit innovative ideas.[8]

Even if Japanese and U.S. firms in the same industries spend comparable resources on R&D and on technology transfer, they allocate those resources quite differently. Japanese firms often gain competitive advantages through a substantial reduction in production costs, whereas U.S. firms frequently invest more in marketing start-up. That is, U.S. firms emphasize marketing strategies over technical performance and production efficiency. The percentage of innovation costs allocated to tooling and manufacturing equipment in Japanese firms is almost 100 percent higher than the percentage in U.S. firms. Finally, Japanese firms allocate about two thirds of their R&D resources to improve process technology, whereas U.S. firms allocate only one third of R&D resources to such efforts.[9]

Differences in the cost of labor and the cost of capital are usually blamed for the decline of U.S. competitiveness. Although in the past these explanations were compelling, since 1980 their significance has faded as these costs have come closer to parity in the leading industrial nations. In this chapter we argue that issues of strategic competitiveness—strategic concerns affecting firm competitiveness that are under managers' direct or indirect control—are becoming more salient to the competitiveness problem. We suggest that the managerial focus on the short term in large firms has resulted from the overemphasis on ROI-based financial controls. We have discussed the effects of financial controls and incentives on managerial risk taking and on the innovation process in M-form firms pursuing a strategy of diversification, primarily through acquisitive growth (chapter 4), as well as the ways that the governance of large M-form firms allowed diversified growth to continue relatively unabated until the mid-1980s (chapter 3). A strong contributing factor to the productivity and technology malaise is managers' unwillingness to bear the costs and risks of long-run innovative product and process development.

Overdiversification and managerial risk aversion have reduced the competitiveness of U.S. firms over the last two decades.[10] The relationship between diversification and R&D investment may be a critical competitiveness issue.[11] For example, Laurence Franko's extensive multinational study of 15 industries in several countries strongly suggests the importance of innovation for competitiveness.[12]

Despite the general consensus that the competitiveness of U.S. firms has declined, there is little agreement as to the exact causes. In this chapter we review traditional explanations that focus on differences in economic structure and on historical and cultural differences. We then move beyond these arguments and suggest that strategic competitiveness issues are amenable to managers' influence and may no longer be dictated by economic structure, culture, or history.

Global Strategic Competitiveness

Figure 4 presents a number of factors affecting strategic competitiveness. We briefly review the influence of economic structure and of historical and cultural factors (dashed arrows) and state why some of these influences may not be as strong as they were in the past. It is also important to note that managers can do little to influence these problems directly. Therefore, our focus is on those strategic issues that managers can affect, specifically, directions for restructuring and strategic refocusing.[13]

Economic Structure Differences

A number of authorities have suggested that the disparity between U.S. and foreign competitiveness is directly related to differences in the respective educational systems, the cost of labor, and the cost of capital.

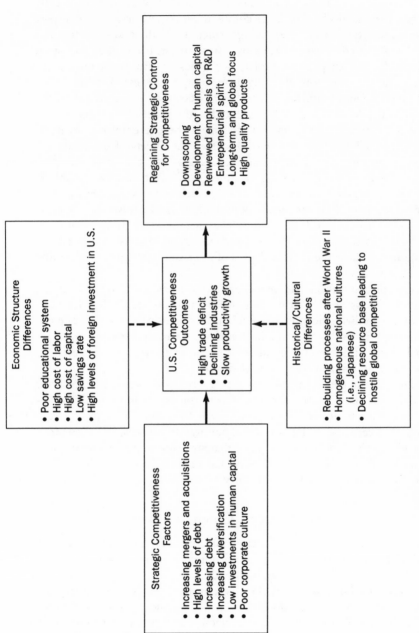

Figure 4. Causes and competitiveness consequences (*Source:* Hitt, M. A, Hoskisson, R. E., & Harrison, J. S., 1991. Strategic Competitiveness in the 1990s: Challenges and Opportunities for U.S. Executives. *Academy of Management Executive* 5(2): 7–22.) Copyright The Academy of Management Executive.

Associated with these problems are the low U.S. savings rate and increases in foreign investment in the United States.

Poor educational system

Deficiencies in the basic educational system in the United States may be a partial cause of lower U.S. productivity growth. It is estimated that approximately 20 percent of adult Americans are functionally illiterate and that more than 25 percent of U.S. high school students do not graduate. In addition, U.S. high school seniors' math skills are significantly lower than those of comparable students from several foreign countries. An example demonstrates the effects of this poor showing: A company built a new plant in the United States with computer-integrated manufacturing and statistical process controls but found that the employees could not operate the equipment because 25 percent of them were illiterate.[14] A special report presented by *Business Week* concluded that the long-term neglect of human capital in the United States is undermining the nation's economic future.[15] Unfortunately, managers have little direct control over the basic educational system, although they certainly may lobby national and local governments for educational reform.

High cost of labor

The high cost of U.S. labor in comparison to labor costs in other nations, especially Pacific Rim countries, is often described as a structural problem affecting competitiveness. Although this may continue to be the case for most of the developing countries in the Pacific Rim, such as Taiwan and Korea, the evidence suggests that labor costs in the United States's major trading partner in the area, Japan, are approaching parity with the United States. The Bureau of Labor Statistics reported that the average cost per hour of wages in 1988 was $13.90 in the United States, compared to $13.14 in Japan. Therefore, low wages no longer provide a distinct competitive edge for the Japanese. In addition, although salaries of top U.S. managers are substantially higher than those of their Japanese counterparts, Japanese middle managers receive higher compensation on average than do those in the United States (Japan = $85,649; U.S. = $56,505).[16] Additionally, high labor costs do not automatically lead to a competitive disadvantage. Some U.S. firms (e.g., Lincoln Electric and Nucor Steel) have been able to use a reward system to produce high efficiency, quality, and innovation. Even though Lincoln, for example, has high labor costs, it also has high labor productivity. Furthermore, the cost of labor is often less than 15 percent of total product cost, so high labor costs alone do not explain the United States's competitive decline.

High cost of capital/low savings rate

Experts argue that U.S. firms must improve their capital investment, with particular emphasis on automation to reduce labor costs. This change is necessary if U.S. firms are to match the productivity growth of foreign competitors. However, it is often suggested that the high cost of capital in the United States discourages investment in capital equipment. Nevertheless, recent evidence suggests that major inputs affecting the cost of capital in Japan and in the United States may be more similar than previously acknowledged.

Kenichi Ohmae has argued that, because of measurement errors, previously reported differences in savings rates for Japanese (16.6%) and for Americans (4.3%) may not be accurate. Using Ohmae's adjustments and adjusting for comparable asset bases, the Bank of Japan estimated the U.S. savings rate to be 14.7 percent and that for the Japanese to be 16.7 percent. Furthermore, the U.S. rate has been increasing.[17] These figures suggest that the cost of capital in the two countries may be closer than earlier estimates showed.

Although his findings are the subject of debate, Milton Friedman has suggested that U.S. trade and budget deficits are a strength rather than a weakness because they have been offset by a surplus in the U.S. capital account. He maintains that U.S. policy has encouraged holders of foreign assets—both U.S. and foreign holders—to add to their dollar assets and notes: "It is a mystery to me why, to take a specific example, it is regarded as a sign of Japanese strength and U.S. weakness that the Japanese find it more attractive to invest in the U.S. than in Japan."[18]

Historical/National Cultural Differences

Some experts have linked the decline of U.S. competitiveness to historical trends in the global economy. Still others attribute the decline to a related factor, namely, cultural differences across national borders.

Rebuilding processes
The relatively low productivity gains made by U.S. firms are often attributed to the post–World War II rebuilding processes in Germany and Japan. The economic infrastructure of these countries was decimated during World War II, but postwar rebuilding processes allowed newer and more productive plant and equipment to replace destroyed assets. Although Germany and Japan may have had a head start in acquiring updated plants and machinery, this advantage has diminished over time and probably accounts for very little new current productivity growth.

Declining resource base
Another view is that the growth rate of the global economy has been declining because of increasingly scarce resources. This decline has created a more hostile environment, especially for mature basic manufacturing industries such as steel, tire and rubber, auto, and home appliances. This trend places increased emphasis on stronger competitive strategy,

either cost leadership or product differentiation.[19] Similarly, at the corporate level, the economics of resource sharing translate into an emphasis on related diversification. Michael Porter suggests that "the environment in most of the developed world is one of relatively slow growth coupled with growing global competition."[20] This slower growth has made competitiveness more difficult to achieve. Although this historical trend has affected competitiveness, American managers now realize that they must compete in global markets to be successful against both foreign and domestic players.

Homogeneous national cultures

Culture has been defined as "the interactive aggregate of common characteristics that influence a human group's response to its environment."[21] It is often suggested that the homogeneity and the work ethic associated with Japanese culture have contributed strongly to the competitive ability of Japanese firms. However, management practices associated with Japanese culture have been changing with continued industrial growth, and the ideals of lifetime employment, a seniority-based wage system, and consensus decision making have been undergoing significant changes. The improving standard of living in Japan means that Japanese firms can no longer compete on the basis of production efficiencies alone; competition from other low-cost producers in South Korea and Taiwan is forcing them to move to more high–end product markets for which the traditional Japanese culture and educational systems are not particularly well suited. Also, incentives used in the past no longer have the same motivational value for a new generation in the Japanese workforce that is less willing to conform rigidly to traditional social norms. These trends, typical of a modern industrialized society, are creating greater similarities between American and Japanese cultures.

Other experts have cited additional reasons for the convergence of Japanese and American cultures. For example, although some individual behaviors within organizations may be different because of differences in national culture, organizational attributes such as structure, rules, and procedures are similar among organizations in different national cultures. This suggests that as a nation industrializes, formal aspects of organizations tend to be similar to those found in organizations in other industrialized nations. Over the long term, these changes are likely to lessen the cultural effects on competitiveness; although behavioral differences are likely to persist because of culture, firm and economic characteristics are likely to converge.[22]

Symbolizing the increasing similarity among Japanese and U.S. firms are the problems experienced by Honda and the firm's reaction to them: "We'd get the people from research, sales, and production together . . . and everyone would say 'Not this' and 'Not that.' We'd talk, but there would be no agreement. . . . Product planning has to be on a tight schedule. But we'd have another discussion, and another study and then more preparation. And finally, the decision would come months later."[23]

This quote emphasizes problems of integration typical of the product development process at an American firm, but the speaker is Honda's CEO, Nobuhiko Kawamoto, describing his frustrations as an engineer developing new products for Honda.

Honda has grown more conservative over time, and its fortunes have suffered as a result. Honda's earnings fell 41 percent for fiscal year 1993 and are expected to decline another 40 percent in fiscal year 1994. Its sales of vehicles have declined, and its share of the passenger car market has dropped both in Japan and in the United States. Honda's 1993 market share in Japan was below 10 percent, down from almost 11 percent in 1992. The reduction in its share of the U.S. market is more dramatic; it fell from a high of 9.9 percent in 1991 to approximately 7.5 percent in 1993.[24] To reverse these trends, Mr. Kawamoto is changing Honda's structure and trying to shake up its corporate culture. For example, he is recentralizing control over the firm's automotive business in Japan and introducing private offices in Honda's communal executive suite at its Tokyo headquarters. Individual responsibility for decisions is being emphasized over group decision making. In short, Honda is moving toward the typical U.S. organizational style, just when many U.S. firms are trying to institute Japanese-style management teamwork. Mr. Kawamato has said he is trying to implement more flexible operations in Honda. Regardless, these moves exemplify the increasing similarity of U.S. and Japanese business operations.[25]

Strategic Competitiveness

Although the factors discussed in the preceding section affect competitiveness, they no longer explain as much of the difference in competitiveness as they have in the past. The good news for U.S. managers is that the remaining strategic factors, those most critical to relative competitiveness, are largely under their control.

An important source of the decline in U.S. strategic competitiveness is poor development of new product and process technologies compared to that in other countries. An indication of this problem is the lack of any significant presence by U.S. firms in the new generation of consumer electronics. For example, in the late 1960s there were as many as 18 U.S. manufacturers of television sets. By the early 1990s, however, there were no U.S. television set producers; most of the top U.S. brands (e.g., RCA, GE, Magnavox) are produced by Japanese and European firms.

There are a number of reasons for this erosion in strategic competitiveness. First, U.S. industry has been slow to translate new technology into commercial success. Second, manufacturing has been emphasized less in the U.S. than in other industrialized countries. Third, fewer resources are being invested in research and development and in technology transfer compared to international competitors. For example, U.S. firms spend approximately 1.8 percent of the gross national product (GNP) on R&D, whereas West German companies spend 2.6 percent and Japanese, 2.8 percent.[26] Furthermore, U.S. firms spend half as much of their R&D budgets on process technologies as do Japanese companies. Japanese firms also spend twice as much as U.S. firms on tooling and manufacturing equipment.

This disparity is demonstrated in the steel industry. While U.S. firms such as Inland Steel and USX have made considerable investments to modernize their manufacturing processes, Japan's Nippon Steel Company spends about $200 million annually on research. Nippon's annual research budget exceeds total R&D spending for the entire U.S. steel industry.[27] It is therefore not surprising that the number of patents issued to large U.S. firms has been declining.[28]

The importance of research and development to strategic competitiveness was demonstrated by a study showing that R&D intensity (company-sponsored research and development expenditures divided by sales) was the principal indicator of sales growth for firms in 15 global industries from 1960 to 1986.[29] Compounding the problem, as we have discussed in previous chapters, diversified U.S. firms have tended to reduce R&D expenditures and to focus on short-term profits. These actions suggest that many U.S. executives have been unwilling to accept the long-term risks of innovation because of the uncertainty of commercial success. These problems are exacerbated by the fact that the overwhelming majority of U.S. R&D investment is concentrated in large firms, the very firms that, in response to economic structure differences, historical trends, and hostile competition, are most likely to reduce the resources allocated to R&D, the area that would likely help them to recover over the long term.

Need to Restructure Large, Diversified Firms

Strategic competitiveness problems are many and complex. Managerial focus on mergers and acquisitions, high levels of debt, large size, high levels of diversification, lack of emphasis on human capital, and poor organizational culture are reflections of these problems, producing lower managerial commitment to innovation and lack of technology development that in turn often harms firm competitiveness.

High levels of corporate restructuring and refocusing in the early 1990s signaled a trend that, if implemented properly, may facilitate improvements in competitiveness by reducing both corporate diversification and company size. Restructuring also creates the opportunity to focus on important implementation concerns, such as the development of human capital and an effective corporate culture.

Government and institutional policies have also affected corporate strategy and competitiveness. Several new government policies contributed to the restructuring frenzy of the 1980s. Government policy changes included antitrust amendments and changes in policy enforcement, new state takeover laws, and individual and corporate tax rate changes. Institutional policy changes included increased activism by institutional investors, more efficient trading exchanges, and requirements that exchanges have more outsiders on key board committees. The costs of takeovers and mergers have also been inflated by innovations in managerial resistance tactics (e.g., golden parachutes). Because these changes and tactics generally increase the cost of takeover or acquisition, the value generated by the merger must be higher to make it worthwhile.

External policy changes, in general, have contributed to the emphasis on related diversification and on creation of shareholder value over unrelated diversification and sales growth. However, pursuing a related diversification strategy by acquisition also reveals information to competitors and makes it difficult to realize competitive advantage. External acquisition financed through the capital markets reveals information to competitors. Government policy changes have created more efficient capital markets, but through these markets a firm's strategy can be exposed to competitors. The ultimate competitiveness solution will not come through acquisition of established assets, which will likely be priced such that little or no value can be gained. Although asset purchases may help in short-run commercialization projects, long-run competitiveness is established through strong strategic control and managerial emphasis on innovation and high product quality. Achieving this kind of emphasis usually requires downscoping from the diversified positions established in the 1970s and the early 1980s.

Restructuring Alternatives

Because of the severity and the pervasiveness of American companies' competitiveness problems, a major reversal of recent trends is required to restore American competitiveness. Many firms have responded to poor global performance in the 1980s by restructuring (rebuilding the strength of a firm by changing its asset structure and resource allocation patterns). Restructuring efforts often involve downsizing (reducing the size of the workforce) and/or downscoping (reducing diversification). Restructuring can also occur through divestments and acquisitions of new businesses (if the purpose is to develop and increase firm health by investing resources in those new businesses). Size reduction, debt reduction and, most important, reduction in diversification should assist managers as they attempt to regain control of their organizations. We suggest that restructuring to strategically refocus on the firm's core businesses, when conducted properly, is a useful step toward regaining strategic control. However, it is important that managers examine their approach to restructuring in order to ensure entrepreneurial renewal. One Harvard business professor, John Gabarro, has argued that firms no longer want to employ old-school turnaround artists who solve problems (e.g., debt costs) only by selling off or closing down operations. They want a new type of manager who cures sick businesses by building their strengths, rather than by bleeding them dry.[30] The remainder of this chapter is devoted to outlining these alternatives.

Change Incentives

One approach to restructuring is to readjust incentives in an attempt to create longer managerial time horizons, especially for division managers. (This alternative is examined in chapter 6.) However, although longer-term incentives can be implemented, one study has found that this approach alone does not fully reduce managerial risk aversion.[31] A related alternative is to reduce the need to focus on entrepreneurial risk taking by reducing the business portfolio to a set of mature stable businesses in which innovation is less important and financial controls are appropriate. Strategic control in such businesses is not as necessary because the firms' business environment is more certain. This scenario, of course, does not resolve the strategic competitiveness problem, although it reduces the information processing required of corporate executives by focusing on a set of unrelated mature businesses.[32] Hanson PLC has been successful in using this approach, which is examined in greater detail in chapter 9. This general approach, however, addresses the symptoms of the problem, not the underlying cause. To deal with the competitiveness problem, a set of incentives must be constructed that motivates executives to take entrepreneurial risks but also guards against managers operating in their own interest. Such an incentive system focuses on long-term performance and integrates divisional performance and overall company performance in determining incentive compensation for division managers. Most important, the incentive system is linked to performance evaluation of strategic actions, rather than short-term financial outcomes.

Agency Problems and LBOs

Restructuring may also be directed at reducing the agency problem (managers who are attempting to optimize their own welfare rather than the firm's) by changing the capital and/or ownership structure (e.g., stock repurchase programs, reductions in debt). Leveraged buyouts (LBOs), while often increasing debt, may also be included in this group. LBOs change the company's ownership from public to private and change the incentives, using free cash flows to make payments on high levels of debt. The LBO restructuring alternative is examined in chapter 7.

Some have argued that taking firms private by having large investment firms arrange for leveraged financing increases efficiency for the recapitalized firm.[33] The recapitalization usually leads to a scaled-down firm that becomes more efficient through divestiture of inefficient assets.

Furthermore, with a realigned incentive structure, owners (and debt holders) are closer to the firm and thus can monitor firm strategy more efficiently, reducing agency costs (the costs of managing the differences in objectives between owners and managers.)

It must also be recognized that increased leverage and businesses dominated by debt holders produce strategic costs. Furthermore, debt holders are traditionally more conservative than are equity holders, and debt is negatively related to R&D investment.[34] Thus, LBOs may serve to increase the efficiency of only mature businesses, where conditions are stable and debt holders prefer investment in businesses that meet cash-flow obligations to service debt. Firms in R&D-intensive industries with rapidly changing technology do not benefit from financial restructuring that increases leverage. This form of restructuring has severe limitations for R&D-intensive industries that are strategically important to national competitiveness.

Strategic Refocusing

In chapter 4 we noted that a strategy of acquisitive growth increases firm debt and size and helps create extensive diversification that in turn decreases innovation activity. However, restructuring divestitures, as described in chapter 8, may reverse the process if the strategic refocusing results in a reduction of debt, size, and diversification. Furthermore, if the strategic refocusing creates stronger strategic control, an improved emphasis on innovation is likely to follow. R&D investment improves after restructuring, without a trade-off in lower performance, unless a firm refocuses on unrelated diversification (see chapter 9).[35] Thus, strategic refocusing that succeeds in reducing debt, size, and diversification, thereby increasing use of strategic control and effective incentives, is likely to improve innovation and, therefore, competitiveness. We emphasized downscoping because it leads to improved strategic control and incentives whereas downsizing often produces short-term efficiency but also lower market share.

International Diversification

International diversification is an offensive strategy that can help meet the competitiveness challenge. (International diversification as a restructuring alternative will be explained in chapter 10.) International diversification has been used as a strategy for achieving increased competitiveness. It has a stronger positive effect on firms' performance than does product diversification. The success of international diversification is, at least, partly the result of capturing the value of innovation and spreading its costs and risks over larger and diverse markets in globally diversified firms. Expansion into international markets provides opportunities for greater returns on innovations and reduces the risk of failure because of the number of different markets in which the innovation may be applied. Furthermore, innovation may help globally diversified firms overcome local disadvantages, giving globally diversified firms incentives to continue to innovate. International diversification also often enhances firm performance because it allows the firm to exploit its core competencies across multiple markets.[36]

There are limits to the positive benefits of international diversification. For example, international diversification increases coordination, distribution, and management costs. It also creates considerable management complexity (e.g., the necessity to deal with trade barriers, logistical costs, cultural diversity, and different access to resources and skills across countries). In addition, international managers may become more interested in currency swaps rather than in product and process innovation. Firms can, however, overcome these limitations and develop a transnational capability that allows them to compete more effectively in international markets.[37]

There are other goals that need to be accomplished during strategic refocusing if restructuring is to create competitive advantage. These include building human capital and creating a strong corporate culture that emphasizes entrepreneurial risk taking and high product quality.[38]

Human Resource Development

When implementing restructuring efforts, special emphasis should be placed on human resources as described in chapter 11. Employees may become concerned about the effects of restructuring efforts on their job security and about their future opportunities with the firm. Because restructuring efforts often include a reduction in the number of middle managers, this concern is real. Restructuring firms must ensure that they retain their best talent, which requires a conscious evaluation of employee ability, along with efforts to reassure top employees about their security and about future opportunities with the firm. Workforce reductions are often made through across-the-board layoffs (e.g., layoffs of 10 percent of employees in each department). While this may be the easiest way to achieve a numerical goal, it is precisely the wrong way to reduce the workforce. Strategic leadership requires that systematic evaluation of all operating areas and personnel be conducted. Only those of the least strategic importance should be cut. Employees working in the firm's core competence should be protected. Furthermore, the most talented employees should be retained, even if they currently work in a function with little strategic importance.[39]

With the decrease in the number of managers comes the need to decentralize authority and responsibility. Employees must become technologically proficient and be able to operate autonomously. Because of the need for cost-effective operations after restructuring, employees will have less supervision and thus will be required to be more self-managing.

This requires a high level of employee skill and knowledge, particularly with the increased sophistication of new technology.[40] Restructuring thus creates a strong need for developing the firm's remaining human capital.

Corporate Culture

When AT&T restructured, as required by federal mandate, it also undertook a dramatic change of its culture at all levels to ensure that it could succeed in a new, highly competitive environment. Because restructuring represents such a drastic organizational change, it is an appropriate time to change or develop a corporate culture that facilitates strategic competitiveness.

The opportunity offered by restructuring can facilitate the development of an entrepreneurial culture. In order to maintain the benefits of restructuring, in the early 1990s GE sought to foster a corporate culture designed to sustain competitive advantage. GE however, found instituting such a change to be difficult and time consuming.

Cultivation of an effective corporate culture includes actions such as developing an entrepreneurial spirit, fostering a long-term and global focus, and reemphasizing product quality. The pursuit of opportunity must be rewarded and the penalty for failure minimized in order to reduce the fear of failure and to heighten the desire to pursue opportunities. In addition, new product champions should be identified, supported, and rewarded.

Long-term and global focus, entrepreneurial spirit, the fostering of human capital, and the promotion of high-quality products are all interrelated; it is the configuration of all these actions/emphases that promotes strategic competitiveness. Often, it is difficult to be successful at one without the others. For example, it is difficult to produce high-quality products without highly skilled employees and managers with long-term goals. Both innovation and high product quality frequently require effective integration of the various functions in activities such as product design to provide information from downline functions such as production and marketing. U.S. firms must produce and market products of equal or better quality than those of their global competitors.

Overview of Restructuring Outcomes

Managers must be encouraged to take risks and must maintain strategic control of the businesses that they enter. If financial rather than strategic control policies dominate, restructuring may allow the firm only to keep pace with the competition. But such a reactive mindset will not produce competitive advantage and likely will lead only to normal or perhaps below-normal profits. However, an offensive strategy that creates value in unique ways often leads to sustained competitive advantage and above-normal profits.

By downscoping (selling off nonessential divisions unrelated to firms' major businesses) firms can create a narrower span of control for top executives, allowing them to reassert strategic control and emphasize their strengths and resources. Rather than fostering techniques to manage information, such as the use of financial controls or portfolio techniques, companies that choose to downscope reduce the amount of information processing required of top-level managers and may also be able to reduce leverage, freeing up cash flows for use in R&D programs and human resource development programs. Downscoping, by reasserting strategic control, also allows implementation of more effective incentives and governance. Finally, the decrease in financial risk associated with debt reduction may also increase managers' willingness to accept the risks of innovative activities.

Although downsizing, in the strict sense of the term, may also provide the opportunity for reduced bureaucratic control and for debt reduction, it may also signal a market retreat (possibly because of foreign competition), instead of restructuring to regain proper strategic control (thereby hurting the firm's stock price). Downsizing may also result in loss of critical employees because retention of the best talent through voluntary programs is often difficult. Our position, therefore, is that the emphasis in restructuring should be on downscoping, rather than on downsizing. Examples of downscoping include Marriott's divestment of restaurants, American Brands' exit from foods, General Mills' withdrawal from retailing, and Allegis's (United Airlines') sale of hotel and car rental businesses.

Summary

Although some U.S. firms have become more competitive (partly because of earlier restructuring efforts), many continue to experience competitiveness problems. The share of the world market controlled by U.S. firms was relatively stable in the 1970s but declined rapidly in the 1980s. Many U.S. firms invested their resources in capital equipment instead of human capital and in acquisitions instead of new technology and product innovations. These actions resulted in a focus on the short term. However, U.S. firms clearly can reverse these trends by taking definitive strategic actions. Diversified firms must restructure and emphasize entrepreneurial cultures, risk taking, and the long term. They must invest in human capital now for returns in the future. There is much opportunity, and U.S. firms can seize it with effective executive action.

There are several implications for managers regarding the competitiveness issue and the need for restructuring:

- "Old" reasons for competitiveness differences (e.g., economic structure, national culture, history) are not as valid as they once were. Rather, managers should focus on strategic competitiveness issues that are under their direct and indirect control.

- The competitiveness problem should not be ignored because there are few, if any, industries where U.S. firms have significant structural advantages.
- The need to restructure and to refocus is paramount. However, simply downsizing (in essence, ceding market share) is not the best way to proceed.
- Because overdiversification has been and continues to be a major problem even after the deconglomeration of the 1980s and the early 1990s, downscoping through strategic refocusing is likely to produce the best results.
- Investment in a strong culture, quality designs, and in human capital is needed to compete in global markets.

Notes

1. *Harvard Business Review.* 1987. Competitiveness survey: HBR readers respond. 65(5):8–11; *Harvard Business Review* 1987. Competitiveness: 23 leaders speak out. 65(4):106–23.

2. Steers, R. M., & Miller, E. L. 1988. Management in the 1990s: The international challenge. *Academy of Management Executive* 2:21–22; *Council on Competitiveness.* 1987. Analysis of U.S. competitiveness problems, America's competitiveness crisis: Confronting the new reality, April:121–126.

3. Franko, L. G. 1989. Global corporate competition: Who's winning, who's losing, and the R&D factor as one reason why. *Strategic Management Journal* 10:449–74.

4. Porter, M. E. 1992. Capital disadvantage: America's failing capital investment system. *Harvard Business Review* 70(5):65–82.

5. Templin, N. 1993. Auto sales rose sharply in late January. *The Wall Street Journal,* February 4:A–2, B–5.

6. Ireland, R. D., Hitt, M. A., & Skivington, J. 1990. The management of R&D: Effects of diversification strategy and environment. *Research Technology Management.* 33(4):37–40.

7. National Science Foundation. 1984. *Patterns of Science and Technology Resources.*

8. Schmookler, J. 1972. *The Size of the Firm and the Growth of Knowledge. Patents, Invention, and Economic Change.* Cambridge, Mass.: Harvard University Press; Hitt, M. A., Hoskisson, R. E., & Ireland, R. D. 1990. Mergers and acquisitions and managerial commitment to innovation in M-form firms. *Strategic Management Journal* (Special Issue) 11:29–47.

9. Mansfield, E. 1988. *A Comparative Study of R and D, Innovation, and Productivity Growth in Japan and the United States: A Final Report.* Working paper, University of Pennsylvania.

10. Hayes, R. H., & Abernathy, W. J. 1980. Managing our way to economic decline. *Harvard Business Review* 58(4):67–77; Hill, C. W. L., Hitt, M. A., & Hoskisson, R. E. 1988. Declining U.S. competitiveness: Reflections on a crisis. *Academy of Management Executive* 2(1):51–60; Hitt, M. A., Hoskisson, R. E., & Harrison, J. S. 1991. Strategic competitiveness in the 1990s: Challenges and opportunities for U.S. executives. *Academy of Management Executive* 5(2):7–22.

11. Baysinger, B. D., & Hoskisson, R. E. 1989. Diversification strategy and R&D intensity in large multi-product firms. *Academy of Management Journal* 32:310–32; Hoskisson, R. E., & Hitt, M. A. 1990. Strategic control and relative R&D investment in large multi-product firms. *Strategic Management Journal* 9:605–21; Hitt et al. 1990. Mergers and acquisitions. Hoskisson, R. E., & Johnson, R. A. 1992. Corporate restructuring and strategic change: The effect on diversification strategy and R&D Intensity. *Strategic Management Journal* 13:625–34.

12. Franko, Global corporate competition.

13. Much of this discussion is based on information from Hitt, Hoskisson, & Harrison, Strategic competitiveness.

14. Stewart, T. A. 1990. Lessons from U.S. business blunders. *Fortune*, April 23:128.

15. Penner, K. 1988. It's time to put our money where our future is. *Business Week*, September 19:140–41.

16. *Houston Chronicle.* 1989. Japan labor costs reported near U.S., April 25:12C.

17. Ohmae, K. 1988. Americans and Japanese save about the same. *The Wall Street Journal*, June 14:30.

18. Friedman, M. 1988. Why the twin deficits are a blessing. *The Wall Street Journal*, December 14:A16.

19. Hall, W. K. 1980. Survival strategies in a hostile environment. *Harvard Business Review* 58(5):75–85.

20. Porter, M. E. 1985. *Competitive Advantage: Creating and Sustaining Superior Performance.* New York: Free Press, 320.

21. Hofstede, G. 1980. *Culture's Consequences: International Difference in Work-related Values* Beverly Hills, Calif.: Sage, p. 25.

22. Adler, N. J., Doktor, R., & Redding, S. G. 1986. From the Atlantic to the Pacific century: Cross-cultural management reviewed. *Journal of Management* 12:295–318.

23. Chandler, C., & Ingrassia, P. 1991. Just as U.S. firms try Japanese management, Honda is centralizing. *The Wall Street Journal*, April 11:A–1.

24. Williams, M., & Kanabayashi, M. 1993. Honda aims to reverse fortunes with retooled Integra, Accord. *The Wall Street Journal*, May 21:B–1, B–10.

25. Chandler & Ingrassia, Japanese management.

26. Young, J. A. 1988. Technology and competitiveness: A key to the economic future of the United States. *Science* 241:313–16.; Clark, K. 1987. Investment in new technology and competitive advantage. In D. J. Teece, *The Competitive Challenge: Strategies for Industrial Innovation and Renewal.* Cambridge, Mass.: Ballinger, pp. 59–81; Cohen, S. S., & Zysman, J. 1988. Manufacturing innovation and American industrial competitiveness. *Science* 239:1110–15.

27. Hicks, J. P. 1989. Lack of spending may doom U.S. steel industry. *Houston Chronicle*, August 7:1B–2B.

28. Mansfield, Comparative Study; Ireland, Hitt, & Skivington, Management of R&D.

29. Franko, Global corporate competition.

30. Dumaine, B. 1990. The new turnaround champs. *Fortune*, July 16:36.

31. Hoskisson, R. E., Hitt, M. A., & Hill, C. W. L. 1993. Managerial incentives and investment in R&D in large multiproduct firms. *Organization Science* 4:325–41.

32. Hitt, Hoskisson, & Harrison, Strategic competitiveness.

33. Jenson, M. 1989. Eclipse of the public corporation. *Harvard Business Review*, 67, (5):61–74.

34. Baysinger & Hoskisson, Diversification strategy.

35. Hoskisson & Johnson, Corporate restructuring.

36. Hitt, M. A., Hoskisson, R. E., & Ireland, R. D. 1991. Global diversification: Interactive effects with product diversification on innovation and performance. Paper presented at the Academy of Management meetings, Miami.

37. Bartlett, C. A., & Ghoshal, S. 1989. *Managing Across Borders: The Transnational Solution*. Boston: Harvard Business School Press.

38. Hitt, Hoskisson, and Harrison, Strategic competition.

39. Hitt, M. A., & Keats, B. W. 1992. Strategic leadership and restructuring: A reciprocal interdependence. In J. G. Hunt & R. Phillips, eds. *Strategic Leadership: A multiorganizational level perspective*. New York: Quorum, pp. 45–61.

40. Miles, R. E. 1989. A new industrial relations system for the 21st century. *California Management Review* 31:9–28.

II

Restructuring Solutions

6

Restructuring Managerial Incentives

During the 1980s, average compensation for chief executive officers in U.S. firms increased by 212 percent. At the same time, factory workers received pay increases averaging 53 percent; engineers, 73 percent; and teachers, 95 percent. For the same time period, the average earnings per share of the Standard & Poors top 500 companies increased by only 78 percent. Therefore, some argue that unless top executives were significantly underpaid prior to the 1980s, the increase in pay during that decade does not seem warranted. On the other hand, some offsetting changes in executive compensation occurred in the early 1990s. The average CEO's salary and bonus fell by 7 percent in 1991 and by 2 percent in 1992. To be sure, this decline occurred during a recessionary period in which corporate profits fell by 18 percent and thousands of managers were laid off. When long-term compensation, including stock options, is added to the mix, however, the chief executives' total pay increased by 26 percent during 1991 and by 46 percent in 1992. That increase may be largely attributable to big gains made by a small group of CEOs. Sixty percent of U.S. chief executive officers experienced reductions in compensation in 1991. Executive pay is not only an important but a controversial issue.[1] Many controversial changes in executive compensation have come in response to firms' lack of competitiveness.

This chapter examines the effects of executive compensation on corporate and division strategic decisions as a restructuring alternative. In particular, we examine the effects of different forms of managerial compensation on corporate diversification and on divisional managers' propensity to take strategic risks. These issues relate directly to the theme of this book—the need to restructure and to downscope. One way to improve competitiveness has been to change managers' incentives. However, without proper downscoping and governance, the effectiveness of this strategy is limited.

Controversy regarding executive compensation is exacerbated by concerns, not only about total cash compensation, but also about the benefits and perquisites that often accompany executive positions. The concerns become greater if an individual catches the "CEO disease." Symptoms include the belief that one can do wrong, a propensity to spend more time outside the firm (e.g., on the board of directors of other companies), a tendency to make all the important decisions, a concern about his or her compensation in relation to counterparts at other organizations, and a wish to hang onto a position too long, often undermining potentially effective successors. Often, as managers move up the ladder, they encounter fewer restraints on their activities. They often have large expense accounts, submit to fewer performance appraisals, and enjoy largely unchallenged power to make decisions. When executives catch the "CEO disease" they may have multiple corporate jets (e.g., the former CEO of R.J.R. Nabisco had 10 planes and 26 corporate pilots on the payroll), large, lavishly decorated executive offices, and other benefits such as golden parachutes (e.g., the former CEO of R.J.R. Nabisco received $53.8 million in the Kolhberg, Kravis, Roberts, & Company facilitated leveraged buyout).[2]

Executive compensation influences managerial action. Over the years, the emphasis in executive compensation has changed from salary to incentives. In recent years executive compensation has particularly emphasized stock ownership and stock options plans. In 1978, 15 percent of top executive compensation was composed of long-term incentive compensation (stock ownership and option plans); by 1988, this percentage had increased to 42 percent.[3] In the 1950s, firms began to introduce incentive compensation in the forms of both short-term bonuses and long-term incentives, both of which were tied to overall corporate performance. In the 1960s and 1970s the move to "divisionalize" firms created the need for compensation packages for both the corporate officers and the divisional managers. Long-term incentives for both groups were focused on overall corporate performance; division managers' incentives were also based on annual divisional earnings (e.g., return on investment). The focus on annual earnings for division managers, of course, helped create a short-term perspective, with the consequences that we have outlined in earlier chapters. Then, in the 1980s there was a movement to restructure divisional compensation plans.

This chapter explores the strategy of restructuring division compensation as an alternate type of corporate restructuring. The purpose of restructuring division manager incentives is to reward longer-term performance. However, such new incentives also have trade-offs. While the primary focus of this chapter is on divisional executives' compensation, we first survey corporate executives' compensation. Divisional executives' compensation has been found to be strongly and positively related to the compensation plans for corporate executives. Examining executive compensation as a restructuring alternative may therefore shed some light on the subject.

Corporate Executives' Compensation

Executive compensation engendered much public debate in the early 1990s. Some of this debate was fueled by several well-publicized cases, such as those of Donald A. Pels, CEO of LIN Broadcasting, and of Steven J. Ross, former CEO of Time Warner. In 1990 Mr. Pels received total compensation amounting to $186,200,000, while Mr. Ross received total compensation amounting to $78,176,000. Both CEOs' compensation was increased by the effects of corporate mergers. Mr. Ross received a $74.9 million bonus on top of his normal pay as a result of the merger between Time and Warner Communications. Similarly, a merger of LIN and McCaw Cellular Communications provided record stock options in LIN for Donald Pels. Questions were also raised about the high pay of some CEOs who traveled with President George Bush to Japan in 1992 hoping to negotiate a reduction in the trade barriers with Japan. The average annual compensation of the U.S. CEOs who traveled with the president was more than $2 million. In comparison, Japanese chief executives average approximately $300,000 to $400,000 per year. This disparity highlighted the Japanese arguments that American executives are overpaid and that the high pay received by U.S. executives has a detrimental effect on the morale of employees.[4]

Many studies have examined the predictors of corporate executive pay. For example, corporate executive compensation is positively related to the size of the organization. Research into the relationship between firm performance and top executive compensation, however, has been inconclusive; it tends to show either a positive relationship or no relationship between the two.

Corporate executives in large firms tend to receive higher amounts of cash compensation than their counterparts in small firms. The positive relationship between corporate size and executive compensation is strongest in relation to base salary. However, there is a relationship between executive bonuses and firm size, as well. Some observers argue that executives decide to diversify their firms in order to lower the risks faced by the firms and thereby to lower their own employment risk. However, the relationship between size and compensation produces another incentive for executives to diversify. Most diversification moves tend to increase the size of the firm. The most common means of accomplishing diversification is by acquisition of other firms. When other firms are acquired and their assets added to the acquiring firm's, it can significantly increase the size of the firm. If firm size is positively related to executive compensation, such moves could be expected to enhance the corporate executives' pay.

One 1989 study found that firm size was positively correlated with chief executive officers' total compensation. This study also found a positive relationship between diversification and size and, in some cases, between diversification and cash compensation. The degree of diversification was found to be positively related to the CEO's cash compensation only in firms where the ownership was highly dispersed. This type of firm is referred to as management-controlled, because there is no concentration of ownership with the power to affect managerial decisions. When managers are able to make decisions without stockholders' interference, they are more likely to diversify their firm and thereby obtain higher compensation.

The same study also showed that firm performance was positively, but not highly, related to CEO cash compensation. In fact, the study showed that only in the management-controlled firms was performance (return on equity) related to CEO cash compensation. The likelihood is that the ROE was used as a primary means to evaluate the performance of managers in these cases. However, in firms that had a large number of outside directors and in which the corporate executives had significant ownership of stock, there was no relationship between ROE and cash compensation. In these firms, the study speculated that other types of evaluations were used.[5]

Pay is often linked to firm size, because it is assumed that the firm becomes more difficult to manage as it grows larger. Undoubtedly, if firm size increases because of diversification, the firm becomes more complex and more difficult to manage. Interestingly, although firm size has been linked to total corporate executive compensation, one study showed that changes in firm size led to only small positive increases in CEO compensation. Therefore, there may be a point of diminishing returns to increases in firm size.[6]

We surmise that firm size, corporate diversification, and, in selected instances, firm performance may be positive predictors of corporate executives' compensation. However, our specific interest herein is in divisional executives' compensation, on which there is far less research.

Divisional Executives' Compensation

Divisional executives' compensation is partly determined by the level of pay of the firm's corporate executives and its determinants (e.g., organization size). The compensation of divisional general managers is based on both market factors and on political and human capital factors. For example, the divisional general manager's cash compensation is highly related to both firm and division size, and his or her bonus is highly related to performance (there is no relationship between salary and divisional performance). Corporate size and performance may be labor-market-related factors, but divisional general managers may also be compensated for political and human capital characteristics within the firm. For example, divisional general managers' compensation is positively related to their tenure both in the firm and on the job. This is assumed to be partly political, because longer tenure allows an incumbent to gain power in the job and in the organization. In addition, the education level of the divisional executive, as well as his or her age, has been found to be positively related to compensation. These are considered human capital variables. Age, for example, affects experience and accumulated knowledge. Therefore, there may be multiple determinants of an executives' compensation.[7]

In evaluating divisional executive compensation as a restructuring alternative, the most important parts are the bonus and the incentive plan on which it is based. The primary focus of this chapter is therefore on alternative approaches for calculating incentive compensation of divisional general managers. Although corporate executive compensation has been changing, change in compensation as a restructuring alternative has focused substantially on division managers. In the mid-1980s divisional long-term incentive plans were proposed as a restructuring alternative to correct the competitiveness problem.[8] The focus of these plans was to reward divisional managers for long-term efforts to maximize shareholder value, as well as current earnings.

Such plans can be based on several alternative approaches. One is to transform the divisions into an independent corporation, as the Coca-Cola Company has done with its Coca-Cola Enterprises (soft-drink bottling) and entertainment companies, and to issue stock on the separate pieces of the firm. This approach was implemented at General Motors, which issued stock for the main company and for its 1980s acquisitions, Electronic Data Systems and Hughes Aircraft.

A second approach is to create "phantom" shares for a particular division. One way this is accomplished is to compare division assets to other publicly traded firms in the industry of focus. These phantom shares, then, have a proxy market value. Another approach rewards both net income growth (ROI) and conservation of capital. In general, these three approaches mirror the key aspects of risk-adjusted rates of return by adjusting the return to stock price through subtraction of the risk-free rate of return (e.g., government bond rate of return). The risk-free rate is considered an inflation adjustment.[9] (The third approach, which rewards both net income growth and conservation of capital, usually lacks a correction for inflation.)

A fourth approach involves issuing stock options on real or phantom shares. This approach creates incentive for managers to take more risk, because options increase in value if the stock carries greater risk. However, managers may not want to take the risk associated with such an incentive, depending on their personal propensity for risk.[10]

Headquarters managers of the parent company may want to change the incentive structure to encourage different behaviors among divisions. For example, executives in an entrepreneurial division needing growth may receive low salaries and limited short-term earnings incentives but significant phantom stock options in order to create more risk taking. A division at a later growth stage may emphasize salary and short-term bonus and play down stock options. The more diversified a firm is, the more difficult it is to create optionlike incentives for division managers. Furthermore, the more diversified the firm, the more difficult it is to implement and manage all long-term divisional incentives. Thus, diversified firms tend to emphasize short-term annual earnings as the central incentive for division managers.

A critical question is how alternative changes in division executive compensation and incentives deal with the short-term focus in corporate America. It is important to understand how division managers' incentives are implemented and how they may affect strategic choices.

Short-Term Division Incentives and Risk Taking

Divisional financial controls frequently are implemented, at least partially, through the use of performance-based incentive compensation schemes, as we have explained. Incentive compensation schemes often have had a short-term orientation and have been based on annual earnings.[11] Division managers traditionally have received incentive compensation for meeting financial performance targets (e.g., specified ROI). The emphasis on financial incentives has been prominent in studies examining division managers. For instance, a number of studies have found a positive association between financial performance-based incentives for managers and the extent and type of firm diversification.[12] This suggests that in highly diversified firms the use of objective financial performance data for control purposes dominates the use of richer and more subjective performance data.

Although any incentive based primarily on financial outcomes can shift risk to the manager, short-term or annual incentives may also induce division managers to reduce long-term investments such as R&D. Because more diversified firms frequently use divisional ROI as a primary criterion in calculating incentive compensation for division managers, short-run profit-maximizing behavior among division managers is encouraged.

If corporate executives set challenging division ROI objectives on which division managers incentive compensation is to be based, division profit accountability implies that the earnings, resources, and career prospects of division managers are dependent on their ability to meet the specified objectives. If they fail to meet them, managers face the prospect of loss of annual earnings bonuses, loss of division resources, and, ultimately, loss of their jobs. It is therefore in the interest of division executives to do everything possible to meet ROI targets. One way to do this is to reduce expenditures that are not essential for the attainment of short-term returns, even though they may be critical for the long-term performance of the firm. Thus, division executives may reduce investments in R&D, market research, and new capital investments.[13] Often, the emphasis on achieving short-term performance targets reflects a strong managerial control orientation. While this may produce improvements in performance and thus increase division manager compensation in the near term, over time a strong control orientation may produce lower performance and reduced compensation for the manager.[14]

Long-Term Incentives and Risk Taking

Although longer-term incentives have become more common for corporate as well as for division managers, only rarely have they replaced short-term financial controls for division managers. Graef Crystal and Mel Hurwich, however, have argued that more long-term incentives for division managers should be implemented to minimize managerial risk aversion.[15] The incentive plans explained earlier in this chapter attempt to link division manager rewards with some form of discounted cash flow that emphasizes value creation for stockholders (in addition to the short-term incentives placed on annual earnings) in order to create longer-term incentives.[16]

These plans evaluate financial criteria over longer time periods with the intention of balancing short-term and long-term incentives. While corporate managers may be able to reduce their employment risk through diversification, division managers have no way of diversifying their employment risk and thus may continue to choose lower risk strategies, even with longer-term incentives.[17]

One study has identified at least three problems with long-term incentives.[18] First, longer-term incentives based on financial criteria are risky for division managers because they can be influenced by factors outside the managers' control. To compensate, managers may be loss averse or overly conservative.[19] Because managers may question the influence they have on the measures associated with long-term incentives, these incentives may not eliminate nor lessen managerial risk aversion.

Second, long-term incentives based on earnings reports may not create true value for the shareholder, and attempting to measure division profit in relation to overall firm market value can be problematic. Although a number of consulting firms have tried to sell the idea of direct measurement of shareholder value for determining incentives, very few companies have implemented the idea at the profit center level.[20] Therefore, it is not clear if available division performance measures are congruent with value creation for shareholders.

Third, the greater the diversity among divisions, the more difficult it is for corporate officers to evaluate the strategic appropriateness of division proposals. Corporate officers don't have the time or, often, the knowledge to understand fully the operational aspects of each division. As a result, they become more risk averse in their evaluation of division proposals for strategic actions and for major resource commitments. Corporate managers may become more risk averse over time because they lose the operational understanding of specific businesses as diversification increases; thus, objective performance controls are emphasized.[21]

This situation is more likely to occur if higher levels of diversification accompany an emphasis on incentive compensation, because strategic control often is deemphasized in more highly diversified firms.[22] In fact, as diversification increases, so does the emphasis placed on division financial performance.[23] Conversely, as diversification increases, the emphasis on overall corporate level financial performance decreases. This implies that corporate emphasis on division financial incentives increases with diversification and that corporate managers may not have the information necessary to implement informed strategic controls to encourage risk taking. Therefore, long-term incentives may be effective to the extent that the corporate officers administering the incentive compensation for divisional managers have an understanding of the requirements for success in the divisions.[24]

Long-Term Incentives: Additional Trade-offs

Incentives for corporate as well as for division managers have evolved from rewards based on overall corporate performance to bonuses based on short-term divisional and overall corporate performance, and tentative steps have been taken to emphasize divisional long-term incentives. These incentives will function properly to the extent that (1) they help division managers feel they have control over the performance evaluated; (2) performance measures are congruent with shareholder wealth creation; and (3) corporate administration of the incentive plan is effective. However, to deal effectively with these problems, the firm often has to accept trade-offs.

First, for division managers to perceive that they are responsible for performance outcomes, the division must be a true profit center. In effect, it must be a stand-alone business. One aspect of such a structure is that all internal transfers (between divisions) may have to be made at market price in order to allow an effective performance evaluation measure to evolve. Of course, having all divisions function as independent businesses may eliminate the opportunity to realize synergy between profit centers. In addition, long-term incentives may create a multicultural corporate environment, a problem if overall corporate culture is important. Graef Crystal observes: "Indeed, the introduction of divisional long-term incentives may cause divisional managers to forget that their parent company owns assets other than theirs."[25]

Trying to overcome a short-term focus through long-term incentives may create other costly administrative problems. Long-term incentives may restrict executive mobility. For example, a division manager who excells in a profitable division may be reluctant to move to a poorly performing division where his or her talents are needed to achieve a turnaround. In addition, although corporate officer compensation plans can be complex, managing a set of divisional plans, even with a small degree of tailoring for each division, increases the management difficulty exponentially. If the division is highly profitable and the corporation is not, it is possible that the divisional executive could receive higher pay than the chief executive officer. It takes a flexible CEO to allow this arrangement. In other instances, the poor performance of the overall corporation may disallow adequate funding for the divisional compensation plan. This may be demotivating for a division manager whose division has performed well in prior year(s). These difficulties may explain why Kenneth Merchant has found that, although many consultants have recommended long-term incentive plans for division managers, few firms have implemented them.[26]

The second problem, creating a match between shareholder wealth and divisional managerial long-term incentives, is related to trade-offs associated with the first problem. To show accurately that divisions create shareholder wealth, a separate stock issue may be necessary, as in the Coca-Cola and GM examples. But, having separate stock issues may lead to difficulties in creating a unified culture, a feeling among division managers that "we are all in this together." Creating phantom shares for each division requires costly information processing for divisional evaluations by corporate executives. To the extent that cheaper information processing can be purchased (e.g., by the use of computers), such incentive systems may be more feasible. However, when the corporate strategy is based on cooperation among divisions to achieve synergy, long-term incentives may conflict with corporate strategy.

Thus, long-term incentives focused on divisional performance lead to creation of an internal capital market that emphasizes separateness among divisions. Group or overall corporate long-term incentives become secondary to the divisional manager, unless the corporate objective is to create cooperation among divisions. Managers may decide that they have no control over their incentive compensation or that bonuses are given subjectively and are vulnerable to bias created by political manipulation on the part of persuasive division managers.

Such manipulation suggests a third problem—inadequate corporate management of the incentive system. If a company is growing by rapidly adding divisions, it is likely that corporate executives will have inadequate operational understanding of most divisions and certainly of the new ones. Rapid divisionalization may also produce decentralization, creating a lack of knowledge of profit center operations that may be exacerbated by geographic distance. Even if it is feasible for corporate executives to learn details of the business, there will be a time lag in doing so.

Furthermore, if most of the new divisions formerly were independent businesses, it is highly likely that some of the division general managers will be former entrepreneurs or independent managers who are unlikely to be interested in playing only a small role in a large corporate bureaucracy. They may therefore resist providing information or perceive corporate officers seeking to understand the business as an intrusion and a threat to their own continued success.

These concerns are likely to produce a deemphasis on long-term incentives, because such incentives require well-informed corporate officers. In such systems, by default, short-term earnings evaluation is emphasized because long-term incentives become too costly to manage. Furthermore, if products have even a small degree of uncertainty (e.g., because of rapid product change), corporate executives must adjust incentives and therefore must take the time to understand the market dynamics. Thus, long-term incentives are more manageable to the extent that product markets are stable.

Although long-term divisional incentives have been recommended as a restructuring alternative, evidence suggests that this approach alone has not been implemented by the majority of firms in need of restructuring. Long-term incentives may not successfully cure firms' competitiveness problem because of the trade-offs in implementing and managing such incentives. Theoretically, division managers' risk aversion may be reduced by implementing longer-term incentives; however, research has shown that although long-term incentives may not lead to reductions in R&D investments comparable to those in firms that emphasize short-term incentives, long-term incentives do not in fact produce more managerial risk taking.[27]

Implementing Divisional Compensation Plans

A compensation strategy should link divisional and corporate strategies with firm resources and core competences. Furthermore, it should be tailored to the needs of the firm and its culture.[28] For example, firms that are dominant or related diversified require a compensation strategy that emphasizes the interdependencies among units. Heavy emphasis on divisional performance may be ineffective for corporate performance if the firm wants to maximize the synergy between businesses yet also allow strong performance in each of the units.[29] On the other hand, in widely diversified firms, strong emphasis on divisional performance as targets for managerial incentives is more appropriate, because in such cases the firm is trying to maximize the performance of each individual division.

Articles in the popular press have called for an emphasis on simplicity in executive compensation plans. They would have compensation largely composed of salary, bonus, and stock options and would limit perks, such as golden parachutes and expensive pensions. There are arguments in favor of granting boards of directors the discretion to reward improvements in important areas such as quality, customer satisfaction, and development of management talent, as well as for stock ownership among executives.[30]

Stock ownership has been emphasized for corporate executives, but we argue that it should be extended to divisional general managers as well, particularly in dominant and related diversified firms. Stock ownership provides incentives for these executives to cooperate with other units and to maximize the performance of the overall firm. Furthermore, incentive pay should be an amount that is meaningful to the executive and that is tied specifically to some level and/or type of performance over which the executive has some control and that is related to challenging but achievable targets.[31]

Not all compensation innovations operate as intended. For example, General Dynamics implemented a new gain-sharing executive compensation plan that provided bonuses to the top 25 corporate managers in amounts equal to predetermined multiples of their salary for each point increase above a base price of General Dynamics shares of stock. As a result of the plan, the 25 top executives earned approximately $24 million in total bonuses during 1991. However, during this same time period, General Dynamics laid off approximately 12,000 employees. In fact, these layoffs actually improved the price of the stock and thereby contributed to the incentive compensation paid to the top executives. These layoffs also contributed to General Dynamics' positive cash position, which attracted investors. Graef Crystal, a compensation expert, has severely criticized this program, and securities analysts worry that it encourages General Dynamics' managers not only to lay off employees but to hoard cash and thereby to forgo future opportunities that may require heavy investments. In short, it may be encouraging General Dynamics' managers to "eat their seed corn."[32]

Summary

As noted at the beginning of this chapter, there has been considerable criticism of executive compensation. Most of this criticism has been leveled at the compensation of corporate executives, because their pay is more visible than that of divisional executives. However, the primary focus of this chapter has been on the effect of restructuring division manager incentives. Research indicates that compensation may have a significant impact on an executive's decision to join and to stay with a firm but that, once hired, executives are not highly motivated by pay; most executives are already highly motivated or they would not have attained the level of position and responsibility that they have. The research therefore leads one to conclude that most top executives define their self-worth by career success and may not require extreme financial rewards to achieve high performance. In fact, many top executives have already achieved financial independence because of prior lucrative compensation and do not need the money. Thus, compensation may have its greatest motivational impact as a symbolic reward. In other words, compensation provides an important scorecard for individuals who have high needs for achievement and for recognition, both of which are common among top executives. While making pay contingent on performance represents an attempt to strengthen the link between performance and reward, the ambiguity in most top executives' jobs disallows a strong expectation on the part of these executives that increased effort will result in improved division performance as measured by the common indicators. These conditions are likely to lead to a weak response among executives to incentive compensation. We should not therefore overplay the importance of compensation as a motivator of executive performance. It is complex and likely a partial motivator of executive effort.[33]

In addition, while many conventional measures of performance serve as only partial reflections of an executive's effort, some measures are also open to manipulation. For example, managers may manipulate choices of actions that affect accounting-based measures of performance in order to increase the value of their bonuses. In fact, one author has argued that, because of the ambiguity in executives' jobs, it may be easier to manage the outcomes to make them look good than to manage the firm to be more successful.[34]

We conclude that executive compensation packages are important but that their ability to affect executive behavior and performance must be kept in perspective. Clearly, compensation plans serve multiple purposes. One of their important roles is to attract and retain effective executives; we do not want to focus only on their potential effect on executive performance and ignore their important effect in the attraction and retention of executives. The structuring of divisional executives' pay packages must have as a goal to attract and retain talented divisional executives. Thus, they may need to include some of the perquisites (e.g., golden parachutes) provided top corporate executives in order to attract and retain divisional executives. Furthermore, it is important to include focus on long-term outcomes and, therefore, on long-term incentives. However, care must be taken in structuring the incentive compensation plan to ensure that it does not produce unintended consequences (e.g., risk-averse behavior). Furthermore, division managers may be tempted to manipulate accounting-based expenses to increase the value of their bonuses. These conclusions lead to the following managerial implications:

- Many executive compensation plans provide incentives (perhaps unintended) for corporate managers to diversify their firms and thereby to increase the firms' size. Thus, corporate incentive compensation should emphasize firm performance over which managers have some control, regardless of firm size or diversity.

- Incentives based on annual ROI may enhance short-term performance but reduce divisional manager risk taking.
- Long-term incentives alone are not adequate. To be most effective, they should be combined with other forms of restructuring, particularly downscoping.
- Long-term incentives also have trade-offs; for example, long-term incentives based on divisional performance may reduce cooperation among related divisions.
- To be meaningful to executives, incentives should be linked to a level and a type of performance that board members can link to managerial action. They should also be based on challenging but achievable targets.

We conclude therefore that restructuring should include some change in corporate strategy, along with a change in long-term incentives, to deal with risk aversion in diversified firms. For highly diversified firms, this usually means refocusing corporate strategy. The first approach used may be a leveraged buyout, as described in the next chapter (chapter 7). Another approach may be voluntary downscoping (see chapter 8). Either approach creates the opportunity for an effective balance between strategic and financial controls. However, strong strategic controls are essential for an effective incentive compensation system as will be explained in the next two chapters.

Notes

1. Byrne, J. A. 1992. What, me over paid? CEOs fight back. *Business Week*, May 4:142–48; Byrne, J. A. 1993. Executive pay: The party ain't over yet. *Business Week*, April 26:56–64.

2. Bryne, J. A., Symonds, W. C., & Siler, J. F. 1991. CEO disease: Egotism can breed corporate disaster—and the malady is spreading. *Business Week*, April 1:52–60.

3. Bennett, A. 1989. A great leap forward for executive pay: Stock options propelled gains by CEOs in '88. *The Wall Street Journal*, B–1.

4. Byrne, J. A. 1991. The flap over executive pay. *Business Week*, May 6:90–6; Abrahamson, J., and Chipello, C. J. 1991. Compensation gap: High pay of CEOs traveling with Bush touches a nerve in Asia. *The Wall Street Journal*, December 30:A–1, A–8.

5. Finkelstein, S., & Hambrick, D. C. 1989. Chief executive compensation: A study of the intersection of markets and political processes. *Strategic Management Journal* 10:121–34.

6. Lambert, R. A., Larcker, D. F., & Weigelt, K. 1991. How sensitive is executive compensation to organizational size? *Strategic Management Journal* 12:395–402.

7. Fisher, J., & Govindarajan, V. 1992. Profit center manager compensation: An examination of market, political, and human capital factors. *Strategic Management Journal* 13:205–17.

8. Rappaport, A. 1986. *Creating Shareholder Value*. New York: Free Press.

9. Crystal, G. S. 1991. Recognizing divisional difference. In F. K. Foulkes, ed. *Executive Compensation: A Strategic Guide for the 1990s*. Boston: Harvard Business School Press, pp. 239–47.

10. Crystal, Recognizing divisional difference.

11. Merchant, K. A. 1989. *Rewarding Results: Motivating Profit Center Managers*. Boston: Harvard Business School Press.

12. Hoskisson, R. E., Hitt, M. A., & Hill, C. W. L. 1993. Managerial incentives and investment in R&D in large multiproduct firms. *Organization Science* 4:325–41; Kerr, J. L. 1985. Diversification strategies and managerial rewards: An empirical study. *Academy of Management Journal* 28:155–79.

13. Jaeger, A. M., & Baliga, B. R. 1985. Control systems and strategic adaptation: Lessons from the Japanese experience. *Strategic Management Journal* 6:115–34.

14. Gomez-Mejia, L. R., & Balkin, D. B. 1992. *Compensation, Organizational Strategy, and Firm Performance*. Cincinnati, Ohio: Southwestern.

15. Crystal, G. S., & Hurwich, M. R. 1986. The case of divisional long-term incentives. *California Management Review* 29(1):60–74.

16. Rappaport, *Creating Shareholder Value*; Brindisi, L. J. 1985. Shareholder value and executive compensation. *Planning Review* 13(5):14–17; Reinmann, B. C. 1986. Does your business create real shareholder value? *Business Horizons* 29(5):44–51.

17. Amihud, Y., & Lev, B. 1981. Risk reduction as a managerial motive for conglomerate mergers. *Bell Journal of Economics* 12:605–17.

18. Merchant, *Rewarding Results*.

19. March, J. G., & Shapira, Z. 1987. Managerial perspectives on risk and risk taking. *Management Science* 33:1401–18; MacCrimmon, K. R., & Wehrung, D. A. 1986. *Taking Risks: The Management of Uncertainty*. New York: Free Press.

20. Merchant, *Rewarding Results*.

21. Haspeslagh, P. 1982. Portfolio planning: Uses and limits. *Harvard Business Review* 60(1):58–73.

22. Baysinger, B., & Hoskisson, R. E. 1989. Diversification strategy and R&D intensity in multiproduct firms. *Academy of Management Journal* 32:310–32.

23. Hoskisson et al., Managerial incentives.

24. Hoskisson, R. E., & Hitt, M. A. 1988. Strategic control systems and relative R&D intensity in large multiproduct firms. *Strategic Management Journal* 9:605–21.

25. Crystal, Recognizing divisional difference, p. 235.

26. Merchant, *Rewarding Results*. p. 46.

27. Hoskisson et al., Managerial incentives.

28. Gomez-Meija & Balkin, Compensation.

29. Gomez-Meija, L. R. 1992. Structure and process of diversification, compensation strategy, and firm performance. *Strategic Management Journal* 13:381–97.

30. Byrne, J. A., Foust, D., & Therrien, L. 1992. Executive pay: Compensation at the top is out of control. Here's how to reform it. *Business Week*, March 30:52–58.

31. Kahn, L. M., & Sherer, P. D. 1990. Contingent pay and managerial performance. *Industrial and Labor Relations Review* (Special issue) 43:107-s, 119-s.

32. Ellis, J. E. 1991. Layoffs on the line, bonuses in the executive suite. *Business Week*, October 21:34.

33. Finkelstein, S., & Hambrick, D. C. 1988. Chief executive compensation, a synthesis and reconciliation. *Strategic Management Journal* 9:543–58.

34. Finkelstein & Hambrick, Chief executive compensation; Healey, P. M. 1985. The effect of bonus schemes on accounting decisions. *Journal of Accounting and Economics* 7:85–107; March, J. G. 1984. Notes on ambiguity and executive compensation. *Scandinavian Journal of Management Studies*, August:53–64.

7

Leveraged Buyouts and Debt as a Restructuring Alternative

Prior to being acquired in a leveraged buyout (LBO) in 1986, Beatrice Food Company had three major businesses — U.S. food, consumer products, and international food — and was arguably the largest packaged food and consumer products company in the United States. In August 1985 the LBO firm Kohlberg, Kravis, Roberts & Company made an offer to buy the company, and, after failing to elicit a white knight (a company, friendly to existing management, that offers a competing bid with the goal of defeating the original offer), Beatrice's board accepted a sweetened offer in February 1986. The deal cost $8.2 billion and was hailed as "the deal of the century." By breaking the company up and selling its assets, KKR expected to produce a windfall of $3.8 billion. However, this windfall was not realized, primarily because Beatrice's balance sheet contained $1.9 billion in intangible assets or goodwill. By 1988 the deal had returned only minimal profits to investors, although KKR had done very well on its fees for negotiating the deal.[1]

In the prebuyout period, sales per employee at Beatrice had declined from $125,950 in 1984 to $113,960 in 1985. After the buyout, however, sales per employee showed substantial progress, moving to $142,450 in 1986 and to $143,368 in 1987.[2] Ostensibly, then, even though investors did not reap the expected windfall, financial efficiency at the company seemed to improve. As of this writing no systematic evidence is available on the performance of units that were sold off, although there is evidence that divested units do not perform as well as expected.[3]

This LBO example is typical of many that took place in the 1980s. This chapter examines leveraged buyouts, another popular restructuring of the 1980s. This alternative, however, is more drastic, because it not only involves modifying managerial compensation incentives but also represents a change in firm capital structure that often is accompanied by asset sell-offs in large firms. Much of the restructuring of large firms through leveraged buyouts in the 1980s was fostered by capital infused through high-yield securities, or junk bonds. Much of this wave of restructuring, the fourth in this century, included vertical and horizontal mergers and marketing line extension acquisitions, as well as sell-offs of unrelated businesses (deconglomeration). The most unique aspect of this activity, however, was the leveraged buyout. LBOs by value increased to 26.8 percent of all merger activity in 1986 from 3.8 percent in 1981, then dropped to 21.7 percent in 1987. The average value of LBOs, however, increased from $31.31 million in 1981 to $137.45 million in 1987.[4]

It is important to note that LBOs composed more than 50 percent of all merger and acquisition activity in the manufacturing sector between 1983 and 1988. LBOs have been most popular in industries that are low-tech (low R&D-intensive) and mature, with stable cash flows. For instance, in the manufacturing sector, LBOs have been more common in nondurable than in durable goods industries. Durables tend to be more cyclical and therefore experience more cash-flow risk. Costs of LBOs in industries that experience cash-flow risk because of long-term investments (e.g., high R&D commitments) tend to be high because the potential liquidity problems raise the cost of capital.

Some have argued that taking firms private by having large investment firms arrange for leveraged financing increases efficiency for the recapitalized firm because the recapitalization usually leads to a scaled-down firm that becomes more efficient as it sheds inefficient assets. Furthermore, it is argued that in this situation a realigned incentive structure puts owners (and debt holders) closer to the firm, making monitoring of firm strategy more efficient.[5] This incentive structure is intended to reduce agency costs, that is, the costs of managing the differences in objectives between owners (also debt holders) and managers. In this chapter we argue, however, that increased leverage and businesses dominated by debt holders also produces trade-offs, especially for firms that need to make long-term investments but experience short-term cash-flow fluctuations. Debt holders are traditionally more conservative than equity holders, and research has shown that in large diversified firms, as debt increases, R&D investment goes down.[6] LBOs may increase efficiency of mature businesses where conditions are stable and where debt holders are likely to prefer investment in businesses that can fulfill cash-flow obligations in order to service debt. R&D-intensive firms with rapidly changing technology are much less likely to benefit from financial restructuring that increases leverage and reduces cash-flow discretion. The purpose of this chapter is to examine the conditions in which financial restructuring through LBOs leads to increased efficiencies and those in which significant trade-offs may occur.

Capital Structure and Corporate Strategy

The increase in financial leverage in the 1980s has raised public policy concerns about the consequences of debt for the economy. New organizational forms relying on unusually high levels of debt have attracted staunch advocates,[7] as well as considerable opposition.[8]

Studies in strategic management have detected relationships between debt, diversification, and research and development. However, most theories of capital structure are largely divorced from strategic concerns. Theories in financial economics historically have focused on tax issues, financial distress costs (e.g., bankruptcy), and the significance of capital structure decisions as signals of management confidence in the future prospects of the firm.[9] Management scholars examining capital structure decisions have treated them largely as a function of management characteristics and behavioral attitudes, rather than of strategic considerations.[10]

While all of these perspectives have contributed to our understanding of capital structure, they have had mixed success in explaining financing patterns or identifying the strategic significance of alternative financing structures. In this chapter we explore the strategic significance of capital structure, focusing on protecting valuable strategies from imitation. This is important because LBOs and changes in debt structure significantly changed during the 1980s. The basic premise is that financial leverage (defined as the ratio of debt to total assets) is unattractive to the extent that disclosing information to capital markets increases the ability of competitors to imitate key resources and firm strategy.

Michael Jensen's "free cash flow" theory proposes a relationship between capital structure, diversification, and long-term investment.[11] Jensen's notion of "free cash flow" suggests that high leverage produces efficiency in terms of more effective capital market monitoring of strategic investments, especially for mature firms. In this chapter, however, we highlight the strategic costs of extensive capital market monitoring. Jensen's theory was originally applied to the capital structure issue by exploring the agency costs of external debt and of external equity.[12] As extended in the free cash flow theory, financial leverage gains strategic significance. Highly leveraged firms are forced to distribute their cash flows to investors, limiting the extent to which major new strategic initiatives can be funded internally. Managers seeking external funding must expose their strategic initiatives to the scrutiny of external capital markets, in essence exposing top management to increased capital market monitoring and thereby limiting management's ability to engage in inefficient empire-building.

The free cash flow notion suggests that diversified firms should be highly leveraged. It assumes that the high costs imposed on the firm by high debt focuses management attention on maximizing returns. Jensen argues that the added discipline of debt is especially useful for firms facing stable or declining demand for their core products. Such firms produce cash in excess of that necessary to maintain competitive viability in their core industries, yet face internal pressures to reinvest earnings rather than distribute them to investors.

With this perspective, investment and financing decisions are no longer separate; rather capital structure is an instrument that constrains the range of corporate and business-level strategies that a firm can pursue. In fact, Jensen argues that LBOs may supplant the traditional corporate form for mature firms producing large free cash flows.[13] Even though the free cash flow theory partially integrates strategic management with capital structure issues, however, capital structure is used to reduce agency costs through better incentives. Furthermore, as we demonstrate in the examples that follow, its application is limited primarily to mature firms.

Examples of LBO

The examples of LBOs that follow are taken from the nondurable goods and the retail trade industries. These examples were selected to illustrate the types of firms and industries most suitable for such transactions. They also illustrate some of the positive and the negative characteristics of LBOs.

Playtex, Inc.

Since 1984, Playtex, Inc. has gone through four leveraged buyouts. In 1984, at the time of the first leveraged buyout, Playtex's family products earned a profit margin of approximately 15 percent, and Playtex's apparel earned approximately a profit margin of 6 percent. After the buyout, profit margins rose to slightly more than 30 percent in 1987 for Playtex's family products and to almost 13 percent in 1987 for Playtex's apparel. At the time of the third buyout in 1988, Playtex's family products had a 28 percent profit margin, and Playtex's apparel had approximately a 15 percent profit margin. The profit margins of both divisions peaked in 1989 at approximately 32 percent for Playtex's family products and approximately 16 percent for Playtex's apparel. However, during the same time, the market share of its primary products declined. Mitch Bartlett, an analyst for Merrill Lynch, suggested that Playtex had not maintained a long-term focus because of its shuttling from one owner to another. In fact, it had lost market share in both its bra and its tampon lines. Furthermore, investment in product development had been reduced. Joel Smilo, the CEO of Playtex during three of its four buyouts (in the last one, he sold the company to the Sara Lee Corporation), defended his record at Playtex by arguing that the firm had created incentives to reduce overhead and had encouraged employees to work smarter. He noted that it had become popular to economize rather than seeking the biggest budget and the biggest staff in the industry. Sara Lee's chairman, John Brown, who purchased Playtex's businesses, offered another viewpoint. He said that Playtex bras represented an extremely good brand but that they may have suffered because of the company's leveraged position. He suggested that Playtex managers did not have the appropriate long-term orientation.

Mr. Smilo was an executive at Playtex in 1984 when Beatrice acquired Esmark, of which Playtex was a division. Playtex was put up for sale shortly after KKR's acquisition of Beatrice in April 1986. Thanks to the ability of Drexel Burnham Lambert, Inc., to sell junk bonds, Playtex's new owners, including Mr. Smilo, borrowed most of the money required to buy the company from KKR. Mr. Smilo paid just $5 million for a 14.3 percent stake in Playtex.

Shortly after the LBO in 1986, Mr. Smilo reduced the Playtex corporate headquarters staff by approximately 23 percent and eliminated the five-year planning process. He also reduced the budgeting and accounting staff. Profit margins were increased by moving much of the manufacturing to the Philippines from Puerto Rico, and prices on the company's tampon products increased by as much as 10 percent a year, double the U.S. inflation rate at the time. Shortly after the LBO, Mr. Smilo also eliminated the development and implementation of new products. He allowed extension of existing lines but ruled out any efforts to diversify into related products. The company sold its Max Factor cosmetics business to Revlon for $345 million, which allowed a reduction in the LBO debt to approximately $650 million. However, in doing so Playtex lost an established brand and business.

In 1988 Mr. Smilo borrowed more money against Playtex's businesses. He split Playtex into two companies and sold parts of each to new buyers, retaining almost 58 percent for himself. This represented the third LBO for Playtex. The new LBOs also were facilitated by junk bonds. Interestingly, investors were willing to put more money into Playtex operations even though the prospectuses for both businesses warned that Playtex's leverage posed significant risk to holders of the notes. This LBO increased the company's debt to almost $1.28 billion, and debt service payments were barely supported by the 1988 profit of approximately $144 million. As a sidelight, Mr. Smilo's original outlay of $5 million in 1986 produced a return of $71.8 million in 1988.

Thereafter, when managers left, Mr. Smilo required that their jobs be left vacant for several months as he tried to squeeze greater profits from the businesses. During this time, both primary businesses continued to lose market share, and in 1990 profit margins declined in the Playtex apparel business; burdened with heavy debt, Playtex apparel earned only $3 million in the first six months of 1991. At this time, Mr. Smilo decided to sell the businesses and did so to Sara Lee Corporation in 1991, saying, "You have to recognize buyouts were bred to be sold." Further-more, he added, "In an LBO, cash flow is everything." During the four buyouts, Mr. Smilo invested $35.6 million and reaped returns of $186.5 million.[14]

The example of Playtex suggests that LBOs may well enhance op-erating efficiencies (Playtex profit margins rose rapidly in the first several years after the first LBO). However, they may do so at the expense of other, longer-term investments. For example, product development and five-year planning at Playtex were eliminated shortly after the first LBO. These cutbacks, along with other actions to create efficiency (e.g., the move of manufacturing to the Philippines), may have been at least par-tially responsible for the reductions in market share over time. Addition-ally, the efficiencies seemed to level off and even deteriorate somewhat after multiple buyouts. Despite this deterioration, the firm was attractive to Sara Lee because it was highly related to some of Sara Lee's own businesses. For example, by combining Playtex with Sara Lee's Bali and Hanes for Her brands, Sara Lee became the largest bra manufacturer and distributor in the United States. Furthermore, the acquisition al-lowed Sara Lee to achieve economies of scale and to refinance Playtex's debt at lower interest rates, thereby reducing the costs of the takeover.

Overall, one may question the value produced by the four leveraged buyouts of Playtex. The last acquisition, by Sara Lee, seems to provide the greatest opportunity to create value. However, the performance of the Playtex LBOs is difficult to assess. The company's operating profits increased significantly after the first LBO but leveled off and/or declined after the later LBOs.

R. H. Macy & Company

In 1985 Macy's was the tenth largest retailer in the United States, op-erating 95 stores in fourteen states, including 23 under the Bamberger's name. More than 75 percent of the stores were located in major shop-ping centers. In 1985 Macy's CEO, Edward S. Finkelstein, believed that a management buyout could help retain key managers and motivate them to keep Macy's on the leading edge of the retail market. The buyout was approved by the board after some negotiation in June 1986, for $3.7 billion.[15]

Macy's sales in the prebuyout period had risen from $4.07 billion in 1984 to $4.37 billion in 1985. This trend continued in 1986 and 1987, when sales were $4.79 and $5.21 billion, respectively. Sales per employee also rose, from $75,280 in 1984 to $76,638 in 1985, $84,841 in postbuy-out 1986 and to $93,043 in 1987. Capital expenditures and operating income also increased in both the pre- and the postbuyout periods. Macy's seemed able to maintain its stature in the retail department store industry, while creating longer-term incentives through ownership for key employees included in the buyout.

Macy's, however, had also acquired considerable debt through the

1986 leveraged buyout and its subsequent acquisitions of the Bullock's and I. Magnum chains. This heavy debt burden proved to be Macy's downfall. In January 1992 Macy's filed for bankruptcy protection because it had been unable to make a crucial payment to suppliers a few days earlier. Macy's had total liabilities of $5.32 billion and assets of $4.94 billion. Almost $4 billion of Macy's debt came from the LBO and the two subsequent acquisitions. Part of its problems stemmed from a general recession, which reduced sales revenue and therefore the firm's cash flow. Without adequate cash flow, Macy's could not meet its high debt payments and other operating costs. As a result, while the firm's operating efficiencies seemed to have increased as predicted with LBOs, its cash flow could not carry the heavy debt load. Although the additional acquisitions were part of the problem, the debt load created through the LBO was a significant contributor.

Playtex and Macy's are representative of firms that have undergone leveraged buyouts. They both represent mature firms in nondurable goods industries, and both seem to have produced increased operating efficiencies after the buyouts. There is not sufficient information to evaluate fully the long-term outcomes of the KKR acquisition of Beatrice. Currently, the evaluation seems equivocal, at best. On the other hand, the long-term outcome for Macy's is less positive. Unfortunately, part of Macy's problems may stem, not only from the LBO, but also from the subsequent acquisitions and the accumulated debt. It indicates one of the potential risks of LBOs to be a strong need for high cash flows to meet heavy debt payments. The risks are particularly acute during economic downturns, as experienced by Macy's.[16]

Below we propose that, in addition to the increased financial distress created by high leverage, there may be more basic strategic concerns with LBOs. They often create high strategic costs and result in strategic tradeoffs.

Capital Structure and Firm Resources

Firms gain competitive advantages and above-normal profits through the efficient acquisition and utilization of resources that other firms cannot imitate. Successful imitation by other firms eliminates competitive advantage and distributes the gain from a strategy to customers. To imitate a strategy successfully, the competitor must possess similar resources, or capabilities that are the functional equivalent of the innovator's. Unless there is a barrier to acquiring the strategically relevant capabilities, the competitor can imitate the strategy of the innovator, rendering any competitive advantage temporary.

To the extent that monitoring of markets removes barriers keeping competitors from acquiring strategically relevant capabilities, the increased monitoring that accompanies debt will be costly to the innovating firm. Potential debt holders often require private information about the firm (e.g., through prospectuses) and information disclosed to capital markets becomes available to others, including competitors. Capital market monitoring arising from reliance on debt financing is costly when (1) information to competitors reduces the cost of imitating resources that provide the basis of a firm's competitive advantage; and/or (2) the firm has not yet established a property right (e.g., patent) to the resource (or configuration of resources) critical for the strategy.

In general, firms that possess strategically important resources that are not currently well understood by competitors and that acquire public debt will suffer strategic information loss by having their operations more widely scrutinized by capital markets. For example, firms with competitive advantages based on detailed buyer information or unpatentable process innovations rely on secrecy to maintain their competitive advantage. The following subsections focus on areas that may suffer strategic costs if a company seeks to take on increasing debt.

R&D and LBOs

Firms in research-intensive industries (e.g., pharmaceuticals) rely on producing a stream of innovations superior to those of their competitors for competitive advantage. Their competitive advantage stems from innovations that are either not yet sufficiently developed to protect from imitation through patents or inherently unprotectable with patents. Therefore, secrecy is critical to such firms. Secrecy is, however, especially difficult to maintain; efforts to do so are impeded by the capital market monitoring associated with high financial leverage.

In addition, as R&D spending increases, financial leverage decreases.[17] In fact, while most observers have argued that debt costs require more free cash flow to cover debt payments, thereby reducing discretionary expenditures, perhaps another reason for reduced allocations to R&D is the inability of the firm to protect the secrecy of new product or process innovations. LBOs in R&D-intensive industries are not likely to add value; in fact, as we have indicated, few LBOs have occurred in these industries. In addition, product development in mature product firms acquired through LBOs (such as Playtex) may be reduced. The lack of new product development may represent part of the reason for the decline in market share experienced by Playtex products.

There are, however, some firms that have increased their investments in R&D after undergoing LBOs.[18] One of the largest LBO firms, Kohlberg, Kravis, Roberts & Company, presented results of seventeen LBOs in which the firm had an equity stake and showed significant positive returns on its investment. Furthermore, KKR suggested that R&D expenditures rose by 15 percent after the LBOs for the seventeen KKR companies. However, others have argued that their data and results are not accurate. A National Science Foundation study found that R&D expenditures declined by an average of 12.8 percent after LBOs, and other studies have found significant reductions and capital spending at firms after LBOs. One study showed that the discrepancy between the KKR figures and those in other studies resulted from the methods used by KKR in making the calculations. The study also found that KKR consistently confused acquisitions with real economic growth. For example, many of the KKR firms continued to acquire companies after the LBO. Thus, while 400 employees might have been laid off as a result of the LBO, another company with 500 employees might have been acquired. In such a case, KKR would report that the LBO had created 100 new jobs, although, in fact, no new jobs had been created but 400 had been lost.[19] Another major study that examined more LBOs than any other study found that after LBOs firms invest less in R&D.[20]

Financial economists have argued that the increased debt from LBOs forces managers to make more efficient choices in their investments. Thus, they are less likely to invest in projects with negative net present value.[21] In effect, what often actually occurs is that managers focus on shorter-term and more applied-research projects, that is, they invest less in basic research and shift resources to applied research that offers more short-term and lower-risk payoffs. This strategy may produce significant positive results over the short term, but the prolonged neglect of basic research may have negative effects on the firm's long-term innovativeness and performance.[22]

Product Life Cycles and LBOs

Firms relying on multiple product introductions in industries where first-mover advantages are important also suffer from information disclosure through capital market monitoring. These firms may find that, before they can begin full-scale product introduction, a quick response by a competitor has destroyed their competitive advantage; goods with short product life cycles and high buyer evaluation costs (such as fashion items) are vulnerable to such tactics.[23] For such companies, success requires multiple product introductions, and those obtaining large market shares early earn important advantages. Most LBOs have occurred in nondurable manufacturing areas, such as apparel, which is subject to rapid changes in style. Many of these LBOs have not been successful.

In 1988 Interco was a furniture producer that had diversified into other businesses, including footwear, apparel manufacturing, and retail sales (furniture and hardware). The firm had good brand names in each of the businesses, including Lane and Broyhill furniture, Converse sneakers and Florsheim footwear, and Ethan Allen and Central Hardware (retail furniture and hardware stores). In 1988 CEO Harvey Saligman feared a possible takeover attempt and sought the help of the investment banker, Wasserstein Perella. The company received a takeover bid of $64 dollars per share but was counseled that the bid was too low. It therefore sought a recapitalization to prevent the takeover by assuming a significant amount of junk-bond debt. Although a leveraged buyout could have been possible, the firm chose the recapitalization.

Almost immediately after the deal was completed, it began to unravel. Operating earnings in 1989 were $227 million, short of the $350 million needed to cover payments on the $1.8 billion debt. Although the firm was able to sell Ethan Allen and Central Hardware, these sales garnered far less than estimated by the investment bankers. A plan was devised to cancel the junk bonds and to replace them with ownership, but creditors had suffered a 90 percent reduction in the price of their bonds and proved unwilling to provide the necessary debt financing. As a result, Interco filed for bankruptcy. This example demonstrates the risk of information disclosure, as well as the default risk inherent in junk bond financing.[24]

Culture, History, and LBOs

Socially complex resources, such as a valuable corporate culture, are especially difficult to imitate because cause-effect relationships are unclear. This ambiguity provides a barrier to imitation when both the firm with the competitive advantage and those seeking to imitate it do not adequately understand the resources that bring about the competitive advantage. Scrutiny of the valuable culture typically does not reveal the investments necessary to duplicate it. Information disclosure to capital markets, therefore, will not lead to imitation.[25]

A corporation's culture may of course be averse to high leverage, and the firm may therefore curtail its use of debt. This attitude is common, for example, in firms with a high percentage of conservative family ownership. However, if the culture is not biased against holding debt and if other issues are equal, firms may not restrict LBOs. On the other hand, other characteristics of the corporate culture (e.g., a focus on innovation or on long-term outcomes) may discourage LBOs because of the their consequences for these factors.

If the historical context of the firm's development provides the basis of an advantage, the advantage may be sustainable because of the difficulty of recreating that framework or its functional equivalent. The unique skills of a founder, for example, may provide the basis of a distinctive and valuable corporate culture or brand identity.

The Walt Disney Company's main competitive advantages stem from the unusual popularity of characters developed over a period of several decades. The careful protection of the use of these characters through aggressive copyright enforcement has precluded imitation, and the historical context of the firm's development impedes imitation with functionally equivalent characters. The affection for Mickey Mouse and the other Disney characters among adult consumers was forged when they were children, an opportunity no longer available to competitors.

For Disney, these advantages mean that close monitoring by capital markets is unlikely to erode its competitive advantage. The need to raise external capital to fund a new theme park, for example, will not provide information to competitors that allows them to imitate Disney's strategy. Other successful theme parks have been developed, in some ways imitating Disney's, but they cannot fully imitate the characters and the special characteristics associated with Disney. Thus, Disney can exploit the tax advantages of debt without being concerned about having competitors imitate its strategies. For firms with competitive advantage derived from a unique historical context, imitation is not facilitated by the information disclosure that may accompany high debt. Thus, for such firms, debt carries low strategic costs. This allowed Disney to recapitalize with more debt in the mid 1980s and prevent a takeover.

Competitive advantages based on reputation, especially when a consequence of the unique historical context in which the firm developed, are similarly not endangered by extensive capital market monitoring. Reputations evolve from buyer experience and thus are difficult to imitate except over long periods of time. If the context in which the experience develops uniquely enhances reputation, imitation may be largely impeded.

IBM, for example, has relied more heavily on its reputation for service and reliability and its ability to penetrate markets than have other computer manufacturers, which often rely on technological innovations to boost sales. The IBM reputation facilitated the development of complementary products by other manufacturers critical to the success of communication goods and allowed IBM to become the industry standard in several markets without being the first mover. This basis of competitive advantage was protected from imitation because it derived from IBM's performance in several markets over many years.[26] Debt did not possess the strategic costs for IBM that it did for competitors, whose success depended on the timely introduction of new products.

In essence, advantages already acquired are not endangered by debt financing. Firms possessing such assets may enjoy the tax advantages of debt with much lower risk of imitation. While its privileged position might have allowed IBM to take on more debt, its conservative culture forced greater reliance on internal financing. IBM also learned that reputation can be fragile; a significant downturn in sales and profits required major changes in corporate strategy and leadership in the early 1990s.

When brand identity is strong and valuable and product life cycles are long, brand identity may provide a source of long-term competitive advantage for the firm. For firms with established brand identities, imitation is difficult. In such circumstances, the strategic costs of leverage are lower.[27]

Dr. Pepper, for example, derives its competitive advantage from a distinctive brand identity refined over 100 years. Competitors' efforts to combat this advantage through the introduction of imitative products (e.g., Coca-Cola's Mr. Pibb) have achieved little success. Given this basis for competitive advantage, imitation is not facilitated through the capital market monitoring associated with high debt. For soft-drink manufacturers that rely on the success of new product introductions rather than on longstanding brand identities, use of financial leverage may carry greater strategic costs than it does for Dr. Pepper. In fact, the Dr. Pepper LBO was quite successful.

Although we have argued that reputation and brand image are not easily imitated, they may be fragile because they are based on stakeholder perception, an intangible (nonphysical) resource. As such, they may not have as significant an effect on capital structure as other tangible and intangible resources.

The fragility of reputation may be affected by short-term actions taken after LBOs to increase free cash flow. For example, Inns of America, Inc., had a reputation for maintaining a clean and secure motel chain in the years prior to its LBO. In fact, it rejected almost 90 percent of franchise applications because they did not meet the firm's standards. However, significant changes occurred after the company was acquired in a leveraged buyout in 1984. Whereas prior to the LBO the firm owned and operated at least 50 percent of its motels, it now owns and operates none of its hotels. It is a totally franchised operation, and the standards for franchisees have been significantly lowered, partly in order to improve free cash flow in the firm.

The reduction in standards for the franchise operators has tarnished the reputation of Days Inns (the franchised name from the parent company). One article noted that travelers using Days Inns motels are more likely than in the past to find stained walls, worn furnishings, and broken air conditioners. In fact, the article reported that Days Inns now ranks near the bottom of some surveys of travelers' satisfaction. Guests and former employees also reported a lack of security and a high incidence of crime and poor maintenance at some locations. Thus, while Days Inns promotes itself as the fastest-growing hotel chain in the United States, adding an average of 20 new properties every month, its occupancy rates were down from approximately 70 percent in 1984 to 60 percent in 1992, or almost 10 percent below the rates at competitors like Hampton Inn and Red Roof Inns.

Many of Days Inns' new properties came from conversions (motels that were part of other chains but lost their franchise because they did not meet company standards). These lower standards have been problematic for the company. In fact, a survey by *Business Travel News* ranked Days Inns next to last among 17 mid-price chains in physical appearance and room quality.[28]

The 1984 Days Inn buyout cost amounted to approximately $570 million, with only $30 million from the investors and the rest financed by junk bonds. In 1989 the firm was sold to the largest franchisee, reaping a profit of approximately $125 million. However, in 1991 Days Inns filed for bankruptcy under the strain of a $700 million debt and high interest rates. In 1992 the firm was purchased for $269 million—less than half the purchase price in 1984 and approximately one third the price paid in 1989. This LBO produced short-term efficiencies but also led to actions that harmed the firm's reputation and value over the long term.[29]

While most researchers have found that LBOs increase efficiency, these efficiencies often are only short-term. In particular, some work suggests that short-term gains in operating efficiencies may be followed by long-term debt-related problems and potential default among LBOs that remain private.[30]

LBOs and Capital Structure

LBOs and capital structure changes may have been positive in some cases, but the positive impact is limited because of high transaction costs (e.g., investment bank fees), trade-offs in innovation, and the inapplicability of LBOs to many business situations. Research suggests that the benefits of LBOs may be restricted to more limited arenas than those suggested by Michael Jensen in his often-cited article, "The Eclipse of the Public Corporation."[31] For example, some research suggests that LBOs offer the most positive outcomes in firms that have a record of generating large and steady cash flows. It is also true, however, that firms acquired by LBOs can typically increase cash flows not only by improving operating efficiencies and increasing sales but also by taking advantage of tax write-offs for increases in depreciation and debt cost.

However, some observers argue that LBOs may be a mechanism for transferring value from shareholders to management as happened in the LBOs at Playtex and Days Inns.[32] The quotes by the CEO of Playtex, Joel Smilo, at the time of the sale of his business to the Sara Lee Corporation suggest that his intentions were to increase short-term returns without investment in the long term. Of course, this may not simply be a function of LBOs; many writers in the popular press and some in academic circles have argued that managers in general tend to focus on the short term. One study has found that managers invest less in projects with long-term payoffs, such as R&D, if they are perceived to reduce annual (short-term) accounting returns.[33] Oliver Williamson has argued that debt governance (or discipline, as used by many financial economists) works mainly on the basis of rules. However, he argues that equity governance allows much greater discretion than does debt governance. He therefore suggests that the use of debt is more effective for financing redeployable assets but that nonredeployable assets (e.g., research and development) should be financed by equity. With LBOs primarily financed by debt, investments in redeployable assets may suffer.[34]

Summary

In this chapter we have argued that heavy reliance on debt may force costly disclosure of sensitive information to competitors. Given the recent trends toward increased debt,[34] this is certain to have an effect on the information disclosed to capital markets. The position developed in this chapter complements other approaches to capital structure. Observations about the interaction of management risk taking and capital structure decisions, along with concerns of financial economists about taxes and potential bankruptcy costs, are important components of a complete understanding of capital structure decisions. Finance researchers have also introduced theories of capital structure that highlight strategic issues. In addition, some have advocated extreme financial leverage for firms that produce cash flows in excess of those required for their core businesses.

The perspective presented herein implies that the relationship between free cash flows and financial leverage may be affected by the nature of the competitive advantage in the core business. Firms for which information disclosure to competitors opens their strategy to imitation by those competitors may prefer low debt despite the presence of high free cash flows. Conversely, firms with attractive investment opportunities in their core businesses may maximize their value with high financial leverage if their competitive advantage stems from unique historical circumstances that are not easily imitated. Reputation is fragile, however, and high leverage may not always work to the firm's advantage.

Because capital structure changed significantly in the 1980s, a view of capital structure that incorporates the strategic implications of such changes is of increasing importance. Although there have been claims that the default risk has been lower than anticipated for junk bonds, restructuring in the 1980s funded by high-yield securities was not as safe as LBOs done earlier in the 1980s.[35] Only 41 LBO deals, or 2 percent, of those completed between 1980 and 1984 defaulted. However, 19 of 78 deals done between 1985 and 1988 defaulted, for a rate of 24 percent. Buyouts during the late 1980s may have been overpriced, and capital structure and management incentives may not have been as focused on the long term as in the earlier period. Probably because of increased default, buyout volume fell from $60 billion in 1988 to $4 billion in 1990. However, the high default rates continued in the 1990s, as exemplified by Macy's and Days Inns, suggesting that theories about the advantages of leverage may be deficient. Although there is merit to the theory that leverage may discipline managers (e.g., by forcing them to cut costs and trim inefficient expenditures in the short run), the need for longer-term perspectives and the problems created by heavy debt loads may offset the gains achieved from increased short-term operating efficiencies.

Furthermore, we suggest that the strategic costs of restructuring through higher levels of debt may produce trade-offs that discourage the use of high-yield securities in capital structure. In addition to the increased risk associated with these securities, there are strategic costs that may prevent others from restructuring using junk-bond financing. In essence, leveraged buyouts are an alternative to unrelated diversification. Unrelated diversification appears to work best when the portfolio focuses on low-technology, mature businesses (see chapter 9). LBO groups such as KKR may be an alternative to unrelated diversification. It appears that LBOs work well for mature product firms that have high cash flows and that are relatively stable. In general, LBOs may help such firms to become more efficient. However, these effects seem largely constrained to an idiosyncratic set of firms. It is not likely that LBOs will be enough to meet the competitiveness challenge faced by U.S. firms as presented in chapter 5.[36]

The following implications for managers are derived from the material in this chapter:

- LBOs as a restructuring alternative may help executives achieve short-term efficiency.
- This strategy can be effective, but only for mature, high-cash-flow industries with assets that are redeployable (e.g., that have alternative uses).
- LBOs may resolve the incentive problem through drastic changes in capital structure but may cause other problems, such as increased risk of bankruptcy.
- Higher levels of debt may be used effectively when history and/or reputation reduce strategic costs, such as the possibility of imitation. However, such barriers may be fragile.

Notes

1. Burrough, B., & Johnson, R. 1988. Beatrice, once hailed deal of the century, proves disappointing. *The Wall Street Journal*, November 21:A1, A8.

2. Yago, G. 1991. *Junk Bonds: How High Yield Securities Restructured Corporate America.* New York: Oxford University Press, pp. 146–48.

3. Woo, C. Y., Dallenbach, U. S., Willard, G. 1991. G.E. spin-off performance: Expectations and evidence. Paper presented at the Academy of Management meetings, Miami.

4. Yago, *Junk Bonds*, p. 111.

5. Jensen, M. C. 1989. Eclipse of the public corporation. *Harvard Business Review* 67(5):61–74; Jensen, M. C. 1986. The takeover controversy: Analyses and evidences. *Midland Corporate Financial Journal* 4(2):6–32.

6. Baysinger, B. D., & Hoskisson, R. E. 1989. Diversification strategy and R&D intensity in large multiproduct firms. *Academy of Management Journal* 32:310–32; Hitt, M. A., Hoskisson, R. E. Ireland, R. D., & Harrison, J. S. 1991.

Are acquisitions a poison pill for innovation? *Academy of Management Executive* 5(4):22–34.

7. Bernanke, B. S., & Campbell, J. Y. 1988. Is there a corporate debt crisis? *Brookings Papers on Economic Activity* 1(1):83–139; Rappaport, A. 1990. The staying power of the public corporation. *Harvard Business Review* 68(1):96–104; Roach, S. S. 1989. Living with corporate debt. *Journal of Applied Corporate Finance* 2(1):19–30.

8. Jensen, Eclipse.

9. Modigliani, F., & Miller, M. 1963. Taxes and the cost of capital: A correction. *American Economic Review* 53:433–43; Miller, M. 1977. Debt and taxes. *Journal of Finance* 32:261–75; Baxter, N. 1967. Leverage, risk of ruin and the cost of capital. *Journal of Finance* 22:395–403; Ross, S. A. 1977. The determination of financial structure: The incentive-signalling approach. *Bell Journal of Economics* 8:23–40; Myers, S., & Majluf, N. S. 1984. Stock issues and investment policy when firms have information that investors do not. *Journal of Financial Economics* 13:187–222.

10. Barton, S. L., & Gordon, P. J. 1987. Corporate strategy: Useful perspective for the study of capital structure. *Academy of Management Review* 12:67–75; Barton, S. L., & Gordon, P. J. 1988. Corporate strategy and capital structure. *Strategic Management Journal* 9:623–32.

11. Jensen, M. C. 1986. Agency costs of free cash flow, corporate finance and takeovers. *American Economic Review* 76:323–29.

12. Jensen, M., & Meckling, W. 1976. Theory of the firm: Managerial behavior, agency costs, and ownership structure. *Journal of Financial Economics* 5:305–60.

13. Jensen, Eclipse.

14. Anders, G. 1991. Odyssey: Playtex goes through four buyouts since 1985, enriching top officer. *The Wall Street Journal*, December 17:A–1, A–5.

15. Yago, *Junk Bonds*, pp. 149–50.

16. Gill, D. 1992. Debt-laden Macy files for bankruptcy. *Houston Chronicle*, January 28:1–A, 6–A; Wolk, M. 1992. Debt proves bane of many retailers. *Houston Chronicle*, January 28:3–C.

17. Baysinger, B. D., & Hoskisson, R. E., Diversification strategy; Guerard, J. B., Bean, A. S., & Andrews, S. 1987. R&D management and corporate financial policy. *Management Science* 33:1419–27; Hall, B. H. 1990. The impact of corporate restructuring on industrial research and development. *Brookings Papers on Economic Activity* 3:85–135.

18. Zahra, S. A., & Fescina, M. 1991. Will leveraged buyouts kill U.S. corporate research and development? *Academy of Management Executive* 5(4):7–21.

19. Long, W. F., & Ravenscraft, D. J. 1991. The record of LBO performance. In A. R. Santez, *The Battle for Corporate Control: Shareholder Rights, Stakeholder Interests and Managerial Responsibilities*. Homewood, Ill.: Business One Irwin, pp. 517–42.

20. Ravenscraft, D. J., & Long, W. F. 1993. LBOs, debt and R&D intensity. *Strategic Management Journal* (Summer special issue) 14:119–35.

21. Fox, I., & Marcus, A. 1992. The causes and consequences of leveraged management buyouts. *Academy of Management Review* 17:62–85.

22. Zahra & Fescina, Leveraged buyouts.

23. Kopp, R. J., Eng, R. J., & Tigert, D. J. 1989. A competitive structure

and segmentation analysis of the Chicago fashion market. *Journal of Retailing* 65:496–515.

24. Anders, G., & Scheadel, F. 1990. Wall Street helped Interco defeat raiders—but at a heavy price. *The Wall Street Journal*, July 11:A–1, A–6.

25. Barney, J. 1986. Organization culture: Can it be a source of sustained competitive advantage? *Academy of Management Review* 11:656–65.

26. Connor, K., & Rumelt, R. P. 1986. *Software piracy*. Working paper, University of California at Los Angeles.

27. Barney, J. 1988. Returns to bidding firms in mergers and acquisitions: Reconsidering the relatedness hypothesis. *Strategic Management Journal* 9:71–8.

28. Helliker, K. 1992. Weak links: How a motel chain lost its moorings after 1980s buyout. *The Wall Street Journal*, May 26:A–1, A–10.

29. Ibid.

30. Fox & Marcus, Causes and consequences.

31. Jensen, Eclipse.

32. Maupin, R. J. 1987. Financial and stock market variables as predictors of management buyouts. *Strategic Management Journal* 8:319–27.

33. Bruner, R. F., & Paine, L. S. 1988. Management buyouts and managerial ethics. *California Management Review* Winter:89–106.

34. Baber, W. R., & Haggard, J. A. 1988. Management use of discrepancy to manipulate financial accounting income: The case of research and development. Working paper, Carnegie Mellon University.

35. Williamson, O. E. 1988. Corporate finance and corporate governance. *Journal of Finance* 48:567–91.

36. Roach, Living with corporate debt.

37. Jensen, M. C. 1989. Active investors, LBOs and the privatization of bankruptcy. *Journal of Applied Corporate Finance* 4(2):61–74.

8

Downscoping

Between 1968 and 1979 General Mills pursued a pattern of growth through acquisition and diversification. Moving from its base in consumer foods, General Mills expanded into toys, games, apparel, specialty retailing, travel service, rare coins and stamps, and restaurants. All acquisitions had well-established national-brand franchises. In 1968 89.5 percent of General Mills' sales were in consumer foods; by 1976, only 61.8 percent of sales were in consumer foods. In 1981 Bruce Atwater became CEO. He realized that corporate strategy was unevenly distributed across industries and product lines and that many product lines were subject to sharp cyclical swings. He also found in the early 1980s that General Mills' diversification strategy was increasingly devalued by the market.

Cyclical downturns in several product lines between 1982 and 1984 led General Mills to announce a restructuring in 1985. Two businesses, Kenner Parker Toys and Crystal Brands (a specialty retailer), were spun off, and other businesses were pared. The restructuring activity was completed by 1988. By the end of 1989, the food business accounted for 71 percent of sales. The other dominant business, restaurants (the Red Lobster chain), was seen as complementary to the consumer foods business; planners assumed that changes in the external labor force (e.g., the increase in dual-career families) would increase the market for the restaurant business and offset any decline in the consumer foods business. Thus, through restructuring, General Mills downscoped, became more strategically focused, and improved its performance.[1]

In chapter 4 we suggested that a strategy of acquisitive growth often creates extensive diversification and increased debt that in turn leads to decreased innovation. This chapter proposes that restructuring divestitures may reverse the process if it results in strategic refocusing (i.e., decreased diversification and stronger strategic control focused on the firm's core businesses). Research presented in this chapter indicates that R&D investment improves in the postrestructuring period when the firm downscopes. Furthermore, downscoping, if managed properly, may not result in a trade-off in performance. Thus, strategic refocusing that succeeds in reducing diversification and in applying strategic control and incentives is likely to improve innovation and subsequent competitiveness. Downscoping, rather than downsizing, is emphasized because downscoping allows improved strategic control, whereas downsizing often emphasizes across-the-board layoffs and ultimately the relinquishing of market share, thereby producing performance trade-offs. Although downsizing may reduce bureaucracy and thereby improve efficiency, downscoping enhances the opportunity for overall strategic improvement in highly diversified firms.

Corporate refocusing of this type, in which large diversified firms in many industries changed their portfolio of assets, was common in the 1980s. More firms, however, downscoped through voluntary divestitures, as in the General Mills example, than chose the more extreme action of taking the firm private through an LBO. This chapter examines the outcome of downscoping and the trade-offs involved. A common misconception is that restructuring involves only downscoping of conglomerates (unrelated diversified firms). Research has shown, however, that firms with intermediate levels of diversification (e.g., related linked firms with mixed related and unrelated components) are more likely to restructure than are firms with other corporate diversification strategies (e.g., related constrained or unrelated types). Firms with all types of diversification, in fact, undertook restructuring actions.[2] The remainder of the chapter describes possible explanations for these actions and reviews the effect of restructuring on R&D activity. Finally, trade-offs of these events are assessed in relation to their effect on future competitiveness.

Restructuring and Diversification Strategy

If a firm has a strong strategic advantage in its primary market, it may have no reason to seek additional diversification. However, if diversification becomes important for defensive reasons, such as reversing poor performance, stimulating new growth, or creating the potential for synergy between separate product divisions, a small amount of diversification may not fully realize these opportunities. Firms considering diversification often implement the multidivisional (M-form) structure, in anticipation of such expansion. As we argued in chapters 1 and 2, the M-form provides information-processing advantages that facilitate continued diversification. Once a firm becomes diversified and implements the

M-form structure, therefore, it may expand diversification to an efficient level; that level will be lower for related and higher for unrelated diversified firms.[3]

When firms exceed certain diversification limits, they suffer reduced performance because ineffective strategic control or overemphasis on financial controls produce poor managerial decisions. As diversification increases, one scholar noted, "a depth-for-breadth trade-off" may occur: "As the capacity to engage knowledgeably in internal resource allocation becomes strained, problems of misallocation and opportunism intrude."[4] Firms may follow a hedging strategy (i.e., hedging against risk) by diversifying into unrelated businesses. This strategy, however, also may produce risk aversion (e.g., reducing investment in R&D or choosing to invest in less risky projects). Although at times such actions may be prudent, they can have negative long-term competitive consequences. In fact, research suggests that low relative R&D investments are related to the competitiveness problems faced by firms.[5]

The problems faced by Pacific Enterprises, a major utility firm on the West coast, exemplify the outcomes of too much diversification. While a number of utility firms diversified their operations in the 1980s, Pacific Enterprises invested more than $2 billion into largely unrelated businesses, such as drug stores, sporting goods outlets, and petroleum operations. In fact, this firm pioneered among utilities in diversifying its operations when it bought pistachio groves in the 1960s. The diversification, however, has had negative effects on the performance of Pacific Enterprises, as the firm's operations outside its core business have performed poorly. For the most part, the profits from its core business have offset the losses from the diversified businesses; however, Pacific Enterprises operated at a net loss in 1991. One analyst at Kidder, Peabody described Pacific Enterprises as a very sick patient with a long expected recovery time. Because of performance problems, the firm has decided to sell many of its diversified operations and to concentrate on its Southern California Gas Company unit, which is one of its most profitable businesses. It may have problems selling a number of its other properties, however. The market for oil and gas properties is weak, as is that for retail operations, which are suffering from problems related to the recession of the early 1990s. Only time will tell if the firm will be able to effectively restructure and achieve positive outcomes.[6]

Chapter 3 suggested that the ultimate reason for restructuring may be poor governance. Lack of strong monitoring by owners (e.g., low ownership concentration), poor board oversight, and excessive free cash flows may allow managers to diversify beyond the point of efficiency for shareholders, although such diversification may be in the managers' best interests (e.g., by reducing their employment risk).[7] Research generally confirms that poor governance, excessive diversification, and poor performance serve as catalysts to restructuring divestitures.[8]

The level of firm diversification often is affected by restructuring.

Restructuring, however, does not always result in a reduction in diversification, because each firm has the opportunity to redirect corporate strategy. In fact, research shows that some firms, after making divestitures, increased their level of diversification, either by divesting businesses highly related to their core business or by acquiring unrelated businesses (using cash from the divestitures).[9] Figure 5 shows that, of the 189 firms studied, most firms (72) decreased their level of diversification in the postrestructuring environment, some (22) firms increased their level of diversification, and others (95) maintained the same level.

Figure 5 also suggests that intermediate diversifiers, related linked firms, are the most likely to restructure. This point deserves explanation because the press has given the impression that highly diversified conglomerates are the most likely to restructure. Related linked, intermediate diversifiers, have both unrelated and related business units and thus may have inconsistent control systems. For instance, related constrained firms that try to achieve synergy among their related businesses to promote economies require different control systems than do unrelated firms. To achieve synergy among related businesses, the organizational arrangements (structure and control systems) should promote cooperation. In unrelated firms, cooperation between business units is relatively unimportant; organizational arrangements that promote independence and competition for resources should produce higher performance. Centralization and other structural arrangements and incentive systems that

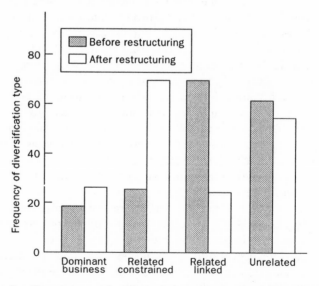

Figure 5. Comparison of pre- and postrestructuring diversification levels (*Source:* Hoskisson, R. E., & Johnson, R. A. 1992. Corporate Restructuring and Strategic Change: The Effect of Diversification and R&D Intensity. *Strategic Management Journal* 13: 625–34.)

promote cooperation are therefore most effective in related business firms, whereas decentralization and structural arrangements and incentive systems that facilitate independence and competition among units are most effective in unrelated diversified firms.

A 1992 study found that centralized control in the corporate office, interdivisional integration, reliance on subjective and objective nonfinancial controls, and emphasis on both corporate and divisional performance in calculating division managers' incentive compensation were positively related to return on assets in related diversified firms. On the other hand, in unrelated diversified firms, decentralization of control to the divisions, reduced reliance on subjective and objective nonfinancial controls, and heavy (or sole) emphasis on divisional performance in determining division managers' incentive compensation were positively related to return on assets.[10]

Related linked firms have characteristics of both related and unrelated diversification. Firms with both related and unrelated diversification components may create inconsistent control systems in promoting restructuring. Such a conclusion is consistent with previous research suggesting that too much integration within unrelated firms creates performance problems. It may therefore be inefficient organizationally to pursue simultaneously synergy to achieve economies of scope associated with related constrained businesses and financial synergy associated with unrelated businesses. This inconsistency suggests why related linked firms may be prime candidates for restructuring.

The problems at Du Pont exemplify the difficulty of managing multiple businesses that vary in their degree of relatedness and in the control systems necessary for them to be effective. Du Pont acquired a number of "promising" high-growth businesses in the mid-1980s. These businesses included electronic products (unrelated to the firm's core business), pharmaceuticals (distantly related to the core business), and agricultural chemicals (highly related to the core business). Unfortunately, Du Pont is not performing well in any of these three businesses, and CEO Ed Woolard is selling them or spinning them off to refocus the firm on its traditional core businesses of fibers, chemicals, and polymers. Du Pont's sales and earnings both declined in 1991 as revenues fell by $1.35 billion and earnings dropped by 39 percent to $1.4 billion, the lowest level since 1985. Return on equity was 8.3 percent, much lower than the 16 percent projected by Woolard in 1989. Du Pont is highly representative of the problems we have been describing. As a result, it is restructuring to refocus strategically on its traditional core businesses.[11]

Restructuring, Corporate Strategy, and R&D Investment

The business press has fostered the idea that the high debt levels associated with acquisitions and sell-offs severely restrict managers' flexibility.[12] High debt forces managers to focus on reducing expenses, including expenditures for R&D and other expenditures with long-term potential payoffs. (This is one of the trade-offs of restructuring with heavy debt, discussed in chapter 7.) One researcher found a negative relationship between acquisitions and R&D investment, primarily because of the debt required to finance the acquisition.[13] If a firm reduces diversification without increasing debt, investment in R&D is likely to increase.

Firms in R&D-intensive industries have strong competitive reasons for maintaining R&D investment at or above the industry average. One study found, however, that firms pursuing growth through acquisition invested less than their industry counterparts in R&D during the postacquisition period. Not only was R&D investment negatively related to acquisition activity, R&D outputs (number of patents) also decreased in the postmerger period.[14] This research also provided evidence that higher debt, increased firm size, and greater diversification contributed to lower levels of R&D investment in acquisitive growth firms.[15] In general, the evidence suggests that multiple divestitures which reduce a firm's level of diversification, size, and possibly, its level of debt should produce greater R&D investment because this action helps managers to reassert strategic control.

If divestitures occur without additional acquisitions, the level of diversification may change. One result of restructuring may be lower and more focused diversification, along with stronger strategic control (allowing more managerial flexibility and an emphasis on long-term performance). Stronger strategic control should produce increased managerial risk taking because division managers perceive that risk is shared more appropriately. As a result, increases in R&D investments may be expected.

Restructuring divestitures may also be executed to build cash reserves in order to make additional unrelated acquisitions. Such acquisitions, of course, may be part of a change in corporate strategy. If restructuring leads to strategic changes that increase the scope of diversification, an accompanying reduction in level of R&D investment may be anticipated. Higher levels of diversification in the postrestructuring period are likely to produce shorter time horizons and more risk-averse actions by division managers. Restructuring activity with no change in diversification strategy or scope is less likely to affect R&D, because most of the controls remain the same. If the divestitures reduce firm size, bureaucratic controls (e.g., rules, policies) may decrease. Furthermore, if resources from the sale of units are used to reduce debt levels, managerial commitment to innovation may increase.[16]

In fact, research has demonstrated that restructuring which reduces diversification is related to increased R&D investment. Restructuring firms trying to refocus strategically on their core business(es) are more willing to take risks. One study indicated that dominant business or related constrained firms in the postrestructuring period were competitive with industry counterparts and, in fact, appeared to be investing more in R&D than the competition. However, R&D investments did not increase for unrelated firms in comparison to industry counterparts in the postrestructuring period.[17]

The Ball Corporation announced plans to spin off its noncore business operations to shareholders, intending to refocus strategically on its glass and metal packaging and aerospace core businesses. In fact, the firm is continuing to invest heavily in its core businesses. For example, it bought additional glass container–manufacturing capacity and negotiated to buy part of Eastman Kodak's Federal Systems Division. By spinning off its noncore business operations, Ball executives expect to concentrate more of their effort and energy on the core businesses and to provide more effective strategic leadership for the firm.[18]

The "R&D factor" may be an important contributor to competitiveness in global markets. In the study reviewed earlier, restructuring appeared to facilitate R&D investment and also led to improved asset utilization ratios and productivity in the postrestructuring period.[19]

Integration

Although downscoping divestitures appear to help U.S. firms be more competitive, this conclusion should be interpreted cautiously. Other research has found that poorly performing firms take greater risks but that they take risks with low expected payoffs.[20] Evidence presented in this chapter on postrestructuring accounting performance (ROA) indicates that performance does not decline. It may be that risk taking in restructuring firms may produce better performance than that undertaken by firms undergoing tactical change through divestiture because of serious unmanageable problems. This conclusion is supported by research showing that layoffs associated with poor firm performance produce a negative stock market response.[21]

The cases of Calumet Farms and Unocal provide evidence the consequences of serious management problems. Although in the early 1980s Calumet was a thriving operation that sold prize yearlings for more than $10 million and an acre of prime bluegrass farmland for $42,000, it later underwent difficult bankruptcy proceedings. In fact, the pending sale of Calumet Farms is expected to net approximately $20 million, one third of the business's worth in the 1980s. Calumet's problems are the result of mismanagement and a $150 million debt. Similarly, Unocal took on a high debt load in 1985 to finance a major stock repurchase to avoid a takeover attempt by T. Boone Pickens. The firm attempted to sell at least $700 million in assets over several years and laid off a large number of employees in order to increase its cash flow and to reduce its debt load. Since 1985 Unocal has sold assets and reduced its debt by approximately $1.4 billion. In 1992, however, its long-term debt was still approximately $4.54 billion. Although Unocal is a related diversified firm, asset sales will continue to reduce its scope of operations. In fact, the intent is to narrow the firm's focus to oil resources and to limit its refining, marketing, transportation, and chemical operations.[22]

Restructuring activity may result in part from increased competition among diversified firms that must have competitive portfolios of businesses. For diversification to be successful, businesses must make acquisitions for strategic reasons, rather than merely to increase size. One theory of diversification holds that dominant business firms may be in a temporary stage between the single business stage and a more diversified (related and unrelated) stage. Thus, there are fewer dominant businesses than single or diversified business firms.[23]

Firms that pursue extensive diversification may ultimately reverse the process and divest businesses to achieve an optimal level of diversification through downscoping. A prime candidate for restructuring may be firms that have both related and unrelated components. The research suggests there are fewer intermediate diversifiers (e.g., related linked firms) after restructuring because firms focus on synergy to achieve economies of scope (e.g., related constrained) or financial economies (e.g., unrelated). As a result, ultimately there may be a trimodal distribution of firms: those that focus on a single or dominant business, those that emphasize a set of related businesses, and those that have a set of unrelated businesses. Diversification must fulfill a competitive strategic purpose; even large diversified firms are subject to competitive influences that, if not managed appropriately, can create the need for more drastic change, such as hostile takeovers or leveraged buyouts by an investment bank.

There are no guarantees that refocusing activity will result in competitive success. Although many firms have improved shareholder value through restructuring, some firms have restructured unsuccessfully; for example, the results of a number of leveraged buyouts have been poor compared to the outcomes of voluntary downscoping and restructuring.

During the 1980s Tenneco restructured its firm and focused strongly on its J. I. Case farm and construction equipment division. In fact, in 1988 Tenneco sold a sizable amount of its oil and gas assets for $7.4 billion in order to reduce its debt, buy back its stock, and prevent a potential takeover bid. In so doing, it shifted the company's strategic focus from energy to the J. I. Case division. While J. I. Case had had net losses each year since 1981, analysts predicted increasing demand. As a result, production was strongly boosted in 1988. Demand, however, did not increase as expected, and serious problems ensued. The firm had sizable inventories in its J. I. Case division and a debt-to-equity ratio of almost 70 percent. In fact, Tenneco was close to bankruptcy when Michael Walsh was hired as CEO. Mr. Walsh made painful reductions in the J. I. Case division, including layoffs of more than 10,000 employees and plant shutdowns.

Even though Tenneco strategically refocused, the decision to focus on the farm and construction equipment market was a poor one. The mere act of strategically refocusing does not guarantee success unless the appropriate business(es) is chosen as the core and the restructuring activity is implemented effectively.[24]

Summary

We conclude that voluntary downscoping with the purpose of strategic refocusing is more likely to produce positive competitive outcomes than are other types of restructuring. Our research showed that R&D investments increased in the postrestructuring period. Restructuring to produce a strategic reorientation appears to correct strategic problems; the majority of restructuring firms narrowed their focus of diversification, although the number of unrelated firms remained relatively constant, and the majority of related linked firms reduced their level of diversification. Restructuring, if done correctly, can stimulate R&D activity, facilitate strategic control, and foster improved asset utilization. As a result, downscoping offers the potential for improved competitiveness. The material covered in this chapter suggests the following managerial implications:

- Firms that are overdiversified should downscope rather than downsize. Downscoping allows improved strategic control.
- Related linked firms are the most likely to need restructuring because of mixed control systems (used with their related and unrelated businesses.) Related linked or a mixture of related and unrelated businesses should be avoided.
- Restructuring should lead to a strategic refocusing on the firm's core business(es). This should allow the reemergence of strategic controls, which produce a longer-term vision (e.g., more investment in R&D) and better asset utilization.
- Strategic refocusing should produce positive outcomes—but only if the appropriate business or set of businesses is selected as the core and if the restructuring is implemented effectively.

Notes

1. Donaldson, G. 1991. Voluntary corporate restructuring: The case of General Mills. *Journal of Applied Corporate Finance* 4(3):6–19.

2. Hoskisson, R. E., & Johnson, R. A. 1992. Corporate restructuring and strategic change: The effect on diversification and R&D intensity. *Strategic Management Journal* 13:625–34; Markides, C. C. 1992. The economic characteristics of de-diversifying firms. *British Journal of Management* 3:91–100.

3. Markides, C. C. 1992. Consequences of corporate refocusing: Ex ante evidence. *Academy of Management Journal* 35:398–412.

4. Williamson, O. E. 1985. *The Economic Institutions of Capitalism: Firms, Markets, and Relational Contracting.* New York: Free Press, p. 289.

5. Franko, L. G. 1989. Global corporate competition: Who's winning,

who's losing, and the R&D factor as one reason why. *Strategic Management Journal* 10:449–74.

6. Rose, F. 1992. Pacific Enterprises faces ocean of diversification woes. *The Wall Street Journal*, February 7:B–4.

7. Hoskisson, R. E., & Turk, T. A. 1990. Corporate restructuring: Governance and control limits of the internal capital market. *Academy of Management Review* 15:459–77.

8. Hoskisson, R. E., Johnson, R. A. & Moesel, D. O. 1993. Divestiture intensity in restructuring firms: effects of governance, strategy and performance. Paper presented at the Strategic Management Society, Chicago.

9. Hoskisson & Johnson, Corporate restructuring and strategic change.

10. Hill, C. W. L., Hitt, M. A., & Hoskisson, R. E. 1992. Cooperative versus competitive structures in related and unrelated diversified firms. *Organization Science* 3:501–21.

11. Weber, J. 1992. Du Pont's trailblazer wants to get out of the woods: Ed Woolard has been shrinking or spinning off businesses he once saw as engines of growth. *Business Week*, August 31:70–71.

12. Deveny, K. 1989. Progress isn't drowning in debt—yet. *Business Week*, June 10:110.

13. Hall, B. H. 1990. The impact of corporate restructuring on industrial research and development. *Brookings Papers on Economic Activity* 3:85–135.

14. Hitt, M. A., Hoskisson, R. E., Ireland, R. D., & Harrison, J. S. 1991. The effects of acquisitions on R&D inputs and outputs. *Academy of Management Journal* 34:693–706.

15. Hitt, M. A., Hoskisson, R. E., Ireland, R. D., & Harrison, J. S. 1991. Are acquisitions a poison pill for innovation? *Academy of Management Executive* 5(4):22–34.

16. Hitt, M. A., Hoskisson, R. E., & Ireland, R. D. 1990. Mergers and acquisitions and managerial commitment to innovation in M-form firms. *Strategic Management Journal* (Special Issue) 11:29–47.

17. Hoskisson & Johnson, Corporate restructuring and strategic change.

18. *The Wall Street Journal.* 1992. Ball Corp. to spin off non-core operations with Peterson chief. August 20:B–4.

19. Nelson, R. R. 1989. Research on productivity growth and productivity differences: Dead ends and new departures. *Journal of Economic Literature* 19:1029–64.

20. Bromiley, P. 1991. Testing a causal model of corporate risk taking and performance. *Academy of Management Journal* 34:37–59; Fiegenbaum, A., & Thomas, H. 1988. Attitudes toward risk and the risk-return paradox: Prospect theory explanations. *Academy of Management Journal* 31:85–106.

21. Worrell, D. L., Davidson, W. N., & Sharma, V. M. 1991. Layoff announcements and stockholder wealth. *Academy of Management Journal* 34:662–78.

22. Stern, G. 1992. Calumet Farm hits the finish line out of the money: Saddled with debts, breeder of Whirlaway and Citation is up for auction. *The Wall Street Journal*, March 26:B–4; Rose, F. 1992. Unocal plans another round of asset sales, job cuts. *The Wall Street Journal*, April 28:B–4.

23. Reed, R. 1991. Bimodality in diversification: An efficiency and effectiveness rationale. *Managerial and Decision Economics* 12:57–66.

24. Lee, S. H. 1992. Tough at the top: Tenneco CEO takes no prisoners in painful restructuring. *The Dallas Morning News*, August 23:H1–H2.

9

Restructuring and the Unrelated Strategy

Assuming managers generally seek to enhance firm value in acquisitions, unrelated acquisitions should not regularly occur. Logically, related acquirers should generally outbid unrelated acquirers in competition for target firms (because they have more to gain, in the form of synergy). Still, unrelated diversification remains a popular corporate diversification strategy. As the evidence presented in chapter 8 suggests, many firms that underwent multiple divestitures to initiate restructuring nonetheless remained unrelated diversifiers. In fact, intermediate diversified firms moved away from their strategy and toward becoming related diversifiers, while unrelated diversifiers often stayed with their strategy. This finding was confirmed by a sampling of firms that was biased in favor of downscoping because the sample firms were overdiversified. Research has also suggested that under some circumstances unrelated acquisitions can produce gains for shareholders, or at least not generate losses. Furthermore, the continued prevalence of unrelated diversification suggests that this strategy is supported by firm stakeholders.[1]

The advantages of a multidivisional structure in the allocation of financial resources has been identified as a reason for unrelated diversification. Resource allocation among divisions by the corporate office may be more efficient than resource allocation in the external market because corporate officers have better information than market analysts and can fine-tune incentives for division managers. Market incentives, by comparison, are rather crude. Market players have two basic choices: sell the equity in a company or try to displace current management. The multidivisional system of internal controls is particularly well suited to unrelated diversification because businesses are kept separate during the capital allocation process (research provides some support for this conjecture).[2] Also, many conglomerate firms are believed to possess an advantage in creating shareholder value through financial synergy.[3] Thus, the central challenge for the unrelated diversifier as it restructures is to manage effectively its current businesses with appropriate controls and to identify acquisition targets that can be effectively managed with those same controls. This approach may allow it to increase shareholder value while avoiding the pitfalls identified with unrelated diversification that we discussed in earlier chapters.

This chapter describes the type of target businesses likely to increase value for an unrelated diversifier, given appropriate controls. It suggests that, although the unrelated strategy continues to be used by firms, its dominant role may be to help police other poorly performing diversified firms or conglomerates. Thus, it is not likely to correct the strategic competitiveness problem described in chapter 5, although it may curtail it in some firms. Although some conglomerates have reduced their level of diversification and adjusted their portfolio to include more mature businesses, this form of restructuring is not considered downscoping. Restructuring the unrelated firm into a more focused conglomerate will not eliminate the competitiveness problem.

Examples of Unrelated Diversified Firms

Hansen PLC is an unrelated diversified company engaged in a wide variety of businesses, primarily in the United Kingdom and in the United States. In the United Kingdom, its businesses include the manufacture of bricks, dry cell batteries, electrical and gas equipment, and tobacco products; the supplying of construction equipment, cement, and house building. Its U.S. businesses include the harvesting and the sale of timber; the manufacture of lumber, garden and industrial hand tools, specialty textiles, housewares, shoes, lighting fixtures, office furniture and supplies, building materials, cement, chemicals, industrial, automotive and consumer and recreational products; and the mining of coal and gold. In the United States, Hansen has owned brand names such as Ball Park (hot dogs), Burger King, Carnation (milk), Spartan (weight-training machines), and Jacuzzi. Ranked by sales, Hansen is among the top 100 industrial firms in the world, with 1991 sales of $13.8 billion. Between 1989 and 1990, it divested approximately 50 businesses or parts of businesses, undergoing a significant restructuring.

Hansen is continually restructuring; it acquires and sells other businesses. Although on paper Hansen is classified in three major business segments (industrial, consumer, and building products), its real business is buying and selling businesses. Hansen's strategy includes buying mature businesses, often ones that are performing poorly, turning around their performance, and selling off the lower performing businesses while keeping the rest. It also restructures and often eliminates large corporate headquarters staffs. In recent years Hansen has been doing more selling than buying. Before 1989, however, it had acquired SCM Corporation, Imperial Group PLC, Kaiser Cement Corporation, and Kidde, Inc. Then, in 1989, Hansen bought Consolidated Gold Fields PLC, and, in 1991, Peabody Holding Company (the largest coal producer in the United States), Cavenham Forest Products, and Beazer PLC.

Hansen focuses on large acquisitions and emphasizes the bottom line by focusing on profitable activities in low-technology industries. This strategy is maintained through tight financial controls, management incentives, and avoidance of risky R&D activity (not required in mature and/or low-technology industries). In following this strategy, Hansen has turned around the businesses of other conglomerates, such as SCM and Kidde. Furthermore, it has achieved its stated goals for growth and for returns to shareholders, apparently by acquiring mature, low-technology businesses requiring minimal R&D expenditures and operating in areas with slow but consistent growth.

Another British firm took a different unrelated diversification approach and failed, at least at first. Thorn EMI PLC had ambitions of being a world force in high-technology markets. In the early 1980s the company bought Britain's largest semiconductor business, pumped cash into its consumer electronics operations, and contemplated a takeover of British Aerospace PLC, the country's biggest aerospace company. Such high-tech businesses are difficult to manage using unrelated business control systems that emphasize financial criteria. Managers need to stay on top of these businesses with strong strategic understanding because of the fast pace of change. In fact, because of its poor ability to control these fast-changing businesses and their consequent poor performance, in 1985 Thorn initiated a four-year restructuring program. It focused on three low-tech businesses: records and music publishing (where it owned the Beatles catalog and recordings of artists such as Tina Turner), appliance and furniture rental (U.S. operation, Rent-a-Center); and light bulb and light fixture manufacturing. Although these businesses are unrelated to each other, they are mature, low-technology businesses with little need for R&D investment.[4] Thorn EMI PLC has done well since its restructuring. Its strategy is now more in line with that of other successful unrelated firms.

Executing the Unrelated Strategy

In the Hansen example restructuring divestitures were executed to build cash reserves for use in making new unrelated acquisitions. Higher levels of diversification in the postrestructuring period are achieved by the acquisition of businesses with risk-averse spending preferences; if restructuring leads to strategic changes that increase the scope of diversification,

an accompanying decrease in level of R&D investment may be anticipated. This line of reasoning is the reverse of that in chapter 8.

Although differences in governance and internal control may affect
corporate strategy, the reverse may also be true, that is, implementation
of a new corporate strategy after restructuring may require a change in
the type of governance. It may be, for instance, that firm managers and
owners agree to focus on a set of unrelated businesses after restructuring.
In this situation, mature businesses not in R&D-intensive industries may
be most appropriate.[5] Such a focus would not require major changes in
board composition, executive compensation, ownership or diversification
patterns, because executives in unrelated firms generally are not rewarded
for risk-taking activity.[6] In this instance, corporate restructuring may
produce temporary downscoping to build a war chest to help finance the
next unrelated acquisition. Thus, an important contingency factor is
likely to be the type of corporate strategy pursued in the postrestructuring period.

Unrelated diversification may emerge if the restructuring activity
does not bring the desired improvement in performance. The relationship between internal controls and strategy may also affect the postrestructuring strategy. If, for example, a firm restructures seeking to implement a related diversification strategy but the new set of businesses
requires different experience and expertise than that possessed by the
firm's current managers, strategic control is less likely to be effective.
Without adequate managerial expertise, financial controls may continue
to be emphasized. Thus, the match between strategy and internal control
arrangements may be affected by important contingency factors related
to the success or failure of the restructuring activity.

Control Systems of the Unrelated Firm

Unrelated diversification strategy appears to work best when the firm can
maintain an advantage over the market. Such an advantage essentially
comes from pursuing strategies with reduced risk. According to two
scholars: "Thus, unrelated product firms can be expected to avoid firms
subject to high environmental uncertainty, such as those engaged in
rapidly changing technology."[7] This implies that the information-
processing demands on corporate executives in unrelated firms who are
responsible for strategic business units engaged in rapidly changing technology and therefore subject to high environmental uncertainty typically
are unrealistic and beyond those executives' capabilities. The implication
is that conglomerates that plan to pursue an unrelated corporate strategy
should limit their search for targets to firms in mature industries that
face placid environments.

As noted in chapters 2 and 3, the hallmark of the diversified firm is
the decomposition of strategic and operational decision making, accompanied by the decentralization of decision making to semiautonomous

divisions. Decomposition and specialization of strategic and operating responsibilities reduce the information-processing requirements on corporate managers and create the need to match business unit strategy with corporate resource allocation processes and reward systems. Some scholars have argued that the corporate-SBU relations must be tailored to the information-processing requirements of the unit's competitive strategy; if the unit and hence the corporation are to be effective, corporate managers need to adapt the methods of mutual coordination, systems of evaluation and control, and levels of decentralization to the information needs of the division. Divisions following different strategic missions and (generic) competitive strategies require specialized information.

One researcher has found that businesses following strategies characterized by relatively high task uncertainty—differentiation and build (i.e., invest and develop business) strategies—experience higher performance to the extent that open and subjective control systems are used. For businesses following strategies characterized by relatively low task uncertainty—cost leadership and harvest (maximize cashflow and divert business) strategies—the reverse is true. These results can be explained by the fact that the information-processing capacity of corporate-SBU dyads is highest when corporate-SBU relations are open and subjective. This requires frequent ad hoc meetings and mid-course corrections to deal with the uncertainty involved. Open and subjective control systems thus provide the information capacity necessary to manage effectively highly uncertain activities. Conversely, for strategies involving low uncertainty, mid-course corrections are less common, and determining the relationship of outcomes to decisions is less complex than it is for more uncertain strategies. Objective control systems emphasizing financial data provide sufficient information to allow managers to operate effectively businesses that follow strategies involving little uncertainty. The greater cost of open and subjective control systems is not justified for such businesses.[8]

Corporate and Business Unit Strategy Implications

An obvious implication is that firms with many business units, each of which is pursuing a different competitive strategy, need to adopt different controls for each type of business unit.[9] Other research suggests, however, that top management's ability to tailor corporate-SBU relations may be constrained by the corporation's overall diversification strategy.[10] In related diversified firms, corporate managers have the option of tailoring corporate-SBU relations to the information-processing requirements of individual SBUs. Where open and subjective information processing is required, corporate-level managers are more likely to have the experience (and the expertise) to review mid-course corrections and to evaluate managers largely on the basis of the quality of their decisions, rather than on the basis of financial outcomes alone. Corporate managers in unrelated firms, however, generally have little firsthand knowledge of the operating affairs of the multiple industries, technologies, or geographic regions. Even in firms engaged in related diversification, top management's ability to gather, process, and interpret the information needed to evaluate division performance accurately and to allocate resources and rewards often is limited. Corporate managers who have small or moderate spans of control in related diversified firms should be better able than their counterparts in highly diversified conglomerates to implement open and subjective corporate-SBU relations.

Assuming managers seek to enhance firm value, we should expect highly diversified firms to avoid the acquisition of new businesses that entail high uncertainty and high information-processing requirements. Such businesses often require mid-course corrections; yet corporate-SBU relations in unrelated diversified firms fail to provide the incentives and information-processing capacity necessary to implement appropriate competitive strategies.

A number of observable business characteristics point to the inherent uncertainty. First, the maturity and the market power of the business may reflect low uncertainty. Young firms are often characterized by a rapidly changing environment and by high risk. The uncertainty typical of young firms implies the existence of high information requirements for success (in order to make effective strategic decisions), a condition unrelated diversifiers will have great difficulty meeting. Firms requiring heavy investments in R&D and in advertising also face relatively large risks; the outcomes of such investments are often unclear and indirect and the salvage value is typically small. The issue is not the acquiring firm's willingness to accept risk but its ability to process the information necessary to manage those risks effectively. A great deal of subjective judgment is necessary to evaluate the merit of research programs and advertising initiatives. Unrelated diversifiers lack the information capacity to make such evaluations as effectively as more focused organizations. The uncertainty inherent in these types of investments implies that unrelated diversified firms will be at a competitive disadvantage compared to related diversified firms in managing businesses in which large investments in R&D and advertising are critical to success.[11]

Some observers have argued that unrelated diversifiers should not pursue service businesses. Service businesses' main assets are the employees who maintain good relations with clients. However, these assets are mobile and may be able to seek employment elsewhere, often taking their clients with them. Thus, acquisition strategies that seek to capture these assets may not prove successful, and many service conglomerates (e.g., Sears, Merrill Lynch, and American Express) have made major divestitures.

Although the economic rationale for unrelated diversification is not strong, a number of scholars have argued that managers prefer growth, seek to diversify employment risk, or fall prey to hubris (e.g., overvaluing their own managerial ability) when formulating acquisition strategies. These motives merely imply that managers may overinvest in inappropriate acquisitions. Managers still possess incentives to select target firms most suited to their expertise and information-processing capacity. A manager with a preference for growth can satisfy that preference with most target firms. Only a manager indifferent to firm value will not seek a target firm that presents the highest profit potential for the acquiring firm. Alternative theories of management behavior do not imply that maximizing firm value is irrelevant to managers, only that it can be a secondary goal. Research has demonstrated that the most efficient unrelated firms select targets that are mature and that require low investments in R&D.[12]

This result may provide a possible explanation for the observation that unrelated diversified firms divest their acquisitions more frequently than do related diversified firms. Because unrelated diversifiers acquire more mature businesses and lack the information capacity to navigate highly uncertain turnaround strategies, relatively high turnover of business units is neither unexpected nor an unambiguous indicator of failure.

Governance of Unrelated Diversification

Chapter 3 suggested that besides functioning as an efficient internal capital market, the M-form structure also provides governance. Oliver Williamson has argued that the M-form overcomes potential problems of managerial opportunism that exist in large functionally-organized (U-form) firms. This suggests that division managers in M-form firms will be more interested in profit maximization than will managers in free-standing U-form firms because the corporate office allocates resources among divisions in the way that it believes will yield the highest potential payoffs.[13] The internal capital market in the M-form firm acts as a governance device that reduces managerial opportunism at the division level and causes division managers to focus on high-yield uses for corporate resources allocated.

Although the M-form may curtail division manager opportunism, it may not bridle corporate managerial opportunism. Chapter 3 explained how governance faced by corporate executives in M-form firms resembles in U-form firms. The M-form without adequate governance may not curtail opportunistic corporate managerial decisions. Of course, some M-form firms may discipline other M-form firms. If ineffective governance and internal controls exist, external capital and labor markets may serve as controls. Furthermore, poor performance can result in takeover opportunities and a reevaluation of firm managers. Some firms thus act as raiders targeting firms where performance deficits occur and/or poor managerial talent exists. This is apparently the role that Hansen played when it bought poorly performing conglomerates such as SCM, Kidde, and Imperial Group. Of course, like other external market participants,

M-form firms that acquire other firms lack low-cost access to internal information and therefore are at a disadvantage compared to internal systems in monitoring corporate executive performance. Furthermore, the high cost of executing takeovers makes this threat appropriate only for poorly performing target firms.[14] Unrelated diversified firms are more appropriate for this monitoring role than are related diversified firms. However, the number of existing unrelated firms in the economy indicates that this strategy is used for many reasons besides the policing of poorly performing firms.

Some have argued that the unrelated firm was created from federal regulation and tax policy. David Ravenscraft and F. M. Scherer have summarized the evidence on antitrust constraints:

> By the 1960s, antitrust constraints on horizontal mergers had become much more stringent, and perhaps in part as a result, the merger wave that peaked in 1968 was preponderantly "conglomerate" in character, that is, involving companies pursuing different, and often totally unrelated, lines of business. The mergers of the 1980s were different again. Antitrust enforcement ebbed, permitting more and larger horizontal mergers. In addition, financial intermediaries had become more free-wheeling in the kinds of mergers they would support, and as one consequence, hostile takeovers rose to unprecedented prominence.[15]

Merger activity leading to conglomerate diversification was encouraged primarily by the Celler-Kefauver Act, which discouraged horizontal and vertical mergers. For example, in the 1973–77 period 79.1 percent of all mergers were conglomerate. However, the conglomerates or highly diversified firms of the 1960s and 1970s became much more focused in the 1980s as constraints on horizontal mergers were relaxed.

Tax law also affects diversification.[16] The activities of some companies may generate more cash than the company can reinvest profitably. Until 1981, because dividends were in some cases taxed more heavily than ordinary personal income, some shareholders preferred that companies retain these funds for use in buying and building companies in high-performance industries. If the stock value appreciated over the long term, these shareholders would benefit by being taxed at the lower capital gains rate. In 1981, however, the top ordinary individual income tax rate was reduced from 50 to 28 percent and the capital gains tax provision was changed so that capital gains would be treated as ordinary income. These changes meant that shareholders would no longer benefit by encouraging firms to retain funds for purposes of diversification. The elimination of personal interest deductibility in 1986 in addition to the reduced attractiveness of retained earnings to shareholders prompted the use of more leverage by firms, which could still deduct interest expense.

These tax law changes may have led to an increase in divestitures of unrelated business units; individual tax rates for capital gains and dividends may have created a shareholder incentive for increased diversification before 1981 but an incentive for decreased diversification after 1981 unless that diversification was funded by debt. No research examining the effects of changes in individual tax rates on diversification levels is available, however. The number of unrelated diversified firms may continue to decrease (with a few exceptions like Hansen Trust and firms that have performed poorly and need to diversify away from their original business). Otherwise, the unrelated strategy may represent overdiversification to accomplish managerial, not shareholder, goals.

Summary

In this chapter we presented information on the restructuring actions of unrelated diversified firms and the divestitures and targets they pursue. We argued that unrelated diversified firms are at a competitive disadvantage compared to related diversified firms in managing businesses involving high uncertainty and will likely be successful only if they acquire businesses with low information-processing requirements. Hansen and Thorn EMI are examples of unrelated diversified firms that have successfully followed a restructuring strategy focused on businesses involving relatively low uncertainty (Of course, Thorn EMI's success came only after unsuccessful attempts followed by some restructuring). Nondiversified firms can also encounter problems. Some single-business firms face risks by focusing on a single market. For example, Federal Express was the market leader in the express mail business. For some time it was able to withstand a number of imitators that entered the market, as well as the challenge of fax machines. Eventually, however, Federal Express, the market creator and leader, fell on hard times. The competition finally caught up, particularly in international operations, where Federal Express had overestimated the potential market and underestimated its competitors. Remaining in one market requires exceptionally well-managed operations compared to those of competitors. It also makes firms vulnerable to technological advances from outside the industry (e.g., fax machines) that provide a substitute product.[17]

This chapter does not discount those who question the fundamental logic of unrelated diversification. Because unrelated diversification entails all of the costs of diversification but by definition generates no synergy (except perhaps financial) within the portfolio of businesses, the economic case for the unrelated diversifying firm remains difficult to make. This chapter suggests that when the managers of highly diversified firms choose, for whatever reason, to use flexible resources to acquire unrelated businesses, they would do well to use the contingency approach suggested. While unrelated diversification strategies can reduce shareholder value, these losses can be minimized and possibly eliminated by acquiring firms that have attributes that fit the information-processing capacities of the unrelated organization. Data suggest that less diversified restructuring firms often outperform conglomerates that restructure but remain conglomerates. While the conglomerates experience smaller losses, they also experience fewer gains. For example, in one annual period, conglomerates experienced a change in profit ranging from a 1 percent average net loss to a 0 percent net gain in any one quarter, whereas other firms operating in specific industries experienced net changes ranging from a 75 percent loss in technology industries to a 203 percent gain in consumer products (cyclical) industries.[18] These data suggest that some conglomerate firms must perform reasonably well to offset the losses of others in order to achieve an average 0 percent change in net profits.

Given our assessment of unrelated diversification, the following managerial implications are relevant:

- With a few notable exceptions, unrelated diversification is driven by poor performance. Firms pursue unrelated diversification initially because of poor performance in a dominant business.
- Successful unrelated diversification requires consistent management with an emphasis on decentralization and strong financial control.
- Corporate managers in unrelated diversified firms should focus on buying and selling assets efficiently, while maintaining strong control over divisional cash flows.
- The focus should be on buying mature, low-technology businesses whose stability allows top managers to focus on buying and selling assets rather than on micromanaging divisional assets.
- Focusing on highly uncertain, technologically oriented businesses produces higher failure rates for the unrelated strategy.
- The rate of divestitures among firms that have tried to pursue acquisitions among service businesses indicates that this strategy may not be viable, even when overlap among client needs exists.
- In general, unrelated diversification should be avoided, except in the special circumstances described in this chapter.

Notes

1. Berkeley, W. M. 1994. Conglomerates make a surprising comeback—with a '90s twist. *The Wall Street Journal*, March 1:A–1, A–11. Williams, J. R., Paez, B. L., & Sanders, L. 1988. Conglomerates revisited. *Strategy Management Journal* 9:403–14.

2. Hill, C. W. L. 1988. Internal capital market controls and financial performance in multidivisional firms. *Journal of Industrial Economics* 37:67–83; Hoskisson, R. E. 1987. Multidivisional structure and performance: The diversification strategy contingency. *Academy of Management Journal* 30:625–44.

3. Leontiades, M. 1989. *Myth Management: An Examination of Corporate Diversification as Fact and Theory.* Oxford, Eng.: Basil Blackwell.

4. Hudson, R. L. 1989. Thorn-EMI sheds its ambitions to be a world high-tech power. *The Wall Street Journal*, June 8:A–15.

5. Dundas, K. N. M., & Richardson, P. R. 1982. Implementing the unrelated product strategy. *Strategic Management Journal* 3:287–301.

6. Hoskisson, R. E., & Hitt, M. A. 1988. Strategic control systems and relative R&D investment in large multiproduct firms. *Strategic Management Journal* 9:605–21.

7. Dundas, K. N. M., & Richardson, P. R. 1980. Corporate strategy and the concept of market failure. *Strategic Management Journal* 3:180.

8. Gupta, A. K. 1987. SBU strategies, corporate-SBU relations, and SBU effectiveness in strategy implementation. *Academy of Management Journal* 30:477–500.

9. Golden, B. 1992. SBU strategy and performance: The moderating effects of the corporate-SBU relationship. *Strategic Management Journal* 13:145–58.

10. Baysinger, B. D., & Hoskisson, R. E. 1989. Diversification strategy and R&D intensity in multiproduct firms. *Academy of Management Journal* 32:310–32.

11. Hoskisson & Hitt, Strategic control systems.

12. Baysinger, B., Turk, T. A., Harrison, J. S., & Hoskisson, R. E. 1989. Information capacity and the characteristics of firms acquired by unrelated diversified firms. Paper presented at the Strategic Management Society meetings, San Francisco.

13. Williamson, O. E. 1975. *Markets and Hierarchies: Analysis and Antitrust Implications.* New York: Free Press.

14. Manne, H. G. 1965. Mergers and the market for corporate control. *Journal of Political Economy* 73:110–20.

15. Ravenscraft, D. J., & Scherer, F. M. 1987. *Mergers, Sell-offs and Economic Efficiency.* Washington, D.C.: The Brookings Institution, p. 22.

16. Turk, T. A., & Baysinger, B. 1989. The impact of public policy on corporate strategy: Taxes, antitrust policy, and diversification clienteles. Working paper, Texas A&M University.

17. Hawkins, C. 1992. Fedex: Europe nearly killed the messenger. *Business Week*, May 25:124–26.

18. *The Wall Street Journal.* 1992. Companies' net income rose 18% as firms gain from restructuring. August 3:A–5,A–6.

10

International Diversification

The strategy of the Sara Lee Corporation calls for obtaining the highest possible market share in nondurable product lines in global markets. Sara Lee is accomplishing this goal largely through acquisitions of firms in other countries. In recent years it has acquired businesses operating in seven different countries with more than $1 billion in annual sales. Most of these acquisitions were in nondurable product lines outside the food business. Sara Lee continues to negotiate for businesses in Italy and Mexico and to search for opportunities in the former Soviet Union. Sara Lee is admired by Wall Street analysts for its global perspective; CEO John H. Bryan foresees the possibility of 4 billion new customers entering the international marketplace and is positioning Sara Lee to service these new customers.

Inside the United States, Sara Lee is known as a food company, primarily for its bakery goods. However, outside the United States, Sara Lee is better known as a manufacturer of apparel and personal care items; it is attempting to become a consumer goods company with mega-brands that transcend product lines and political boundaries. In fact, it is increasingly moving into other nondurable goods for earnings growth; more of its 1991 operating profit was generated by sales of nonfood goods than by sales of food products. Its changing product mix helped Sara Lee achieve a 31.8 percent compounded annual return on its common stock during the 1980s, the best among *Fortune* magazine's 100 largest corporations in the United States in 1991.

Sara Lee's strategy has been to identify and develop or to acquire nondurable product lines needed by most people, build them to be number one (or possibly number two) in their markets, and then expand each product line under a single label. For example, in 1979 Sara Lee acquired Hanes, which primarily made women's hosiery. It then expanded the Hanes line to include men's and boys' underwear, as well as women's and girls' underwear. The Hanes brand is also used with scarves, gloves, and socks.

Sara Lee is an excellent marketing company. In fact, marketing is the core competence of the corporation. The executive vice president of marketing for a competitor, Fruit of the Loom, forecasts that promotion will become increasingly important as consumers depend more on mass merchandiser retail outlets where people shop primarily for price and for perceived value. Sara Lee should be effectively positioned to take advantage of this market.

Sara Lee is both product and internationally diversified. Its product diversification is related but in separate industries. However, it builds on its core competence of marketing for success in all its markets. The results have paid off handsomely. In 1991 Sara Lee had sales of $12.4 billion, net income of $535 million, and earnings per share of $2.15, in each case a significant increase over the preceding year.[1]

In this chapter we explain the importance of moving into global markets, the benefits of doing so, the interaction of international and product diversification, and the limits to the benefits of such activities. Understanding the global competitiveness puzzle requires that we examine the effects of international diversification by firms.[2] For our purposes, we define international diversification as an expansion across country borders into geographic locations that are new to the firm. While international markets yield new opportunities, they also present increased competitive challenges from international and domestic competitors. Furthermore, they increase the complexity of managing the corporation. While firms may choose to diversify internationally for a number of reasons, the primary goal is to gain a sustainable competitive advantage. To accomplish this, international diversification should afford a firm opportunities to perform more of its activities internally.[3] It should also further the exploitation of interrelationships among different business segments and geographic areas or among businesses in related industries. Thus, international diversification may produce economies of scale, scope, and/ or experience. Furthermore, internationally diversified firms may be able to gain competitive advantage by exploiting differences in national resources, flexibility, and bargaining power from a multinational network.[4] The advantages of international expansion are shown by the experience of Sara Lee. Clearly, Sara Lee is identifying market needs and diversifying both its product lines and its geographic markets to take advantage of market opportunities. It seems particularly adept at leveraging its core competence in marketing to gain advantages in the markets entered.

International Diversification, Product Diversification, and Performance

The research on the relationship between product diversification and firm performance has been largely mixed. It is clear that firms can over-diversify. In earlier chapters we concluded that early diversification efforts may actually enhance performance up to some point but that continued diversification generally leads to decreasing returns for the firm. As a result, there may be a neutral relationship between product diversification and performance when examined over time; however, extensive diversification that produces overdiversification is likely to reduce the firm's overall performance.[5]

International Diversification

International diversification offers several advantages over product diversification. It often produces higher performance. Product diversification may be motivated by a company's poor performance or expected poor performance, which can lead to a desire to reduce future risk by diversifying into new product areas. In contrast, international diversification is usually motivated more by anticipated market opportunities.[6] There have been several reasons given for the positive relationship between international diversification and firm performance. International diversification has been found to help stabilize returns by producing economies of scale, scope, and/or experience. Multinational firms that are able to integrate globally, that is, to integrate across country borders by standardizing products and production and coordinating critical resource functions such as R&D, may be able to achieve optimal economic scale and amortize investments in those critical functions over a broader base.[7] International diversification thus allows a firm to exploit its core competencies or distinctive firm capabilities.[8] An example is Sara Lee's ability to exploit its core competence in marketing across product and international market boundaries. Resource sharing and learning among global firms' multiple international operations facilitates the exploitation of core competencies to produce synergy.

Another example can be found in the Nestlé S.A. Company, head-quartered in Switzerland. While most people think of Nestlé as a food company, it may soon have big pharmaceutical and skin care businesses. The firm has continued to grow, partly through effective management of its multiple international operations, partly through acquisitions that help exploit its core competencies to produce synergy. For example, it attempted to take over L'Oréal S.A., which would fit easily into Nestlé's skin-care business. Nestlé's CEO, Helmut Maucher, is attempting to link the food, health, and skin-care businesses. He suggests that good nutrition, health, and skin care are all related, which justifies research into new products that would combine technologies. For example, Nestlé is involved in a joint venture with Baxter International's Clintec Nutrition

Company. This joint venture combines Baxter's hospital supply expertise with Nestlé's food experience to produce nutritional and food products to be used for hospital patients. Nestlé is using the relatedness to produce synergy.

Furthermore, Nestlé is promoting speed and creativity in its innovation process. In 1991, Nestlé reorganized its product management system. The company is now heavily decentralized, with powerful country managers who make the primary and critical marketing and product formula decisions. Its performance supports the actions being taken. Nestlé reported sales of SFr 50.49 billion and net income of SFr 2.47 billion in 1991. Both figures represented increases of approximately 10 percent over those for the preceding year.[9]

It is not uncommon for a firm that is profitable in its home domestic market to expand into international markets to utilize the competitive advantages enjoyed in the domestic market more effectively. The profitability gives the firm the resources to invest in the new assets required for expansion into international markets. Such firms are often able to access more efficient labor pools and to benefit from global scanning for competition and market opportunities. As a result, they may have more efficient and competitive operations and therefore produce higher returns for their investors and better products for their customers than domestic firms.[10]

Evidence of the fact that firms diversify internationally to seek market opportunities made possible by profitable operations in domestic markets is shown by the number of small firms that are enjoying much success in international markets. The Vita-Mix Corporation, based in Ohio, has been manufacturing and marketing a high-powered blender for 70 years. However, in 1991 the firm's executives saw opportunities in global markets. They hired an international sales manager and have seen exports climb to 20 percent of the firm's $20 million annual sales. Vita-Mix has more than doubled its number of employees and is using advances in technology (800 phone numbers, fax machines) to allow the export business to grow and a seven-day-a-week schedule. Another example is Sharper Finish, Inc., a Chicago-based manufacturer of commercial laundry equipment. It maintains contact with 300 distributors in 30 separate countries, and exports account for 60 percent of its total annual sales. Yet another Chicago firm, Midwest Tropical, Inc., a designer aquarium manufacturer, is exporting its product to Japan. Its international sales have grown dramatically in the last few years and increased by approximately 30 percent in 1992 alone.[11] We conclude that international diversification usually produces higher firm performance than domestic product diversification.

Product Diversification in Multinational Firms

While it is interesting to compare the effects of international and product diversification, many multinational firms are also highly product diversified. It is therefore important to understand the interrelationship between product and international diversification. The combination of international and product diversification is sometimes referred to as global diversification.[12]

Product diversified firms may be able to enhance performance by diversifying internationally. They do so by achieving some of the benefits of international diversification and by capturing synergies of product diversification. Related diversified firms must exploit the interdependencies across their businesses to achieve the desired synergies. International diversification can facilitate this process by helping firms to achieve economies of scale and scope and by encouraging resource sharing and emphasis on core competencies across business units. One study has shown that firms which were both product diversified into related business areas and internationally diversified were able to achieve greater profit stability than product diversified firms that were not internationally diversified, suggesting that international diversification reduces risk by stabilizing returns. This is important because interrelated businesses produce risk; one business failure may affect the performance of other businesses with which it is interrelated.[13] Furthermore, international firms pursuing related product diversification have been found to outperform those pursuing unrelated product diversification.

Another study showed that international diversification helped firms achieve favorable risk-return profiles with high returns and low risk by reducing the variance of exposure and increasing the variety of investment opportunities.[14] International diversification may also facilitate performance in unrelated product diversified firms. Research has shown that unrelated diversified firms that were also internationally diversified had higher profit growth than those that were not internationally diversified. In unrelated product diversified firms, international diversification facilitates the exploitation of economies of scale and scope, thereby promoting greater profit growth. Unrelated product diversified firms often cannot achieve economies of scale in domestic markets, but expansion into new international markets can help them achieve such economies. In addition, international diversification may help unrelated firms achieve unique synergies that competitors find difficult to imitate, in addition to the financial synergy that is the most common benefit attributed to unrelated diversification.[15]

Diversification and Innovation

In earlier chapters we discussed the fact that highly product diversified firms often are less innovative. These reductions in innovation may lead to lower competitiveness and lower firm performance over time.[16]

International diversification, in contrast, may facilitate innovation. It provides the potential for firms to achieve greater returns on their innovations by providing larger and/or more numerous markets in which to sell the new products or over which to spread the cost of new processes. Thus, international diversification provides incentives for firms to innovate. In addition, international diversification may be necessary to generate the resources necessary to sustain a large-scale R&D operation.[17] In industries where technological obsolescence is rapid, companies often lack the money to develop new technologies and to provide the capital-intensive operations required to take advantage of them. Firms operating only in domestic markets find such investments especially difficult because it takes them longer to recoup the original investment, and it may in fact be impossible to recover the entire investment before the technology becomes obsolete. International diversification improves the firm's ability to appropriate value from innovation.[18]

International diversification may also facilitate innovation in product diversified firms. The incentives for innovation in internationally diversified firms may partially offset the disincentives for innovation in product diversified firms. For example, movement into international markets lowers the risk of innovation in any particular business, as we have noted, by making investment in R&D more attractive, even to risk-averse division managers, because their risk is spread across larger markets. The opportunity to gain profits from innovation before the technology becomes obsolete or is imitated by competitors may overcome the disincentives to assuming risk.

While international diversification has many benefits for both innovation and performance, trade-offs exist. International diversification requires facing risks and overcoming potential barriers, such as trade barriers, cultural differences, and differences in trade laws. As a result, internationally diverse firms are complex and difficult to manage, and continued international diversification may at some point produce costs that exceed the benefits.

Limits to International Diversification

Early product diversification efforts may produce positive returns, but these returns often level off and even turn negative as diversification increases. Research has shown a similar pattern for international diversification, although the apex of the curve is at a much higher point than that for product diversification.[19]

There are several characteristics of international diversification that increase its complexity and make it difficult to manage. Broad geographic dispersion increases coordination and distribution costs, and there may be multiple coordination and distribution problems. To derive the benefits of economies of scale and of scope requires coordination and an ability to distribute goods efficiently across international markets, which may be stymied by different government regulations and trade laws across countries. Furthermore, there are logistical costs, problems with cultural diversity, and various other intercountry differences, such as access to

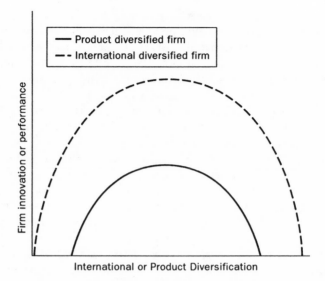

Firm innovation or performance (y-axis)

International or Product Diversification (x-axis)

— Product diversified firm

-- International diversified firm

Figure 6. Alternative relationships between international or product diversification and firm innovation or performance

raw materials and human resource skills. Expenditures for employee wages and capital equipment may vary considerably across countries. These differences greatly increase the risks associated with decisions to allocate resources across the various products/markets in which the firm operates. As a result, it is difficult for headquarters executives to establish and maintain strategic control in internationally diversified firms.

To achieve the benefits of international diversification, the firm must achieve integration of its various international operations, while at the same time allowing local operations the autonomy required to respond to their markets. This is exceedingly difficult to do. If firms use centralized organization structures to achieve integration, they may sacrifice the ability to respond effectively and efficiently to local market changes. On the other hand, developing decentralized structures that allow more effective response to local markets can mean sacrificing integration. Coordination in such businesses often increases geometrically the information processing required of corporate executives.[20] As a result, the relationship between international or product diversification and innovation or performance is likely to resemble an inverted U, as shown in Figure 6. Multinational firms that are also product diversified have inverted-U relationships to performance and innovation, but the change in slope occurs much more rapidly. In other words, the height of the curve (the point at which the slope in the relationship with innovation and performance turns negative) is lower for product diversified multinational firms than for nonproduct diversified multinational firms. This relationship is also depicted in figure 6. When the slope of the relationship between international diversification and innovation and performance turns negative, the firm may need to restructure.

Restructuring Internationally Diversified Firms

The complexities involved in managing both international and product diversification simultaneously may require restructuring to allow more effective management of the enterprise in order to improve performance. One way of doing so is to maintain international diversification while reducing product diversification and refocusing on the firm's core businesses. Samsung, a successful business group in South Korea, provides an excellent example. At one time Samsung was a producer of products ranging from sausages to ships. However, in 1992 Samsung began a restructuring designed to reduce the number of different businesses in which it operated and to concentrate on its core businesses of machinery, electronics, and chemicals. Samsung's CEO, Lee Kun-Hee, noted that the days of emphasizing growth and size over quality were at an end. In addition, he declared that Samsung would specialize by moving more heavily into capital- and technology-intensive industries. Since 1989 Samsung has divested $3 billion worth of businesses, and it continues to consolidate groups of related businesses and to restructure. The expectation is that the Samsung electronics business will be the flagship of the firm. Even this business is complex; it entails the production and the distribution of color televisions, VCRs, and microwave ovens. Samsung is also attempting to compete in the multibillion-dollar market for semiconductor chips. As part of its restructuring, the firm invested approximately $2.2 billion in a state-of-the-art microchip processing plant. As of October 1993, Samsung had the highest global market share in 1-megabit DRAM chips; its goal is to beat the Japanese in the 64-meg DRAM market. In addition, it has developed a joint venture with Hewlett-Packard to design and develop a sophisticated, reduced-instruction-set computing (RISC) microprocessor for HP's popular line of workstations.

Samsung still faces important challenges. For example, experts continue to question its R&D and design capabilities. While the firm has been highly efficient in the manufacture of memory chips, it continues to depend on U.S. or Japanese firms for the technology used in the manufacturing process. The firm must make improvements in its technology development to continue to support its full line of products. While Samsung's R&D budget is large by Korean standards, it is still small compared to that of its major Japanese and U.S. competitors.

Another challenge faced by Samsung is that of managing its global operations. The company expects to quadruple sales by the year 2000 to $200 billion. This level of achievement requires a large and excellent top executive group, and it may also require a major change in the Korean management style. Of course, the company's restructuring and its refocusing on primary product areas should help Samsung maintain the strategic control systems that will be vital to the continued development of new technology and to the establishment of the global integration necessary to reach its goals.[21]

Other examples of restructuring in multinational firms are General Electric in the 1980s and Japan's Nippon Steel. Interestingly, while GE was a large multinational firm, it also was a highly product diversified firm in the early 1980s, when Jack Welch became CEO. One of Welch's first critical moves was to focus the firm's resources on fewer businesses. He divested several of GE's unrelated businesses and organized the remaining diverse sets of businesses into three broad groups of core businesses — high technology (e.g., medical systems, aircraft engines), electronics and electrical equipment (e.g., lighting, appliances, motors), and services (e.g., credit, information, and construction). He sold off businesses that were unable to become one of the top two in their markets. While the restructuring often refocused GE's efforts on making its U.S. plants more competitive, eventually it led to an increased emphasis on international diversification for the existing sets of businesses. While GE's financial performance improved considerably over time, it also experienced tremendous internal turmoil because of the company's inability to establish effective and appropriate structures to manage its operations. While the restructuring efforts seemed appropriate, the implementation of those efforts was less successful.[22] (We discuss implementation in chapter 11.)

While it has not been obvious to many outside Japan, Japanese firms have also faced restructuring pressures and have been undergoing restructuring activities. The pressures behind some of these restructurings are somewhat different from those that led to restructurings in the United States and possibly in other countries. For example, Japanese businesses in the 1980s and early 1990s faced problems of excess personnel and intense pressure to take initiatives to correct trade imbalances with other countries. One important issue in Japan has been the need to reduce the workforce. This is a critical concern, given the Japanese cultural norm of maintaining lifetime employment. Tactics such as loans of workers to suppliers, subcontractors, and industrial customers, along with early outplacement and reliance on attrition, only deferred the problem. Nippon Steel, for example, needed to reduce its workforce by 3,500 in the late 1970s but needed a reduction of an additional 19,000 by the end of the 1980s. It is still trying to figure out how to best do so in the 1990s. The firm, operating in a mature industry, could no longer rely on export growth to maintain full employment and had few growth opportunities in its core businesses. As a result, it could grow only by diversifying into new markets. The Japanese often prefer to move into new businesses by internal development, but this often requires more time than seems acceptable. As a result, a number of Japanese firms are restructuring by diversifying their product lines through mergers and acquisitions. Some

of the restructuring being conducted in Japanese firms is thus the opposite of the restructuring actions being taken in the United States and in
other countries.

Nippon Steel restructured substantially, engaging in both related and
unrelated product diversification in the 1980s and the 1990s. It significantly reduced its emphasis on its primary steel business and invested
heavily in new businesses, such as new materials and chemicals, electronics and information systems, biotechnology, and leisure development services. Much of the new business development came from internal development and from shifting from the steel core business to the other
businesses, particularly those with related technologies.[23]

There is a Japanese market for corporate control, much like that in
the United States and in other countries. Between 1980 and 1986, Japan
had an average of 8.8 combinations per 10,000 incorporated businesses.
During this same time period, the United States experienced 8.2 combinations per 10,000 incorporated businesses. Most of the mergers and
acquisitions in Japan were of much smaller size than those in the United
States. For example, Nippon Steel was formed out of a merger between
two major steel companies in Japan in 1970. In addition, although traditional Japanese corporate governance system formed a barrier to many
international acquisitions by Japanese firms, these firms became global
bidders in the acquisition market. It is interesting that direct Japanese
foreign investment has shifted from Asia to the United States and western Europe, and the primary mode of investment has become acquisition.

Multinational firms must also restructure, but the form of the restructuring may vary, depending on the type of firm, its headquarters
country, and the industry of its core business. Samsung and GE restructured by divesting unrelated product diversified businesses and by refocusing on core businesses, as well as by continuing the international
expansion of those core businesses. Nippon Steel exhibited the opposite
type of restructuring; because of the mature and declining steel industry
in Japan and worldwide, it searched for new product markets and therefore acted to diversify the product markets in which it operated.

The implementation of international diversification and restructuring in these complex multinational firms involves other important factors, including the ability to understand the strategic intent of competitors and employ managers from different countries.

Understanding Strategic Intent in Global Markets

In order to succeed in international markets, executive officers must understand the strategic intent of competitors and of key managers in
charge of international operations within the firm. Firms seeking to
achieve strategic control must ensure that managers of international strategic business units share a common vision with corporate headquarters.
To do this, firms seek to control the norms and the premises underlying

the strategic decisions made in these international operations. Gaining such control requires an understanding of the differences in decision premises and in decision models used by managers in different countries.

It may be even more important to understand the strategic intent of competitors. The ancient military strategist Sun Tzu argued that it is critical to understand the mind of the enemy before the battle. Many have argued that competitor analysis is important in order to seek and gain a competitive advantage. One of the first objectives of such an analysis is to develop a profile of the nature and the likelihood of success of strategic moves each competitor is likely to make. It is also important to understand and to predict competitors' probable responses to the firm's own strategic moves.

Understanding the strategic intent of competitors in global markets is complex and more difficult than understanding competitors' intent in domestic markets. It is complicated by the differences in culture, experience, and business conditions across country boundaries.[24] Sun Tzu suggested that others can see the tactics used by competitors, but none can see the strategy out of which a successful battle occurs. That strategy becomes apparent only with retrospective analysis.

Without appreciation of competitors' strategic intent, firms entering international markets may be doomed to a perpetual game of catch-up. This game of catch-up has been quite obvious in many U.S. domestic markets and global markets in which U.S. firms have competed.[25] It is perhaps most evident in the U.S. television manufacturing business. In 1991 Jerry Pearlman, CEO of Zenith Electronics Corporation, the last U.S. manufacturer of televisions, noted that his firm spent much of the 1980s trying to combat cutthroat competition from Japanese and South Korean manufacturers. Because of continuing net losses in the television business, Zenith gave up. Pearlman said that if he couldn't beat them, he would join them, and he sold a stake in Zenith to Lucky-Goldstar Group from South Korea.[26]

It also may be important for firms to understand the strategic intent of their partners in joint ventures and other strategic alliances, as well as of the suppliers to whom they outsource. Some foreign joint venture partners and suppliers may use the opportunity to learn the market and eventually become competitors. Some people have argued that Japanese companies have often entered joint ventures in order to learn the technology of their U.S. partners. There has been a proliferation of cooperative strategies among international competitors and among firms headquartered in different countries. For example, Caterpillar has linked up with Mitsubishi, and Hewlett-Packard, as noted earlier, with Samsung. Of course, U.S. firms also have certain strategic goals when they enter joint ventures. Some have entered joint ventures with Japanese firms to weaken the Japanese invasion of U.S. markets and to learn Japanese management systems. The linkages for a number of these firms may thus have been based on a defensive strategy. Gary Hamel has suggested that these alliances may present a danger to U.S. firms who form partnerships with foreign firms.[27] He argues that Japanese firms are better learners than their western partners, perhaps because of firmer control, a strong internal labor market (among Japanese firms), and cultural differences. The Japanese, for example, have a strong collective orientation that is different from the individualistic focus in the United States. American managers may prefer decentralization and an emphasis on financial evaluation, but collective learning may be more difficult in diversified firms in which decentralization and financial control are emphasized.

Managers from difference cultures also may have different strategic approaches. A 1990 study showed that there were differences in the strategic decision models used by top U.S. executives and by top South Korean executives. While focused on the same strategic decision, the U.S. and South Korean executives utilized different criteria and weighted the criteria differently in making their decisions. Differences in culture, experience, stage of industrialization of the home country, ownership structure of businesses, natural resources, and relationship between business and government all influence the strategic decisions made by executives in different home countries.[28]

The problems that can arise when joint venture partners have different strategic orientations and intents is demonstrated in the conflicts that arose in the joint venture between GM and South Korea's Daewoo Corporation. In 1986 GM and Daewoo launched a joint venture to build a car in Korea to be sold in the U.S. domestic market. The automobile was designed by GM's German Adam Opel unit. The venture had trouble from the beginning. There were management conflicts and operational disputes. GM's methodical and lengthy decision-making process did not match well with Daewoo's style (rapid decisions made by only a few top executives). Resolution of conflicts over issues was therefore difficult. Neither firm fully understood the other's strengths and weaknesses at the beginning of the venture, and the partners failed to assess jointly their goals and methods when it was obvious that the conditions were different than expected. The strategic orientation and intent of the executives of these two corporations represented a misfit, and the joint venture was a failure.[29]

The need to understand fully the strategic intent of competitors is also evident in the current competition in the global airline industry. It is projected that by the year 2000 global passenger airline traffic will almost double from the levels of the early 1990s. It is also expected that there will be fewer competitors by the turn of the century. As of this writing, American and United Airlines are positioning themselves to be major international carriers, and these airlines are expected to be the primary beneficiaries of the current competition in the U.S. domestic market. Interestingly, neither American nor United even flew overseas before 1982.

Foreign airlines are observing the actions of American and United and evaluating alternative maneuvers. For example, British Airways, KLM Royal Dutch Airlines, and Northwest Airlines are considering the development of a holding company or consortium to coordinate marketing, scheduling, and other operations on a global basis. Their intent is to cooperate in order to compete against American and United. The two competitive weapons that have been highly effective in the United States, frequent flyer programs and control of computerized reservation systems, may not help American and United to gain a competitive advantage in the international markets.[30] Given the expected competitive battles for the new and growing global market, it is critical that firms understand the strategic intent of their competitors and be able to predict expected competitive moves.[31]

Those firms that are able to understand the strategic intent of their competitors, of the key managers in their own operations, and of venture partners are more likely to succeed and to prevent the need to restructure. And firms that are most able to understand the strategic intent of their competitors are those that have maintained a focus on their core business and/or have restructured to do so. Furthermore, those firms that have maintained a strong integration among their operations, along with the decentralization necessary to allow flexibility in their local markets, are likely to perform well over the long term.

Summary

This chapter has examined the effects of international diversification on firm innovation and performance. We noted that product diversification may initially have positive effects on performance, but negative effects on performance are increasingly likely as diversification increases. There has been considerable evidence to suggest a negative relationship between product diversification and innovation, whereas international diversification has been found to be positively related to both innovation and performance and may even facilitate higher levels of innovation and performance in product-diversified firms.

International diversification, however, also creates complexity in the organization, especially for central headquarters. There is need for global coordination and integration, which are difficult to achieve because of the differences in cultures and operations among local markets. The autonomy necessary for the flexibility to compete in local (national) markets further exacerbates the problems of achieving integration. There are many other reasons that it is difficult to manage internationally diversified firms. These headquarter controls limit the ability to manage international operations effectively, suggesting that continuing international diversification will eventually lead to lower innovation and performance and create the need for restructuring.

We discussed several examples of restructuring. Both GE and Samsung restructured by divesting unrelated businesses in order to downscope and to refocus on core businesses. After so doing, both firms are better able to maintain or to reinstitute strategic controls that promote innovation and higher performance. A number of firms in Japan have been restructuring in the opposite manner. For example, Nippon Steel, operating in a mature and declining industry, was faced with the need to diversify its product line and did so. Many Japanese firms have begun to diversify by making acquisitions, both within Japan and in other countries. Each of the restructurings described was necessary, but each achieved a different degree of success. The GE changes brought only moderate success because of problems with implementation (structure and culture). The restructurings at Nippon and Samsung have not been completed and thus await final evaluation.

Understanding the strategic intent of the firm's competitors, joint venture partners, and its own managers of international operations may be critical in the success of international diversification. This is an important issue for multiple firms because many markets can be considered global. Many American businesses, including Sara Lee, Rohm and Haas, Mellon Bank, Cooper Industries, Dexter, and Herman Miller, are beginning to appoint international members to their board of directors.[31] The employment of foreign directors may be helpful in fostering understanding strategic intent of foreign competitors and in implementing international diversification.

The information examined in this chapter suggests the following managerial implications:

- International diversification can help firms increase innovation and increase profits. As a result, managers should give strong consideration to strategic moves into international markets to gain economies of scale, scope, and/or experience.
- While product diversification is likely to produce higher performance only in the early stages of related product moves, international diversification can enhance the performance potential of product diversification.
- International diversification can also be used by managers to obtain a more favorable risk-return profile.
- International diversification can improve a firm's ability to appropriate value from innovation, even in product diversified firms.
- Managers must take care not to overdiversify internationally. International firms are complex and difficult to manage, and at some point the costs of managing such operations exceed the benefits.
- International firms may also have to restructure to downscope their product diversification and/or to reduce the number of international markets served.
- To be effective in international markets, managers must understand the strategic intent of competitors, joint venture partners, and employed managers operating outside the home country.

While international diversification has multiple potential benefits, it is also quite difficult to implement. Therefore, much effort must be focused on implementation to realize the benefits of international diversification.

Notes

1. Gibson, R. 1992. Sara Lee mulls purchases to satisfy hunger for growth: Global strategy calls for gaining top share in nondurable product lines. *The Wall Street Journal*, April 14:B–4.

2. Hitt, M. A., Hoskisson, R. E., & Harrison, J. S. 1991. Strategic competitiveness in the 1990s: Challenges and opportunities for U.S. executives. *Academy of Management Executive* 5(2):7–22.

3. Rugman, A. M. 1979. *International Diversification and the Multinational Enterprise*. Lexington, Mass.: Lexington Books.

4. Porter, M. E. 1985. *Competitive advantage*. New York: Free Press; Kogut, B. 1985. Designing global strategies: Comparative and competitive value-added change (Part I). *Sloan Management Review* 27:15–28; Hitt, M. A. Forthcoming. Comment on the evolution of multinational corporations: Integration of international diversification and strategic management. In B. Toyne and B. Nigh, eds., *The State of International Business Inquiry*. Columbia, S.C.: University of South Carolina Press.

5. Hoskisson, R. E., & Hitt, M. A. 1990. Antecedents and performance outcomes of diversification: A review and critique of theoretical perspectives. *Journal of Management* 16:461–509; Markides C. C. 1992. Consequences of corporate refocusing: Ex ante evidence. *Academy of Management Journal* 35:398–412.

6. Buhner, R. 1987. Assessing international diversification of West German corporations. *Strategic Management Journal* 8:25–37; Geringer, J. N., Beamish, P. W., & De Costa, R. C. 1989. Diversification strategy and internationalization: Implications for MNE performance. *Strategic Management Journal* 10:109–19; Rugman, *International Diversification*.

7. Caves, R. E. 1982. *Multinational Enterprise and Economic Analysis*. Cambridge, Eng.: Cambridge University Press; Kobrin, S. J. 1991. An empirical analysis of the determinants of global integration. *Strategic Management Journal* (Special Issue) 12:17–37; Kogut, Designing global strategies.

8. Hamel, G. 1991. Competition for competence and interpartner learning within international strategic alliances. *Strategic Management Journal* 12:83–103; Lei, D., Hitt, M. A., & Bettis, R. 1992. Development and application of core competencies in global firms: Organizational learning and organizational context. Working paper, Southern Methodist University.

9. Browning, E. S. 1992. Nestlé looks to realms beyond food for the future: Swiss company maps takeovers, including skin care, pharmaceuticals. *The Wall Street Journal*, May 12:B–4.

10. Grant, R. M., Jammine, A. P., & Thomas, H. 1988. Diversity, diversification, and profitability among British manufacturing companies, 1972–1984. *Academy of Management Journal* 31:771–801; Kotabe, M. 1989. Hollowing out of U.S. multinationals and their global competitiveness. *Journal of Business Research* 19:1–15; Kobrin, Empirical analysis.

11. Holstein, W. J., & Kelly, K. 1992. Little companies, big exports. *Business Week*, April 13:70–72.

12. Kim, W. C. 1989. Developing a global diversification measure. *Management Science* 35:376–83; Vachani, S. 1991. Distinguishing between related and

unrelated international geographic diversification: A comprehensive measure of global diversification. *Journal of International Business Studies* 22:307–22.

13. Kim, W. C., Hwang, P., & Burgers, W. P. 1989. Global diversification and corporate profit performance. *Strategic Management Journal* 10:45–57; Kay, N. M., & Diamantopoulos, A. 1987. Uncertainty and synergy: Towards a formal model of corporate strategy. *Managerial and Decision Economics* 8:121–30.

14. Kim, W. C., Hwang P., & Burgers, W. P. 1993. Multinational diversification and the risk-return tradeoff. *Strategic Management Journal* 14:275–86.

15. Harrison, J. S., Hitt, M. A., Hoskisson, R. E., & Ireland, R. D. 1991. Synergies and post acquisition performance: Similarities versus differences in resource allocations. *Journal of Management* 17:173–90.

16. Hoskisson, R. E., & Hitt, M. A. 1988. Strategic control systems and relative R&D investment in large multiproduct firms. *Strategic Management Journal* 9:605–21; Baysinger, B. D., & Hoskisson, R. E. 1989. Diversification strategy and R&D intensity in large multiproduct firms. *Academy of Management Journal* 32:310–32; Hitt, M. A., & Hoskisson, R. E. 1991. Strategic competitiveness. In L. W. Foster, ed., *Advances in Applied Business Strategy*, vol. 2. Greenwich, Conn.: JAI Press, pp. 1–36; Hitt, Hoskisson, & Harrison, Strategic competitiveness.

17. Kobrin, Empirical analysis; Kotabe, N. 1990. The relationship between off shore sourcing and innovativeness of U.S. multinational firms: An empirical investigation. *Journal of International Business Studies* 21:623–38.

18. Kotabe, off shore sourcing; Teece, D. J. 1986. Profiting from technological innovation. *Research Policy* 15:285–306.

19. Grant et al., Diversity, diversification; Geringer et al., Diversification strategy.

20. Kogut, Designing global strategies; Prahalad, C. K., & Doz, Y. L. 1987. *The Multinational Mission: Balancing Local Demands and Global Vision*. New York: Free Press; Bartlett, C. A., & Goshal, S. 1988. Organizing for worldwide effectiveness: The transnational solution. *California Management Review* 30:54–74; Barlett, C. A., & Goshal, S. 1989. *Managing Across Borders: The Transnational Solution*. Boston: Harvard Business School Press; Lei et al., Development and application.

21. Nakarmi, L., Gross, N., & Hof, R. 1992. Samsung: Korea's great hope for high tech. *Business Week*, February 3:44–45.

22. Barlett & Goshal, Managing across borders.

23. Kester, W. C. 1991. *Japanese Takeovers: The Global Contest for Corporate Control*. Boston: Harvard Business School Press.

24. Prahalad & Doz, *Multinational Mission*; Park, D., & Hitt, M. A. 1991. Executive effects on strategic decision models: Examination of strategic intent. Paper presented at the Strategic Management Society meetings, Toronto, Canada.

25. Park & Hitt, Executive effects on strategic decision models.

26. Therrien, L., & Nakarmi, L. 1991. Zenith wishes on a Lucky-Goldstar. *Business Week*, March 11:50.

27. Hamel, G. 1991. Competition for competence and inter-partner learning with international strategic alliances. *Strategic Management Journal* (Special Issue) 12:83–103.

28. Hitt, M. A., Tyler, B., & Park, D. 1990. A cross-cultural examination of strategic decision models: Comparison of Korean and U.S. executives. *Proceedings of Academy of Management*, August:111–15.

29. Treece, J. B. 1991. Why GM and Daewoo wound up on the road to nowhere. *Business Week*, September 23:55.

30. Nomani, A. Q. 1992. Global dogfight: World's major airlines scramble to get ready for competitive battle. *The Wall Street Journal*, January 14:A–1,A–9.

31. Lublin, J. S. 1992. More U.S. companies venture overseas for directors offering fresh perspectives. *The Wall Street Journal*, January 22:B–1.

11

Implementing Restructuring and Exercising Strategic Leadership

Kodak has undergone restructuring four times since 1982 — and it continues to do so. The company operates businesses in photography, chemicals, business machines, and pharmaceuticals. Since 1982 Kodak has reduced staff, divested businesses, and realigned its remaining businesses. Four times top executives have promised a new focus, greater efficiencies, and increased earnings. In fact, however, Kodak has reported tremendous variability in profits and in employee numbers. Its profits have increased by as much as 70 percent in some years and decreased by as much as 45 percent in others. The firm dropped to a low of 121,000 employees in 1986 and then in 1988 reached a high of 145,000 employees. In 1991 Kodak had an operating profit of $2.5 billion, compared to $1.88 billion in 1982 (1991 and 1982 are comparable because they both occurred during recessions). Adjusting for inflation, Kodak's 1991 earnings were 5.7 percent below those for 1982. In 1992 the firm made only $1.07 billion on sales of $20 billion. This level of earnings was termed unsatisfactory by Kodak's CEO and was only marginally better than the company's earnings of $1.05 billion in 1991, before the latest round of restructuring changes were implemented. Kodak's restructurings thus do not appear to have produced dramatic improvements in performance.

According to industry analysts, Kodak's most significant problem is its continuing investment in its cash cow (the basic photography business) in the hope that it will become a growth business. One analyst has suggested that "if you feed a cash cow you do not increase growth, you get a fat cow." Another analyst has argued that Kodak has spent a lot of its cash flow from its good businesses on its poor businesses. Kodak's acquisition of Sterling Drug, Inc., for example, was accomplished by adding approximately $350 million in interest to Kodak's annual debt costs. In 1991 Sterling Drug earned $379 million in profit, a gain of only $29 million over the debt cost incurred in its purchase.[1]

The Kodak example suggests that restructurings do not necessarily produce better performance. Kodak's acquisition of Sterling (an international pharmaceutical company) may have represented an attempt to expand internationally. However, achieving international growth with unrelated products is difficult, as we discussed in chapter 10. Some firms may restructure to reduce their level of product diversification (i.e., downscope, as was discussed in chapter 8) and use the new resources to expand internationally. Movement into international markets, however, represents no guarantee of success. In fact, implementation of international diversification often is more complex than implementation of domestic strategies. Yet effective implementation is critical to the success of any strategy; the decisions on how to restructure and how to implement these restructurings may be critical to the overall effectiveness of the restructuring.

The topic of this chapter is the implementation of restructuring decisions. In particular, we emphasize the advantages of downscoping over downsizing and the need to maintain strategic leadership and control.

Downscoping and Downsizing

Corporate downsizing refers to the divestiture of businesses and/or the reduction in size of current businesses, often accomplished through employee layoffs. Downscoping, in contrast, refers to the process through which firms reemphasize their core businesses. Firms often accomplish downscoping through divestiture of businesses unrelated to their primary or core businesses, sometimes accompanied by selected employee layoffs in order to improve efficiency. Effective downscoping may employ both divestitures and selected layoffs in unrelated businesses but at the same time seeks continued growth in the firm's primary core businesses. We advocate downscoping, rather than downsizing, as a restructuring strategy.

Workforce reductions have become an integral part of modern organizational environments. In the late 1980s and early 1990s, thousands of jobs were eliminated in private and public organizations. Unlike earlier workforce shrinkages, which generally were in response to economic downturns and often affected only those in blue-collar and less skilled jobs, the workforce reductions in the 1980s and 1990s reflect a pervasive trend toward reduction of white-collar and executive jobs. In 1990 approximately 70 percent of the new jobless were white-collar workers. We need to understand these workforce reductions and their implications.

Some observers in the media have suggested that these workforce reductions are not a restructuring, but rather a bloodletting. One important example is the General Motors Corporation announcement of a workforce reduction of 74,000, along with the closing of 21 plants over a four-year period; others include the workforce reductions at IBM, Xerox, Kodak, Procter & Gamble TRW, and UNISYS.[2]

The elimination of jobs has occurred in numbers unprecedented since the Great Depression of the 1930s. It has been suggested that the 1980s were a period of excess and that we are now paying for that excess; in fact, one analyst stated that "not since the reckless 1920s has America experienced such a collective abdication of responsibility with such long-term consequences."[3] Many firms have argued, however, that the downsizings of the 1980s and the 1990s were necessary in order for them to become "lean and mean" and therefore, efficient. The question then becomes whether these firms have been achieving efficiency as well as other goals of downsizing. Results from a survey published in *The Wall Street Journal* provide answers to this question. The survey found that 89 percent of those firms that were downsizing had as a goal reducing expenses. However, only 46 percent suggested they had achieved this goal. Another 71 percent suggested that their intent was to improve productivity, but only 22 percent of the respondents said they were meeting goals for increasing productivity; 67 percent said their goal was to increase competitive advantage, but only 19 percent noted they had reached this goal. Finally, 32 percent named increasing innovation as a goal, but only 7 percent claimed to have achieved this goal, while 83 percent gave increasing profits as a goal, but only 32 percent had achieved it.[4] Downsizing, therefore, does not necessarily improve corporate fortunes as intended. Chapter 5 indicated that restructuring is necessary to correct problems of strategic competitiveness, but the way the restructuring decisions are implemented may be critical to whether the firm achieves its goals and in fact becomes more competitive.

Intended and Unintended Consequences

Restructuring has many potential outcomes, positive and negative, intended and unintended. Intended positive outcomes might include increased efficiency, potential regeneration of organizational success, decreased costs, improved productivity, improved quality, enhanced competitive advantage, inculcation of new basic values (culture), and the creation of new sources of synergy within the organization. These positive intended outcomes may not all be realized. In addition, there may be potential unintended consequences, including increased employee turnover, lower employee commitment and loyalty to the organization, survivor guilt, insecurity and depression, overemphasis on penalties for ineffective decisions, managerial risk aversion, resistance to change, emphasis on short-term outcomes, and reduced innovation.[5]

Beyond the effects on individual employees, which also affect organizational outcomes, restructuring is likely to produce a pervasive crisis-oriented atmosphere.[6] In this atmosphere, rewards for good decisions may be overshadowed by the penalties for poor decisions.[7] If penalties for ineffective decisions are emphasized, managers may become more risk averse. As a result, they may sacrifice strategic, long-term thinking to focus on current crises and short-term returns. In such an environment, managers may limit their data-gathering and decision-making activities to those that offer protection and increase survival. Although the intent of restructuring is to enhance organizational regeneration and competitive advantage, some outcomes may be dysfunctional. In some situations, the organization may experience a lack of long-term planning and innovation, increased scapegoating, resistance to change, and debilitating conflict.

Negative outcomes may be avoided and anticipated through proactive efforts. As a result, strategic leadership should be emphasized during restructuring decision making and, in particular, during implementation of the restructuring. This represents a significant challenge. Managers often must design and implement restructuring actions for immediate impact but also preserve long-term goals to enhance competitive position, organizational growth, and survival.[8] In fact, the stock market often reacts positively (that is, shareholders achieve positive returns) when layoffs are announced for purposes of restructuring or consolidation unrelated to financial performance; when layoffs occur because of financial reasons, the market reacts negatively (shareholders achieve negative returns). Strategic layoffs may reduce costs and at the same time preserve long-term strategic goals and produce overall positive consequences. This outcome occurs only with the exercise and maintenance of strategic leadership.[9]

Maintaining Strategic Leadership

Strategic leadership in the firm may have dissipated before the need to restructure is perceived. In a firm in need of restructuring, incentives for both corporate and division managers may have created risk aversion for an extended period of time. Managers who have a propensity to take appropriate risk may have already left the organization if they had other opportunities, while those who sought change through high risk taking may have been fired. There may also be some who have accepted the short-sighted system to avoid job loss. The central causes of restructuring, then, may have substantially dissipated strong strategic leadership. In support of this position, one study found that the board of directors was least likely to initiate restructuring if top managers had strong strategic control of the firm.[10]

As was noted earlier, recent workforce reductions have increasingly focused on members of mid- and upper-level management. There are three common approaches to handling reductions in managerial personnel—early retirement programs, elimination of layers of middle management, and across-the-board layoffs. Each of these alternatives presents potential problems. Offering early retirement inducements reduces the control of the firm in determining who will leave; some of the individuals who take the early retirement option may be people that the firm does not want to lose. Across-the-board layoffs imply that there is little evaluation of the relative importance or contribution of the different units and executives to the organization's strategic mission. Such an approach assumes that all units are equally important, which is unlikely to be accurate. The implementation of across-the-board layoffs thus may harm the performance of units critical to the firm's strategic mission and objectives. The third option, the elimination of middle-management layers, is designed to develop a "lean machine." However, it also reduces the number of experienced managers available to fill top executive positions when they become available and reduces the reservoir of talent available for future development. It may also encourage strong performers to leave because they are likely to find employment opportunities elsewhere. Because of these shortcomings, firms must search for other means of reducing the workforce, including managerial and professional positions, that maintain the integrity of units important to strategic objectives and that allow the firm to retain the talent to exercise effective strategic leadership in current and future periods.[11]

Strategic leadership requires managers to handle the ambiguity of multiple and complex functions and to manage through others.[12] It requires anticipation, vision, flexibility, and the ability to empower others to create strategic change.[13] It therefore entails what is commonly referred to as transformational leadership (i.e., leadership that produces major change in the organization). Some analysts argue that those executives who exercise strategic leadership must have a ten- to twenty-year vision and therefore must develop the cognitive abilities and the mindset necessary to deal with complex decisions they will face.[14] The integrity of this level of cognitive abilities must be maintained in planning restructuring activities. Firms involved in restructuring must continue to develop lower-level managers and to nurture in them the appropriate mindset for undertaking strategic leadership, either immediately or in the future. Mentoring of the remaining middle managers to ensure that they develop an appropriate cognitive map with which to deal with the complex decisions required of strategic leadership is critical to the long-term success of restructuring efforts.

The maintenance of strategic leadership requires that workforce reductions be accomplished with thorough planning and effective decisions. This means that thorough evaluation of units and of managers and professionals must accompany restructuring decisions and workforce reductions. Units critical to the strategic mission and managers and professionals with the strongest potential for becoming effective strategic leaders in the future must be buffered from workforce reductions to the extent possible, especially in light of the evidence that strategic leadership may have already deteriorated before the decision to restructure.

One example in which the maintenance of strategic leadership was quite difficult but extremely important is in the layoffs and plant closures at GM. As was noted earlier, General Motors has begun the closing of 21 plants and will reduce its workforce by 74,000 by 1995. It also plans significant reductions in capital spending. Although at one time GM was a prime example of a successful corporation, it apparently was unable to manage "life at the top of the market." With the changes announced by its chief executive officer, GM will become a much different corporation. Some of GM's workforce reductions are being accomplished through attrition and retirements. The company instituted a hiring freeze in 1992 and is selling nonautomobile assets. One thing is clear: By the end of 1995 GM will be a much smaller company, although it will still be a large, major corporation. The means by which it implements its restructuring may be critical to whether it remains a strong and viable corporation into the twenty-first century.

Because of significant competition, primarily from foreign automakers, GM's share of the U.S. automobile and truck market decreased from approximately 50 percent (in the mid 1970s) to almost 33 percent (in 1993). As a result, it has had significant idle plant capacity. The plants closed in the early 1990s had the capacity to produce 2 million cars and trucks annually. The reduction leaves GM with the capacity to produce more than 5 million cars and trucks per year; the company plans to use 100 percent of its remaining capacity after the completion of the plant closures.[15] The future of GM will be determined by the exercise of strategic leadership during and after its restructuring efforts.

Exercising Strategic Leadership

As was noted in the previous sections, restructuring efforts often have unintended, negative consequences. It is difficult to maintain strategic leadership during restructuring because the actions involved, such as layoffs among middle management, often result in elimination of future leaders. On the other hand, the effectiveness of restructuring decisions can be achieved only with effective leadership. For example, effective strategic leadership would continue investment in development of new technology and in the continuous development of employee skills. This is most likely to occur under the downscoping and restructuring scenario recommended in chapter 8 and is least likely to occur in downsizing efforts designed to promote efficiency and a "lean and mean" organization without recognition of the continued development necessary for future growth and survival.[16]

Strategic leadership involves the balancing of short-term needs with long-term growth and survival. It involves making downscoping decisions regarding the divestiture of businesses unrelated to the firm's core business and the reduction of selected workforce units and people on the basis of their contribution to the firm's strategic objectives. Finally, it involves continued investment in innovation and human capital—the continued development of and investment in core competencies and human capital and the fostering of a strong organizational culture.

Core competencies

Research suggests that the nurture and maintenance of core competencies can provide a basis for competitive advantage.[17] Core competencies represent the skills, capabilities, and knowledge on which organizational learning is focused and often relate to functional skills such as marketing and R&D.[18] For example, R&D would be recognized as a core competence at Merck, as would marketing and promotion at Philip Morris and development and transfer of innovation to the market at 3M. A company's ability to develop and utilize a core competence across separate businesses, markets, and geographic locations may be distinctive and difficult for competitors to imitate. As a result, it may help create a sustained competitive advantage.[19]

The development and application of a firm's core competencies can facilitate the management of interrelationships among businesses and may be particularly important in firms that have multiple international operations. (Resource sharing is particularly complicated in internationally diversified firms.) The use of core competencies as a means of sharing resources across businesses may help integrate businesses operating in different geographical markets across country borders.[20] Of course, sharing of tangible resources can be complicated, but the sharing of intangible resources (knowledge or skills such as core competencies) represents a special opportunity in global firms. Development and application of core competencies may help implement international diversification, described in chapter 10.

The utilization of core competencies can reduce the complexity of information processing by executives. When firms emphasize core competencies, top executives have fewer different resources and markets on which to concentrate for strategic decisions. Rather, they can make strategic decisions that utilize and emphasize the advantages of selected core competencies.

During restructuring, executives must be careful not to harm existing core competencies in the organization. These core skills should be buffered from major disruptions during downsizing and/or downscoping actions. For example, individuals whose skills are critical for the core competencies should be protected from layoffs, and units and businesses in which core skills can be applied to the greatest advantage should be maintained. If these steps are taken, the streamlined organization, after restructuring, should have a stronger emphasis on the application of core competencies.[21]

Human capital development

Several scholars and practitioners have argued that the development of human capital is critical for strategic competitiveness. U.S. firms have on occasion invested millions of dollars in new technical equipment, only to learn that there was a shortage of skilled labor to operate that equipment. The importance of human capital is shown by the fact that one third of the growth in the U.S. gross national product from 1948 to 1982 is attributed to increases in the education level of the workforce; 50 percent of the growth resulted from technological innovation and knowledge that depended heavily on education. Only 15 percent of the growth was attributed to increased investment in capital equipment.[22]

Effective management development programs represent one means by which human capital may be developed and maintained. It is important to note that firms moving from a domestic to a global strategy require shifts in cognitive and strategic orientation. Furthermore, the cognitive abilities that are necessary in the exercise of strategic leadership require continued emphasis and development. Management development programs may facilitate the development and maintenance of the necessary skills but are rarely sufficient as the primary or single source of human capital development in restructuring organizations. Mentoring programs and careful assignments of individuals to jobs for developmental purposes may also be necessary. Reward and incentive systems should be designed to maintain a balance between long-term decision making with a reasonable amount of risk assumption and decision making focused on the short-term (see chapters 6 and 8).

Development programs facilitate communication among employees and help construct a common vision for the organization. They promote cohesion, act primarily as a socialization agent, and help inculcate a common set of core values. They can also influence organizational flexibility by helping managers to develop the critical skills necessary for an effective response to competitive challenges.[23] It should be recognized, however, that the change affects the effectiveness of employee skills. Many restructuring efforts not only eliminate jobs but change other jobs. The elimination of management layers and of other professional jobs often adds new responsibilities to the remaining professional and managerial jobs and therefore increases the skill requirements of those jobs. Furthermore, if the organization continues to develop innovation, new skills will be required to develop and implement those innovations in the organization. In addition, restructuring that eliminates management layers leads to larger spans of control and, often, an increase in decentralized authority; employees must become more self-managing. This can be accomplished effectively only if the remaining employees have the necessary skills to perform the newly added responsibilities.

Unfortunately, in restructuring efforts one of the first expenses to be cut often is human resource development programs. For example, when Phillips Petroleum Company acquired significant debt to fend off a takeover attempt by the corporate raider T. Boone Pickens, the firm had to reduce other expenditures. One of its first actions was to eliminate its corporate training and development function. This is an example of short-sightedness in restructuring efforts.

Organizational culture

Organizational culture is a system of shared meanings and values among the organization members.[24] Restructuring presents both opportunities and problems for modifying the corporate culture. Restructuring presents the opportunity to change a structure but also sometimes creates a crisis in which individuals resist change. The opportunity thus exists for changing culture, but the change also may encounter resistance. (If the current culture is appropriate, care must be taken to maintain that culture when implementing restructuring decisions.) One of the dangers managers face is the tendency to respond to resistance to change with defensive leadership behaviors, sometimes referred to as quick-fix or cookbook solutions. The application of strategic leadership may help in changing a culture by first creating a vision and infusing the organization with it. Then, commitment to the vision must be mobilized and the change implemented and institutionalized. Of course, this process involves shaping and reinforcing the new culture.[25]

Lee Iacocca was successful in creating a strategic vision for Chrysler and implementing change during the early 1980s. He did so by organizing a management team that helped develop and implement the vision and that created a process through which to inculcate and reinforce the new values at Chrysler.[26]

As was noted earlier, restructuring actions often disrupt an organization's culture. Downsizing and downscoping actions can produce uncertainty and job insecurity, making surviving employees risk averse and short-term-oriented. However, culture also offers a means of controlling the premises of employee's behaviors and attitudes. For example, a reward system consistent with new cultural norms can be a powerful means of achieving control.[27] After restructuring actions are completed, the culture should be managed to promote the pursuit of opportunity through rewards and to minimize the penalty for failure. Rewards should be consistent and based on individual achievement and innovation. In short, the culture should promote diversity and individuality and reward risk taking rather than risk avoidance. If it is to do so, rewards must be based on long-term, rather than short-term, performance (unless the short-term approach is appropriate).[28]

Strategic control systems

For rewards to be based on long-term performance, organizational control systems must be reviewed to ensure they are in tune with long-term needs. One study of large diversified firms concluded that focus on acquisition strategies results in an emphasis on financial controls based on short-term goals.[29] In order to focus on long-term performance, restructuring firms should utilize strategic controls that focus on the content of strategic actions, rather than on their outcomes. When Jack Welch became CEO of GE, he decided to restructure in order to regain strategic control. He sold off some units and reorganized others in order to restructure the approximately 47 separate businesses into 14 strategic business units. As a result, his span of control was reduced by 26 general managers, and he was better able to exercise strategic control over the remaining 14 SBUs.

Restructuring designed to downscope normally results in fewer and more similar operating units. This situation provides an opportunity to reinstitute strategic control. With a smaller span of control and with units designed to be more similar to the core business, top executives can control the strategic actions and behaviors of the various units' executives instead of focusing primarily on financial outcomes. The use of strategic controls has been found to promote a longer-term focus and more innovation over time.[30]

The use of strategic controls should be integrated with reasonable operating autonomy for the different units. Autonomy allows these units the flexibility necessary to undertake strategic actions to achieve competitive advantage in their respective markets, while strategic controls not only ensure appropriate strategic behaviors but also promote sharing of both tangible and intangible resources among interdependent units. Strategic leadership provides the opportunity to achieve operating autonomy and the exercise of strategic controls.

The reorganization of Hewlett-Packard in 1990 illustrates this point. Although HP had undergone structural changes after entering the computer business, the 1990 restructuring was badly needed in order to restore the firm's competitiveness. The once highly successful firm was suffering from slow decision making, conflict between product divisions, and increased costs. One reporter referred to the firm as a dinosaur watching fleet-footed mammals steal its nest eggs. The firm was largely decentralized but without integration between the divisions. While the decentralization allowed more innovation, it also created redundancies and poorly integrated product lines; a number of the independent divisions created new computers that were not well integrated with each other. The computers required a complex integration of disparate technologies, components, and software. There was clearly a need for more effective integration among the related product divisions.

Hewlett-Packard's CEO, John Young, instituted significant restructuring actions. He eliminated excessive layers of management and replaced the leadership of product development groups with strong individuals who could cut through the red tape. He integrated computer product groups along their markets and reorganized the sales force to solve acute marketing problems.

The changes required revisions in the company's organizational structure, and in its culture as well. For example, the restructuring produced a reduction of 3,000 jobs in 1990 and of 2,000 more by 1992. This loss of jobs was significant because Hewlett-Packard claimed never to have fired anyone prior to this time. In fact, excess employees either found new jobs within the firm in three months or were assigned new posts, albeit sometimes at lower ranks and pay. The firm thus became less paternalistic with the restructuring changes. It also became much more aggressive in its marketing and advertising of new products, such as workstations. The changes in structure were especially dramatic because they accomplished the necessary integration of units while at the same time maintaining unit autonomy. These changes boosted HP's earnings, along with the stock price in 1991 and 1992. There is much optimism at Hewlett-Packard for success in the 1990s.[31]

Building a New Organization Structure

Many large diversified firms employ variations of the multidivisional (M-form) structure. Often such structures are designed to provide maximum autonomy to each of the multiple product divisions within the firm. At one time, M-form structures were thought to be highly efficient for large multiproduct firms. In fact, some scholars have argued that M-form structures are excellent at generating efficient, low-cost production and distribution of products. On the other hand, others have noted that M-form structures may not be efficient in the promotion of innovation. In fact, smaller and less diversified firms without M-form structures may be more effective innovators because they are able to develop and utilize tacit skills (skills that are idiosyncratic to a particular firm).[32] It is interesting that Hewlett-Packard apparently utilized a form of the M-form structure prior to restructuring. Its product divisions were allowed considerable autonomy. There was, however, little or no coordination, which in turn produced a complex mixture of noncomplementary products. In fact, resource sharing and nurturing of core competencies are difficult to achieve within M-form structures because the M-form overemphasizes divisional autonomy. Some alterations of the M-form structure may be necessary and should be implemented along with restructuring decisions.[33]

Differentiated and Integrated Structures

The primary alteration of the M-form structure required is that necessary to achieve integration of different units. Clearly, each product division must be allowed appropriate autonomy to take necessary actions to compete effectively in its market. There is, however, a need for some means of integrating each division's actions with those of other divisions. This is particularly important when the products are related because achieving synergy among related products requires integration. There is also a need to promote resource sharing among product divisions that have complementary products and/or processes. Finally, promoting the economies of applying core competencies and utilizing them to achieve competitive advantage requires integration. Research suggests that M-forms able to accomplish this integration, called cooperative M-forms, achieve higher levels of performance than other types.[34] There are several means of achieving integration in these types of organizations: loosely coupled systems, integrators, and loosely structured multiunit teams.

Loose coupling

Loosely coupled systems allow units to act independently but at the same time to respond to the overall organization needs. The differentiated units have the autonomy to deal with their own environment but also act in concert with other units as the need arises. Such organizations require simultaneous centralization and decentralization.[35] Loose coupling may be facilitated by shared values (or a common culture), subtle leadership, and focused attention.

A strong corporate culture can promote normative integration and thus provides a subtle means of centralization.[36] In conjunction with corporate culture, subtle leadership from top corporate executives provides centralized direction and coordination but grants flexibility and discretion to the divisional units. Subtle leadership thus entails the provision of a centralized vision and a means of facilitating the application of that vision throughout the organization. This is generally accomplished by providing strategic direction and by using strategic controls in conjunction with an incentive compensation system. Finally, focused attention requires selecting targets, focusing resources on those targets, and taking action. The choice of targets may be incorporated into the central vision. In addition, if the achievement of targets or goals requires coordination across separate units (a superordinate goal), focused attention will facilitate integration across those units.

Top executives play a key role in the integration of separate units. They help develop the premises for a strong corporate culture, provide subtle leadership through a central vision, and focus attention by selecting goals whose achievement require coordination across units. These are all subtle means of achieving integration across diverse units.

Integrators

Achieving integration across multiple diverse units may require formal structural mechanisms in addition to loose coupling. Coordination between units may be facilitated by the use of integrators, individuals who occupy formal positions with the express purpose of facilitating and achieving coordination across units. To be effective, integrators must be knowledgeable about the various units' idiosyncratic markets, environmental demands, and technologies. Because of the complex knowledge required and the difficulty of achieving coordination among diverse units, integrators are most effective in coordinating small numbers of units. For example, prior to its acquisition by Beatrice Foods, Samsonite was encountering problems in coordinating manufacturing and marketing efforts in its furniture division. An integrator position was established to facilitate communication and to coordinate decisions between the manufacturing and the marketing functions. The integrator was so effective that the position became unnecessary after slightly over one year; the person in the integrator position was promoted in recognition of excellent work in achieving integration between the two functions. If the number of divisions or units is high, integration may be more effectively achieved through other complex structural mechanisms, such as multiunit teams.

Multiunit teams

Multiunit teams are composed of members representing each of the diverse units or divisions in which coordination is important. The goals of these teams are the same as those of integrators—to promote and to facilitate coordination among the diverse units.[37] These unit representatives should be key managers who have the authority to commit their units to critical decisions. These teams help promote synergy among the units. The chairperson of the multiunit team might be a corporate executive who can infuse the team with the central vision or, perhaps, an integrator who reports to the corporate office. These multiunit teams should facilitate the sharing of resources and the application of core competencies across units.[38]

Multiunit teams have been employed effectively for many years by Boeing in the design and the manufacture of aircraft. Teams may also create problems, however, by slowing the decision-making process, as they did at Hewlett Packard. Teams need strong leadership; one way to provide this is to give the team leader budgetary control over team projects.

Building Tacit Knowledge and Skills

Tacit knowledge and skills help the firm to customize its strategies and to develop and maintain competitive advantages. This knowledge is idiosyncratic and cannot be easily replicated or imitated outside the firm.[39] Tacit knowledge and skills therefore help the firm pursue customized strategies that are difficult to imitate by competitors. The key is the ability to develop and to apply tacit knowledge and skills to different products and markets.

The importance of tacit knowledge and skills is likely to grow in the future. The primary value added for many products and services derives less from actual production and distribution than from specific technological and asset improvements (e.g., customized product offerings, technological change, and styling and image). This is particularly true as assets become less tangible. However, M-form structures do not facilitate the development of tacit knowledge and skills unless there is a strong internal labor market. This internal market encourages employees to invest in firm-specific rather than in generalized skills because the skills can be used to take advantage of career opportunities inside the firm. This can create problems for U.S. firms; compared to other economies, such as Japan's, the U.S. economy has a strong external labor market that encourages the development of generalizable skills, which are transferable to other organizations.

Integrators and multidivisional teams are generally effective in promoting the development and the application of tacit knowledge and skills. Alterations of the M-form structure aimed at facilitating integration should promote the development of tacit knowledge and skills.[40]

Global Restructuring

In chapter 10 we discussed the relationship between international diversification and product diversification. We noted that many firms are choosing to diversify internationally rather than to diversify their product lines. Furthermore, we suggested that many of the firms that choose to diversify internationally rather than to pursue product diversification often achieve higher performance and more innovation. Many firms are both product and internationally diversified; these complex organizations are difficult to manage effectively. Even international diversification at some point becomes too difficult to manage effectively and has a negative effect on innovation and performance. As a result, firms that are product and internationally diversified reach a point at which restructuring is necessary. Restructuring a firm that is both product and internationally diversified is of course more complex and more difficult than restructuring a product diversified firm in domestic markets.

The principles of restructuring are the same. It is important to refocus the firm on its core businesses and markets. The firm should attempt to take advantage of the economies of scale and scope provided by international diversification, but it may have to refocus not only its product orientation but its orientation to international markets. In other words, in addition to divestiture of unrelated product divisions, it also may have to sell off businesses and/or move out of markets that for idiosyncratic reasons are unprofitable. (It must be recognized that movement out of a particular market may preclude or erect strong barriers to reentry at a later time.) Again, the decision rules discussed earlier in this chapter and in chapter 8 apply to this type of restructuring decision. Managers must perform careful analyses of product divisions, geographical markets, and individuals in those divisions in order to make effective restructuring decisions. In addition, the implementation of those restructuring decisions requires strategic leadership and the other characteristics we have described in this chapter.

The restructuring should be focused on achieving a transnational capability, the ability to manage both integrated and country-specialized firms across country boundaries.[41] Implementation of both expansion and contraction requires a careful understanding of the cultures and the business practices within each country in which operations exist. Because cultures and other idiosyncratic characteristics of a country can affect management decisions and practices in that country, implementation of restructuring decisions in an internationally diversified firm is especially complex.[42] For example, partial divestitures of divisional assets and/or layoffs of personnel may be problematic in Asian cultures with collective and communitarian values, such as lifetime employment. Many of these cultures also place an emphasis on harmony, unity, and sincerity, so layoffs may be especially difficult and demoralizing, not only to those employees who lose their jobs, but also to the survivors. Although implementation of restructuring in domestic businesses also creates problems, implementing such decisions in international operations may require careful evaluation and even more sensitivity.

The restructured international firm must promote local responsiveness that requires decentralization and autonomy while at the same time achieving coordination across the geographically differentiated businesses.[43] As a result, the need to maintain differentiation and integration remains strong in internationally diversified firms but is more complex and more difficult to achieve.

Summary

Making the decision to restructure a firm is complex. Restructuring decisions alone, however, cannot be successful without effective implementation. The primary focus of restructuring decisions should be downscoping, rather than downsizing, although downsizing often is a component of downscoping actions. Such restructuring actions often have intended and unintended consequences. For the most part, the intended consequences are positive, but the unintended consequences often are negative. It is critical that the unintended consequences be managed so that they do not offset the positive intended outcomes. To achieve this balance requires that firms maintain strategic leadership after restructuring. The development, maintenance, and implementation of core competencies are critical. Even with cost reductions, the firm must also emphasize human capital development. In fact, restructuring firms may need to increase the emphasis on human capital development because they must operate with fewer people and larger spans of control. There is less slack, and many employees must take on new responsibilities after restructuring has been implemented; they must have the skills necessary to perform those tasks effectively. In addition, there will be fewer individuals prepared to take on key executive positions when they become available. Emphasis on the development of these remaining individuals is therefore important.

Another potentially important variable in the exercise of strategic leadership is organizational culture. If leaders can develop and maintain a strong culture that promotes shared values, that culture can provide a means of simultaneous decentralization and centralization. Shared values provide a subtle means of centralization. Those managers who share the same values are more likely to make complementary decisions, even though they may be operating in different units. In addition to helping the firm to maintain shared values, top executives in restructured firms should try to develop and implement strategic control systems. Part of thee rationale for downscoping or for strategic refocusing is to enhance the opportunity to utilize strategic rather than financial controls. (Whereas financial controls often promote short-term oriented and risk-averse behavior on the part of division managers, strategic controls promote more appropriate risk taking behavior with a long-term orientation.)

In order to exercise strategic leadership in the ways we have described, the firm must develop an organization structure that facilitates strategic leadership. It needs to develop a structure that is differentiated (and decentralized) but also integrated. Means of achieving integration include using loose coupling, integrators, or multiunit teams. In complex organizations, all three types of structural processes may be utilized. They often represent alterations of the multidivisional structure.

The alteration of the M-form structure through the application of loosely structured multiunit teams helps to promote the development and the application of tacit skills and knowledge, which may be necessary to develop strategies that cannot be easily imitated by competitors, thereby promoting the firm's competitive advantage.

Finally, many large firms are both product and internationally diversified. Restructuring decisions in such firms are more complex. While we noted in chapter 10 that international diversification may be desired over product diversification because of its positive effects on innovation and performance, there are limits to such diversification. International diversification is highly complex to manage. Past some point, additional international diversification may produce downturns in innovation and performance. In such cases, global restructuring may be required. We also suggested, however, that restructuring decisions and implementation in international operations may require special knowledge and sensitivity to the cultures and operations in different markets. Restructuring internationally diversified firms may be even more complex than restructuring product diversified firms in domestic markets.

There have been a number of successful restructuring efforts; Xerox, Goodyear Tire and Rubber, General Dynamics, Burlington Northern, and Honeywell have effectively restructured and have experienced a performance turnaround recognized in the stock market. For example, the stock price of Goodyear Tire and Rubber increased from a low of slightly below $20 a share in 1991 to a high of more than $60 a share in 1992.

W. R. Grace & Company, one of the largest U.S. conglomerates, decided to downscope. Its goal was to refocus on its core chemical and healthcare businesses. As of this writing, it plans to divest over $1.5 billion of assets in this restructuring effort and hopes to obtain 10 percent annual earnings growth and 20 percent return on equity by 1995. This will be no easy task because it has 28 separate businesses with more than 100 different product lines. Furthermore, W. R. Grace's long-term debt has increased dramatically in recent years to 54 percent of total capital. The company borrowed to finance capital spending and dividend payments because cash flow had been negative since 1986. The firm obviously needed restructuring. The success of the restructuring at W. R. Grace may largely depend on how carefully the executives follow the guidelines set forth in this chapter for implementation of their restructuring decisions.[44]

In conclusion, it is not enough for firms to decide to downscope. To achieve long-term positive results, they must also effectively implement downscoping decisions. The information in this chapter suggests the following managerial implications:

- Emphasize downscoping over downsizing.
- Increase (rather than decrease) emphasis on human capital development.
- Rebuild and maintain strategic leadership, and foster a strong positive culture.
- Emphasize strategic control to balance with financial control in order to reduce risk aversion.
- Stress core competencies.
- Realign structure to reinforce core competencies through integrating mechanisms (loosing coupling, integrators, and multiunit teams).

Notes

1. Rigdon, J. E. 1992. Kodak changes produce plenty of heat, little light. *The Wall Street Journal*, April 8:B–4; Maremont, M., & Lesly, E. 1993. Getting the picture: Kodak finally heads the shareholders. *Business Week*, February 1:24–26.

2. Johnson, H. 1991. These latest layoffs aren't restructuring, they're bloodletting. *Houston Chronicle*, December 22:5E.

3. Johnson, Latest layoffs.

4. Bennett, A. 1991. Downscoping doesn't necessarily bring an upswing in corporate profitability. *The Wall Street Journal*, June 4:B–1,B–4.

5. Hitt, M. A., & Keats, B. W. 1992. Strategic leadership and restructuring: A reciprocal independence. In R. L. Phillips & J. G. Hunt, eds., *Strategic Leadership: A Multi-Organization Level Perspective*. New York: Quorum Books, pp. 45–61; Brockner, J. P., Davey, J., & Carter, C. 1988. Layoffs, self-esteem and survival guilt: Motivational, affective and attitudinal consequences. In K. S. Cameron, R. I. Sutton, & D. A. Whetten, eds., *Readings in Organizational Decline*. Cambridge, Mass.: Ballinger, pp. 279–90; Wheeler, K. G., Gray, D. A., Gia-

cobbe, J., & Quick, J. C. 1990. Organizational and human resource results of corporate restructuring problems, pitfalls and benefits. Paper presented at the Academy of Management meetings, San Francisco.

6. Cameron, K. S., Kim, M. U., & Whetten, D. A. 1988. Organizational effects of decline and turbulence. In Cameron, Sutton, & Whetten, *Readings*, pp. 207–24.

7. Whetten, D. A. 1988. Sources, responses and effects of organizational decline. In Cameron, Sutton, & Whetten, *Readings*, pp. 151–74.

8. Cameron, K. S., Freeman, S. R., & Mishra, A. 1990. Effective organizational downsizing: Paradoxical processes and the best practices. Paper presented at the Academy of Management meetings, San Francisco.

9. Worrell, D. L., Davidson, W. N., & Sharma, V. M. 1991. Layoff announcements and stockholder wealth. *Academy of Management Journal* 34:662–78.

10. Johnson, R. A., Hoskisson, R. E., & Hitt, M. A. 1993. Board of director involvement in restructuring: The effects of board versus managerial controls and characteristics. *Strategic Management Journal* (Special Issue) 14:325–41.

11. Hitt & Keats, Strategic leadership.

12. Byrd, R. E. 1987. Corporate leadership skills: A new synthesis. *Organizational dynamics* 16:34–43; Hambrick, D. C. 1989. Guest editors' introduction: Putting top managers back in the strategy picture. *Strategic Management Journal* (Special Issue) 10:5–15.

13. Byrd, Corporate leadership skills.

14. Hunt, J. G. 1991. *Leadership: A new synthesis.* Newbury Park, Calif.: Sage; Hambrick, Guest editors' introduction.

15. Ingrassia, L., & White, J. B. 1991. GM plans to close twenty-one more factories, cut 74,000 jobs/capital spending. *The Wall Street Journal*, December 19:A–3,A–14; Templin, N. 1993. Auto sales lose sharply in late January. *The Wall Street Journal*, February 4:A–2,B–5.

16. Clark, K. 1987. Investment in new technology and competitive advantage. In D. J. Teece, ed., *The Competitive Challenge: Strategies for Industrial Innovation and Renewal.* Cambridge, Mass.: Ballinger, pp. 59–81; Young, J. A. 1988. Technology and competitiveness: A key to the economic future of the United States. *Science* 241:313–16.

17. Hitt, M. A., & Hoskisson, R. E. 1991. Strategic competitiveness. In L. Foster, ed., *Applied Business Strategy.* New York: JAI Press, pp. 1–36; Hitt, M. A., & Ireland, R. D. 1985. Corporate distinctive competencies, strategy, industry, and performance. *Strategic Management Journal* 6:273–93; Hitt, M. A., & Ireland, R. D. 1986. Relationships among corporate level distinctive competencies, diversification strategy, corporate structure and performance. *Journal of Management Studies* 23:401–16; Prahalad, C. K., & Hamel, G. 1990. The core competencies of the corporation. *Harvard Business Review* 68 (May–June):79–93.

18. Lei, D., Hitt, M. A., & Goldhar, J. D. 1992. Generic strategies, complementarities and organization design in global manufacturing firms. Working paper, Southern Methodist University.

19. Barney, J. B. 1988. Returns to bidding firms and mergers and acquisitions: Reconsidering the relatedness hypothesis. *Strategic Management Journal* (Special Issue) 9:71–78.

20. Lei et al., Generic strategies; Gupta, A. K., & Govindarajan, V. 1984. Business unit strategy, managerial characteristics and business unit effectiveness at strategy implementation. *Academy of Management Journal* 27:25–41; Gupta, A. K., & Govindarajan, V. 1986. Resource sharing among SBUs: Strategic ante-

cedents and administrative implications. *Academy of Management Journal* 29:695–714; Porter, M. E. 1985. *Competitive Advantage.* New York: Free Press.

21. Hitt & Keats, Strategic leadership.

22. Nussbaum, B. 1988. Needed: Human capital. *Business Week,* September 19:100–02; Hitt & Hoskisson, Strategic competitiveness.

23. Nussbaum, Needed; Miles, R. E. 1989. A new industrial relations system for the 21st century. *California Management Review* 31:9–28; Hitt & Keats, Strategic leadership.

24. Kerr, J., & Slocum, J. W., Jr. 1987. Managing corporate culture through reward systems. *Academy of Management Executive* 1:99–107.

25. Tichy, N. M. 1987. Training as a lever for change. *New management,* 4(3):39–41; Tichy, N. M., & Ulrich, D. O. 1984. SMR forum: The leadership challenge—a call for the transformational leader. *Sloan Management Review* (Fall):59–68; Tichy, N. M., & Devanna, M. A. 1986. The transformational leader. *Training and Development Journal* 40(7):27–32.

26. Westley, F., & Mintzberg, H. 1989. Visionary leadership and strategic management. *Strategic Management Journal* (Special Issue) 10:17–32.

27. Kerr & Slocum, Managing corporate culture.

28. Hoskisson, R. E., Hitt, M. A., Turk, T., & Tyler, B. 1989. Balancing corporate strategy and executive compensation: Agency theory and corporate governance. In G. R. Ferris & K. M. Rowland, eds., *Research in Personnel and Human Resources Management,* vol. 7. Greenwich, Conn.: JAI Press, pp. 25–57.

29. Hitt, M. A., Hoskisson, R. E., Ireland, R. D., & Harrison, J. 1991. The effects of acquisitions on R&D inputs and outputs. *Academy of Management Journal* 34:693–706.

30. Hitt, M. A., Hoskisson, R. E., & Ireland, R. D. 1990. Mergers and acquisitions and managerial commitment to innovation in M-form firms. *Strategic Management Journal* (Special Issue) 11:29–47; Hoskisson, R. E., & Hitt, M. A. 1988. Strategic control systems and relative R&D investments in large multiproduct firms. *Strategic Management Journal* 9:605–21.

31. Yoder, S. K. 1992. Hewlett-Packard is too busy to notice industry slump. *The Wall Street Journal,* May 11:B–3; Yoder, S. K. 1992. A 1990 reorganization at Hewlett-Packard already is paying off. *The Wall Street Journal,* July 22:A–1,A–10.

32. Williamson, O. E. 1985. *The Economic Institution of Capitalism.* New York: Free Press; Hitt et al., Mergers and acquisitions.

33. Lei et al., Generic strategies.

34. Hoskisson, R. E., Hill, C. W. L., & Kim, H. 1993. The multidivisional structure: Organization fossil or source of value? *Journal of Management* 19:269–98.

35. Weick, K. E. 1982. Management or organizational change among loosely coupled elements. In P. S. Goodman and associates, eds., *Change in Organizations.* San Francisco: Jossey-Bass, pp. 322–38.

36. Kilmann, R. H., Saxton, M. J., & Serpa, R. 1986. Issues and understanding and changing culture. *California Management Review* 27:209–24; Weick, K. E. 1987. Organizational culture as a source of high reliability. *California Management Review* 29:112–26.

37. Hitt, M. A., Hoskisson, R. E., & Nixon, R. D. 1993. A mid-range theory of interfunctional integration, its antecedents and outcomes. *Journal of Engineering and Technology Management,* 10:161–85.

38. Lei et al., Generic strategies.

39. Nelson, R., & Winter, S. 1982. *An Evolutionary Theory of Economic Change.* Cambridge, Mass.: Belknap Press.

40. Argyris, C. 1983. Action science and intervention. *Journal of Applied Behavioral Science* 19:115–40.

41. Bartlett, C. A., & Ghoshal, S. 1988. Managing across borders: New strategic requirements. *California Management Review* 30(1):54–74.

42. Hitt, M. A., Tyler, B. B., & Park, D. 1990. A cross-cultural examination of strategic decision models: Comparison of Korean and U.S. executives. *Proceedings: Academy of Management,* August:111–15.

43. Bartlett & Ghoshal, Managing across borders; Bartlett, C. A., & Ghoshal, S. 1991. Global strategic management: Impact on the new frontier of strategy research. *Strategy Management Journal* (Special Issue) 12:5–16.

44. Sandler, L. 1992. Restructuring plays payoff nicely. *The Wall Street Journal,* February 5:C–1,C–2; DeGeorge, G. 1991. The word at Grace: If it's not selling, sell it. *Business Week,* December 16:57–58.

12

Learning from the Past and Looking to the Future

Merck & Company, Inc., develops, manufactures, and markets products in human and animal health and in specialty chemicals. It produces highly related products that are largely undiversified from the point of view of base technology and product development. Unlike many U.S. firms, Merck avoided the merger/acquisition craze of the 1980s, as well as the popular "leveraging up" among large firms, and instead focused its effort and its resources on internal research and development and on maintaining the quality of its products.

Merck has chosen to diversify internationally rather than through its product line. The results of Merck's strategy, which differed from that of many U.S. firms during the 1980s, are phenomenal. In the five years from 1987 to 1991, Merck experienced an annual growth rate in sales of 14.1 percent for a total increase of 70 percent. Its net income grew at an annual rate of 23.6 percent for a total increase of 134 percent and its earnings per share increased by more than 100 percent from $2.23 per share to $5.49 per share during this same five-year period. In a survey of 750 independent pharmacists, Merck was rated first among 42 pharmaceutical manufacturers in six different categories, including product quality. Even more impressive, Merck was rated as the most admired corporation in America for six straight years in *Fortune*'s reputation survey.

Clearly, Merck has been one of the best managed and most successful corporations, not only in the United States but in the world. Merck has been able to achieve such high levels of performance by maintaining its focus (not diversifying), avoiding mergers and acquisitions, eschewing major debt (its debt-to-equity ratio in 1991 was .10, extremely low among large U.S. corporations), emphasizing R&D to provide for future growth, and diversifying internationally to build a global network and market.[1] If all U.S. firms operated in the same manner as Merck, there would have been little need for us to write this book on corporate refocusing. Merck has been an exemplar for U.S. and foreign firms.

Many U.S. firms are the antithesis of Merck. We have provided examples throughout this book of firms that have overdiversified, participated heavily in the mergers and acquisitions binge, and used extraordinary levels of debt to finance growth (chapter 4) or restructuring (chapter 7). These strategies and actions have produced organizational structures and control systems that promote short-term and risk-averse behaviors on the part of corporate and division managers. This chapter provides a summary of the problems affecting strategic competitiveness and outlines our recommendations for overcoming competitiveness difficulties.

Diversification, M-form Structure, and Agency Concerns

During the 1960s and 1970s many large firms followed a corporate strategy of diversifying their product lines, often moving into unrelated product markets. The diversification trend extended into the 1980s, but federal tax laws and guidelines on enforcement of antitrust laws changed in a way that led firms to reduce their level of diversification. The changes in tax laws, promotion of leverage by prominent scholars, and innovations in the capital markets instead promoted strategies of growth through mergers and acquisitions financed largely with debt. Many firms that were highly diversified (overdiversified, to use Markides's term)[2] and/or had acquired a large number of businesses experienced performance problems during the 1980s. The 1980s were a period of intense foreign competition, which only exacerbated the performance problems. A period of restructuring, beginning in the early 1980s and continuing into the 1990s, followed.

The history of diversification as a strategy was chronicled by the business historian Alfred Chandler. Chandler noted that as firms began to grow and diversify their operations, they adopted the multidivisional or M-form structure to help them manage their diversified businesses.[3]

The M-form structure provides benefits for managing diverse businesses. It allows decentralization of authority for operational decisions from corporate to division managers, who have more expertise and information regarding such operations. According to Oliver Williamson, this structure is quite efficient and promotes profit maximization by division managers. Williamson also argues that M-form structures establish an internal capital market that reduces managerial opportunism, by creating the opportunity for appropriate monitoring, which is not necessarily available in freestanding firms with dispersed ownership.[4] As we reported in earlier chapters, however, the evidence on the performance of M-form firms is decidedly mixed; the M-form structure, while providing benefits, also has disadvantages. One of those disadvantages is that it promotes short-run profit maximization at the expense of long-term performance if diversification is not kept in check. There are also corporate control problems, particularly with highly diversified firms. In fact, several analysts have argued and empirically verified that highly diversified firms with multidivisional structures often emphasize financial over strategic controls, tending to promote short-term, risk-averse strategies on the part of division managers.

Given the problems stemming from overdiversification and the potential disadvantages of the multidivisional structure, it is legitimate to ask why firms continue to diversify. One of the reasons offered by many scholars can be classified as agency problems. The notion that managers act as agents for the owners in managing corporations and that the public corporation provides an efficient separation of ownership and managerial control dates back to the classic work *The Governance of Corporations* by Berle and Means, (1936). However, agency problems more recently have been popularized by Michael Jensen.[5] Essentially, whereas shareholders can diversify their risk by spreading their ownership across several different firms, managers cannot diversify their risk in a similar way. Their risks are tied to their employment and can be managed only by diversifying the product line of the firm. Diversifying the product line, Jensen argues, is not in shareholders' best interests, because shareholders can more efficiently diversify their own stock portfolios. Nonetheless, because ownership is separated from control, managers are able to develop strategies to diversify the product lines, thus operating more in their own interests than in those of the shareholders. Furthermore, product diversification provides an easy way to promote growth and thereby increase the size of the firm, which is also in managers' best interests; most research shows that firm size and executive compensation are positively related and that managers who are able to increase the size of the firm are likely to receive higher compensation.[6] Executives therefore have at least two incentives for increasing the product diversification of the firm. As a result, many large firms in the United States and abroad participated in the diversification binge. However, Merck avoided such diversification and there are clear differences between its performance and that of many other large U.S. corporations.

There are times when it is appropriate to diversify a product line. First, as we noted in chapter 9, some firms are able to manage unrelated diversification effectively. It may be appropriate to diversify if the firm is able to manage its diversification effectively. Furthermore, firms in dying industries may need to diversify to maintain their viability and shareholder value. One example is the U.S. tobacco industry. Because of all of the health problems associated with the use of tobacco products, the Philip Morris Company has diversified into other consumer product businesses; in fact, one of the reasons given for Philip Morris's choice of Michael A. Miles as CEO was his ability to continue the firm's diversification away from the tobacco industry. Mr. Miles was formerly head of Kraft General Foods, one of the major product divisions within Philip Morris. He beat out William Murray, a 21-year veteran of the tobacco business.[7]

Research by Richard Reed suggests that there are two main types of firm strategy—a dominant business approach, such as that by Merck, and a more diversified approach. He suggests that once a firm moves beyond a certain level of diversification and implements the M-form structure, it will expand diversification to an effective and efficient level. The diversification level probably will be lower for related and higher for unrelated diversified firms. It should also be noted that C. C. Markides's research suggests that there is an optimal level of diversification for each firm. This level of diversification varies by firm and is based on the firm's ability to gain synergy effectively from diversification and thereby manage the diversification to achieve maximum performance.

The most critical issue in the management of large and diversified firms is the ability to maintain strategic controls. Our research, and that of others, strongly suggests that firms emphasizing financial controls often, focus on short-term and risk-averse strategies. Firms that emphasize strategic controls, however, are able to maintain longer-term strategies within their different product divisions, avoid debilitating managerial risk aversion, and continue to invest in long-term and risk-balanced projects. Firms that use strategic controls tend to invest more in R&D and in maintaining the efficiency of their operations, often through capital investments. This is important because research has shown that firms are better able to compete in global markets if they invest more in R&D. Of course, the importance of R&D varies by industry. For example, in the pharmaceutical industry, it is quite important. It is interesting to note that the top performer in the global pharmaceutical industry, Merck, invests more money in R&D, both in total dollars and in percentage of total revenues, than any other firm in the industry. In 1991, Merck invested almost $1 billion in R&D, representing approximately 10 percent of all research spending by U.S. pharmaceutical companies and 5 percent of all research investment by pharmaceutical companies throughout the world.[8]

Research, ours and others', has shown that corporate governance of large firms has been problematic. One of the biggest difficulties has been the inability of boards of directors to control managerial actions. In this book we provided prime examples of the results of this problem, one of which is General Motors. In fact, GM's recent restructuring and downsizing are the direct result of management and corporate governance failures in past years. However, it is interesting to note that the restructuring decision was forced by GM's board of directors, specifically, by outside board members. There is, then, a renewed emphasis on the use of the board of directors to maintain more effective control of management decisions and actions.

Mergers, Acquisitions, and Their Effects

Mergers and acquisitions have been a popular corporate strategy for many years. Because of the multiple incentives outlined in this book, they were particularly popular in the 1980s. Many analysts argue that restructuring through acquisitions, some based on the market for corporate control, has led many corporations to operate more efficiently. There are, however, multiple trade-offs. First, most acquisitions create larger firms, unless all of the acquired assets are eventually sold off. While size can create some economies (e.g., economies of scale in purchase and manufacture of products), mergers also create difficulties in the management of the operations, particularly if they entail related products. It is difficult to diversify by developing new but unrelated products through internal research and development; it is often easier to enter a new market by purchasing a firm that is already operating in that markets. Acquisitions, therefore, often produce increased diversification.

Research has shown that increased diversification often produces reduced investments in research and development.[9] In addition, many acquisitions are financed partially or largely through debt. Large firms and those with more debt have been shown to have lower investments in R&D.[10] Recent research has shown that acquisitions, as well as large size, diversification, and heavy leverage, have a negative effect on investment in R&D.[11]

Managers spend much time and effort in making acquisitions, detracting from their ability to oversee and to manage the ongoing operations of the firm. Because acquiring firms are often large and complex and require much managerial attention, this inattention frequently produces inappropriate control systems (e.g., emphasis on financial and bureaucratic controls and deemphasis on strategic controls) and inadequate attention to the strategic management of the firms. In shifting to financial controls, other managers within the firm reduce commitment to innovation and emphasize risk-averse strategies and short-term profit maximization. Given the importance of R&D to the competitiveness of many firms, this shift may be one reason that firms following an acquisition strategy have been unable to show performance gains; in fact, a number have produced poorer performance after acquisitions.

One example of such an unproductive merger is that of a major competitor of Merck, Bristol-Myers Squibb. In 1989 Bristol-Myers merged with the Squibb Company, becoming the second largest pharmaceutical company in market share in the United States. The merger was expected to increase the company's earnings growth by 19 to 20 percent annually. However, three years after the merger, the firm continued to struggle with a host of problems that threatened its continued growth. In fact, its

growth rate in 1992 was in single digits rather than in the expected double digits. Before the merger, many people in the industry viewed Squibb
as being better at research and development than Bristol-Myers; Squibb
was acknowledged to be entrepreneurial, willing to take risks, and to have
a strong team spirit. Bristol-Myers, in contrast, was known to be more
formal and hierarchical. Attempting to merge these disparate cultures
produced problems and led to turnover in the merged R&D operation.
Many of the research scientists in Squibb's R&D labs were unhappy that
their programs were eliminated or given to Bristol's R&D people.[12]

Merck, in contrast, largely avoided acquisitions. In fact, a recent
Merck annual report suggested that many firms in the industry sought to
grow through mergers and acquisitions and paid a premium to do so,
whereas Merck sought to strengthen its product lines, expand its markets, and broaden its research programs by making sizable investments
in R&D. It emphasized internal development as a primary source of future growth.[13]

Evidence shows that firms in other industries that avoided the "urge
to merge," as did Merck, are prospering. For example, while other global
advertising firms were preoccupied with paying off debt acquired to finance acquisitions, the Leo Burnett Company prospered through quiet
development of its strong international business. By 1991 it had operations in 46 different countries, and 42 percent of its $3.58 billion in
revenue came from outside the United States. Similarly, Coopers and
Lybrand avoided the merger craze within its industry and prospered. Between 1988 and 1991 its international billings increased by 78 percent to
$4.1 billion, or 66 percent of the firm's total revenue. These firms have
been able to avoid the problems created by acquisitions.[14]

Many scholars have argued that the market for corporate control
produced a large number of acquisitions in order to create more efficient
firms. This seems to have been an argument blind to the unforeseen
significant trade-offs. It is also possible that the acquired firms were not
undervalued, as was argued by many financial economics scholars, a point
that, if true, suggests inefficiency in the market for corporate control.
For example, a 1993 study examined the acquisitions made by eight
prominent corporate raiders, including Carl Icahn and T. Boone Pickens.
The theory underlying these raiders' activities and their public pro-
nouncements suggests that they bought controlling interest only in firms
that were highly undervalued. After taking control, they supposedly initiated significant actions to increase the efficiency of those firms and thus
to increase their value. The study found, however, that in approximately
50 percent of the cases, the raiders bought controlling interest in firms
that were performing well above the average in their industry and thus
may not have been inefficient or undervalued. This may be one of the
reasons that some of these corporate raiders' acquisitions (e.g., Carl
Icahn's TWA) have performed poorly.[15]

Alternative Governance Mechanisms

A popular tool for managing agency problems, particularly in the 1980s, has been executive incentive compensation. This type of compensation helped improve executives' total compensation considerably during that decade; during those years average compensation for chief executive officers increased by 212 percent, considerably above the level of cost-of-living increases during that period and well above the salary increases received by other employees, such as engineers (73 percent increase) and teachers (95 percent increase). During those same years, the average increase in earnings per share of the Standard and Poors top 500 companies increased by only 78 percent. We noted in an earlier chapter that executive pay is not only an important but also a controversial issue; much attention has been paid in the press to highly paid (some would argue overpaid) U.S. corporate executives. Obviously, executive compensation influences managerial action, and thus it is an important potential governance device. Our argument is not that generous executive incentive compensation is wrong but that it has been tied to the wrong objectives. Research has shown that much executive incentive compensation has been linked to maximizing short-term returns, often the returns of individual divisions, sometimes at the expense of overall corporate performance. In some cases, such as those of Donald Pels at LIN Broadcasting and Steven Ross at Time Warner, CEO compensation has been highly publicized. This pattern of high total compensation continued into 1992, when Thomas Frist received almost $126 million after Hospital Corporation of America went public following a leveraged buyout in 1989.[16]

Our argument is that incentive compensation should be based on long-term performance and should provide appropriate incentives to invest in projects that have at least balanced risk. Furthermore, managers should be encouraged to own stock in the firm. These incentive programs must be based on strategic controls and must allow flexibility. Without strong strategic control by corporate officers, division managers will feel that their strategic proposals need to be low-risk because the proposals will be judged by their financial outcomes only and not by the quality of their strategies. Incentive compensation programs must be based partially on divisional performance but also must take into account corporate or group performance if they are to encourage cooperation among divisional managers (when it's important to). Finally, a compensation strategy should link divisional and corporate strategies with firm resources and core competencies and should be tailored to the needs of the firm and its culture.[17]

Other mechanisms for managing agency problems are leveraged buyouts and changes in the capital structure of a firm. In fact, Michael Jensen predicted the demise of the public corporation and suggested it would be replaced by LBOs.[18] However, Alfred Rappaport has suggested that Jensen's arguments were premature and that the public corporation is here to stay.[19] In any case, ownership needs to be focused for managers to stay in line. The best mechanism for achieving this appears to be increasingly concentrated ownership among institutions.

According to Jensen's free cash flow theory, high leverage creates benefits of efficiency by imposing discipline on managers. Large amounts of debt considerably limit managers' actions. Jensen is concerned that without the discipline imposed by debt, managers will use the funds inappropriately (in ways that do not benefit the shareholders). This argument ignores the potential trade-off costs of debt. As was noted earlier, research has shown that firms with high debt loads have lower long-term investments, such as R&D, than their competitors with less debt. Furthermore, firms with high debt loads do not reinvest in maintaining the basic structure of operations.

Because of Jensen's arguments and because of innovations, such as junk bonds, in the capital market, many firms took on extraordinary debt in the 1980s. The effects of such actions are evident in the increased number of bankruptcies among large, highly leveraged firms. Jensen argues that bankruptcies are not bad. A firm following Jensen's theory, however, may find itself out of business when it could have enjoyed continued viability without excessive debt.

Debt can be useful in helping firms to develop and improve their growth over time. Firms must, however, maintain a balance of debt and equity and continue normal and important investments required to maintain a competitive advantage. Except in unusual circumstances, firms should not take on extraordinary debt. We conclude that LBOs can be useful, but only in specific cases and in only a few industries (e.g., mature and declining industries). LBOs are not a panacea; high debt has significant trade-off costs that are often greater than the benefits of the discipline it provides.

Proof that debt is not a panacea is shown by Merck. Merck has had a very low debt-to-equity ratio, and yet it been an excellent corporation. Merck's managers have not needed debt to discipline their actions. They have invested for the long term, and the firm is reaping the benefits of their actions. In fact, had Merck taken on heavy debt in earlier years, its investments in R&D and its extensions into the global market might have been curtailed. As a result, its performance would have suffered.

Downscoping and International Diversification

Because of overdiversification, the merger and acquisition craze, and the use of extraordinary debt, many firms have had to restructure in the late 1980s and the early 1990s. Some firms sought to downsize their operations to reduce their expenses and to pay off portions of their debt. While downsizing can increase short-term efficiency, we argue that the appropriate type of restructuring is downscoping, which enables firms to strategically refocus on their core businesses and to regain strategic control of their operations. We argue that, if implemented correctly, downscoping does not necessarily produce a trade-off in performance. Strategic refocusing reduces the level of diversification by divesting primarily unrelated units in order to refocus on core businesses. This step allows the reestablishment of strategic control. Incentives can then be applied to improve the overall innovation of the firm and thus its subsequent competitiveness. In contrast, downsizing actions often emphasize across-the-board layoffs and the relinquishing of market share. Whereas downsizing may reduce the size of the firm and deemphasize bureaucratic controls as well as improve efficiency, downscoping enhances the opportunity for overall strategic improvement of the firm. While we might expect that downscoping occurs primarily with conglomerates (unrelated diversified firms), in chapter 8 we noted that firms with intermediate levels of diversification (e.g., related linked firms with mixed related and unrelated businesses) are more likely to restructure than are other types of diversified firms. These hybrid firms often have control systems that are inconsistent. In reality, all types of diversified firms have undergone restructuring.[20]

Restructuring that results in downscoping is likely to reduce the diversification level and the size of the firm. The divestitures, in turn, produce cash that can be used to reduce debt. Each of these actions can have a positive effect on long-term investments, such as those in R&D. The reduction in diversification allows a reduced emphasis on financial controls and an increased emphasis on strategic controls, while the reduction in firm size limits the use of bureaucratic controls and allows a return to strategic controls. Reduction in debt increases managers' flexibility, allowing them to invest funds with a longer-term perspective and strategy.[21] Research has also shown that downscoping not only facilitates investments in R&D but also improves asset utilization ratios and productivity.[22]

International diversification has often been used as a substitute for or a supplement to product diversification. We argue that, in many cases, international diversification allows a firm to continue its growth but also to continue its focus on core businesses. If implemented correctly, it allows the firm to maintain strategic control but also to achieve increased growth and development through access to international markets. Merck provides an example of this strategy. Merck expanded internationally rather than through diverse product lines and, in fact realigned its marketing structure to take greatest advantage of its products and markets on a global basis. As a result, Merck has captured 5 percent of the global pharmaceutical market.

Research has shown that international diversification can facilitate innovation. It provides the potential for firms to receive greater returns on innovations, because they have access to larger and/or greater numbers of markets in which to sell new products or over which to spread the cost of new processes. As a result, international diversification provides incentives for firms to innovate. In addition, international diversification may generate the resources necessary to sustain the large-scale R&D operation that is necessary, for example, in the pharmaceutical industry.[23] International diversification can also help firms achieve greater economies of scale and scope; it encourages resource sharing and an emphasis on core competencies across business units. Firms operating only in domestic markets may find major investments in new plant and equipment or in R&D difficult because it takes longer to recoup the original investment; in fact, the investment may not be recoverable before the technology becomes obsolete. International diversification improves the firm's ability to appropriate value from innovations and/or other major long-term capital investments.

There are limits to the positive effects of international diversification, however. For example, there are potential management problems with trade barriers, diverse cultures, and different trade and tax laws. Because of this, internationally diverse firms are complex and difficult to manage. We argued in chapter 10 that international diversification may at some point produce costs that exceed its benefits. We cannot assume that benefits from international diversification are infinite and always exceed the costs of such diversification. In fact, in recent years some internationally diversified firms have had to restructure (examples were provided in chapter 10).

Another critical issue for firms operating in global markets with strategic alliances, a common means of expanding internationally, is understanding the strategic intent of both competitors and joint venture/strategic alliance partners. In fact, some joint ventures have produced poor results because the partners have failed to understand each other's original strategic intent. We must better understand the cultures and the potential strategic cognitive models that foreign nationals hired by the firm to fill key executive positions bring to their jobs. Some international firms are better than others at learning through joint ventures because of the firm's culture. While international diversification has many benefits, there are, therefore, trade-off costs that must be effectively recognized and managed.

Unrelated Diversification

While we emphasize the importance of restructuring in order to downscope and the benefits of international diversification, some firms are able to effectively implement unrelated diversification. In limited instances, these firms may restructure with the intent of increasing the unrelatedness of the various businesses in their portfolio.[24] As was noted earlier in this book, the multidivisional structure provides certain advantages in the allocation of resources among unrelated diversified firms. In fact, research suggests that building cooperative structures in related diversified firms and competitive structures in unrelated diversified firms produces the best performance.[25]

One of the primary advantages of unrelated diversification is the ability to achieve financial synergy (optimum allocation of financial resources). One example of a successful unrelated diversified firm is Hansen PLC, discussed in chapter 9. Essentially, Hansen PLC is in a continual process of restructuring. It regularly acquires and divests businesses, thereby changing its portfolio. In fact, the primary purpose of Hansen PLC is buying and selling businesses. It often buys mature businesses that are performing poorly and makes changes to improve their performance, later either selling off the the revitalized firm or keeping the best parts and selling the rest. Hansen PLC operates in low-technology businesses that do not require long-term investments (e.g., R&D) and in which emphasis on maximizing financial returns, even in the short term, has no major long-term negative effects. It often chooses businesses in industries with slow but consistent growth.

Firms with unrelated diversified businesses often follow a strategy much like a portfolio strategy. In other words, the firm manages its businesses like a portfolio, buying and selling those businesses as its primary purpose. These firms also often pursue a strategy of maintaining a resource advantage over the market, primarily by maintaining lower risk. They avoid high-growth and rapidly changing technology and service industries. This reduces the requirements for information processing on the part of corporate officers in order to maintain appropriate strategic control of the businesses. Research has shown that the relations between corporate and divisional management that are open and based on subjective evaluation produce the highest levels of corporate performance.[26] Maintaining open and subjective evaluations in unrelated diversified firms requires managers to process too much information. We emphasize that although some unrelated diversified firms can be successful, the opportunities for success in such firms are limited and require careful attention.

Implementation

It is one thing to formulate an appropriate strategy and another to implement it effectively. We argued in chapter 11 that implementation is a critical issue and that effective implementation of restructuring strategies is complex and difficult. Restructuring often requires the divestment of certain businesses and the reduction of costs and increases in efficiency throughout the organization. In achieving these goals, there are likely to be employee layoffs, sometimes of significant proportion. The choice of businesses to divest and employees to lay off and the means by which these decisions are implemented may foretell the success of the restructuring.

It is not uncommon for firms to accomplish major layoffs by across-the-board reduction in the employee workforce. We argue that this approach is wrong because different units, businesses, and functions within the firm vary in importance to the success of the firm. For example, core businesses and core competencies should be largely buffered from the layoffs. While these units should be required to increase the efficiency of their operations, they should not suffer in the same proportion as other businesses and functions in the firm.

Furthermore, it is critical that strategic leadership be exercised and maintained during and after the restructuring. This requires evaluating carefully the firm's human resources and ensuring that top-quality employees remain with the firm. It may also require that the firm increase, rather than decrease, its expenditures for the training and development of human resources. After restructuring, firms will have fewer employees; those remaining will have to undertake increased responsibilities and will require the skills to perform those responsibilities effectively. The firm will need to retain high-quality employees and to ensure that they have the necessary skills to perform the jobs to which they are assigned.[27]

Restructuring firms may also have to change their structure, adapting their multidivisional structure in order to have a differentiated and yet integrated organization form. This may require emphasis on loose coupling, partially through a strong corporate culture, cultivating a central vision throughout the firm and focusing attention on selected goals. It also may entail the use of horizontal structural devices, such as integrators and multiunit teams, that have been advocated by analysts for decades but largely ignored in many large firms.[28]

Finally, we argue that firms must continue to develop tacit knowledge and skills in order to customize and implement its strategies. Such knowledge and skills are idiosyncratic to the firm and cannot be easily replicated or imitated by competitor firms. These types of knowledge and skills can be developed on the job or through formal development programs. Because these types of knowledge and skills are not valuable outside the firm, the firm must encourage employees to develop and utilize these skills by providing a strong internal labor market within the company.

As we noted earlier, some globally diversified firms must also restructure. The key to effective international restructuring is the development of a transnational capability. Even more important is the ability to build and to coordinate the diverse units across country boundaries. This requires effective integration and cooperation. Fostering these qualities requires a combination of appropriate development programs (to inculcate important skills and a common set of core values), effective incentive compensation programs (that encourage not only entrepreneurial efforts within each business and country but also cooperation across units for the benefit of the corporation), and structures that facilitate integration and cooperation across diverse units.

Concluding Observations

In this book we have emphasized that many firms overdiversified, grew too large, and acquired too much debt. As a result, they were forced to restructure. It is important that they be effectively restructured. We argue that for most firms, effective restructuring requires strategic refocusing in the form of downscoping. Downscoping reduces the level of diversification within the firm's manageable limits and refocuses the firm on its primary core businesses, allowing it to regain strategic control. This type of restructuring reduces the size of the firm, thereby deemphasizing bureaucratic controls that may inhibit firm efficiency. Furthermore, divestment of low performing businesses and/or units unrelated to the firm's core businesses produces cash flow that can be used to reduce a firm's debt to more manageable levels.

In addition, we argue that acquisitions made as a strategic end rather than as an appropriate means to an end are likely to produce negative trade-off costs that offset their benefits over the long term. We want to emphasize that an acquisitive growth strategy is not necessarily inappropriate if the acquisitions are chosen carefully to ensure synergy within the firm. This usually requires the acquisition of highly related businesses that can be easily integrated into the firm because of their common cultures (unlike the Bristol-Myers and Squibb merger). Furthermore, much emphasis must be placed on achieving an effective integration of the two units (that is, integrating the acquired firm into the acquiring firm). The main message of this activity, both divestiture and acquisition, is that diversification also requires specialization. Without such specialization firms will be confronted by an international competitor willing to contest for market share. Diversification must therefore contribute to competitive advantage; otherwise, it will eventually lead to downsizing or loss of market share.

We also strongly emphasize the importance of innovation and entrepreneurial efforts in order to maintain or regain strategic competitiveness. This emphasis goes beyond industries, such as pharmaceuticals, that emphasize research and development. Even in industries where R&D does not play a strategic role, new process innovation and other entrepreneurial efforts can help firms gain strategic competitive advantages. Firms must provide quality, whether in the products they manufacture or in the services they provide, in order to be globally competitive.

Firms may choose to diversify internationally as a substitute for diversifying through products. For many firms, this can be a positive strategy, as it was for Merck. Even international diversification, however, has its limitations.

Finally, we argue the importance of implementation of the restructuring decision. It is not enough to develop the correct strategy. It also must be effectively implemented. Buffering and emphasizing core competencies, building and maintaining strategic leadership, and reemphasizing strategic, rather than financial, control are critical elements in the effective implementation of restructuring decisions.

These strategic implementation actions are being reinforced by other forms of governance. Institutional investors are more assertive as their investments in firms grow, making it more difficult to shift investment strategies. Boards of directors, particularly external board members, are becoming more active as shareholders are more vocal. These changes place greater pressures on managers to make effective strategic decisions for the firms. Changes in government policy regarding interpretation and enforcement of antitrust laws in the early 1980s produced emphasis on related, rather than unrelated, diversification. Concomitant changes in tax laws, however, fueled acquisition strategies financed primarily by debt. Government policy changes also facilitated a more active market for corporate control; some activity was positive, and some had negative outcomes. Ultimately, however, the competitiveness solution is based not on restructuring of corporate assets through the market for corporate control but on strategic control and managerial emphasis on innovation and product quality. Governance in Japan, characterized by patience and focus on the long term, has contributed to Japanese firms' competitive advantage. Michael Porter has called this the capital advantage.[29]

A Look to the Future

Large U.S. firms have become too diversified. This development has been fostered by weak governance within M-form structures and by an emphasis on nonstrategic acquisitions. As international competition increased, large U.S. firms suffered because of their overdiversification and their lack of focus. Even after the restructuring of the 1980s and the early 1990s, additional changes are needed. Many large firms remain too diversified. We therefore predict that downscoping activity will continue. In chapter 1 we used GE as an example of the positive results of downscoping thanks to the strong strategic leadership of Jack Welch. However, what is the strategic specialization of GE? Is the current main competitive weapon Jack Welch himself, who maintains three different groups of businesses through the force of his presence? GE is still diversified. We predict that the level of diversification at GE will not be competitively sustainable in global markets over time and that if GE does not downscope further, it may eventually experience performance difficulties in the face of global competition.

In June 1993 Kodak announced the need for yet another restructuring. The dominant theme in its restructuring announcement was the layoff of personnel, along with some divestiture of assets. In essence, Kodak is downsizing again. Kodak is overdiversified as a result of its large acquisitions in the 1980s. It should have downscoped sooner, but executives have been reluctant to do so. Strategic leadership was apparently lacking, and human resource potential is being lost through downsizing. As a consequence, Kodak's board of directors hired a new CEO in 1993.

Reactive downsizing, over time, will lead to further erosion of U.S. firms' competitive position. Large size is often needed in global markets to produce products on a global scale. Downsizing, therefore, may harm a firm's ability to complete in global markets. Downscoping does not necessarily require shrinkage of market share; it implies focusing on businesses where competitive advantage is sustainable in domestic or global markets.

Downscoping also facilitates emphasis on innovation and entrepreneurial action. With strong strategic leadership, downscoping can provide buffering and support for and emphasis on core competencies. It also supports an emphasis on human capital and continuous improvement in physical (e.g., manufacturing) assets. In addition, downscoping facilitates carefully planned international diversification. If downscoping does not become the main approach to restructuring, strategic competitiveness will continue to erode.

We believe that current governance structures are adequate to accomplish this if owners and boards are freed from some current regulatory restrictions. For instance, restrictions barring institutional stockholders (e.g., mutual or pension funds) with significant blocks of shares from sitting on boards should be lifted because the presence of such major shareholders on corporate boards will increase the pressure on other board members to act decisively. In addition, stock ownership among board members should be promoted. Board members with significant ownership positions have been shown to prevent overdiversification and faster downscoping.[30]

Once downscoping has been accomplished, better managerial strategic control and corporate governance are likely to result. Managers have fewer businesses unrelated to the firm's core competencies to lead, and governance can be more effective because the board of directors has fewer businesses to oversee and is more likely to exert strategic control in place of reliance on financial outcomes. This type of governance facilitates managerial risk taking. Strategic leadership must be mastered to implement appropriate strategies effectively.

While some of the U.S. firms that restructured in the late 1980s and the early 1990s strategically refocused through downscoping, others downsized or restructured by other means (e.g., by acquiring significant debt through LBOs) that produce short-term gains but long-term deficiencies. We are optimistic that some U.S. firms will experience a turnaround and be highly competitive (that is, gain competitive advantage) as we approach the twenty-first century. Other restructuring firms that have not appropriately focused on their core business(es), invest less than their competitors in R&D (because of significant debt), have lost significant human resources through downsizing, and have reduced their emphasis on development of strategic leadership are likely to experience severe problems in the late 1990s. We therefore foresee a two-tier business system developing in the United States. The top tier will include firms like Merck that have "done it right" all along and those that are experiencing a renewal because of downscoping and strategic refocusing. The second tier will include those firms that did not downscope (but should have) or that restructured in inappropriate ways. These firms will experience continued decline.

It is unclear what will happen to GE and to Kodak. Kodak is currently undergoing one of several restructurings it has undertaken since the 1980s. Unfortunately, it does not seem to be refocusing, and the prospects for a turnaround do not appear to be good. On the other hand, GE CEO Jack Welch has recognized that his firm has problems and is attempting to effect a major culture change. Only time will tell whether this will lead to the necessary refocusing to position GE for the twenty-first century.

As we noted in the opening of this chapter, if all firms were like Merck, there would have been little need to write this book. Unfortunately, there are few firms like Merck. Many firms are still overdiversified, too large, and debt-laden. We have provided recommendations on how executives can make the changes necessary to regain and to exercise effective management of their firms. We must cast off the arguments for and our fascination with mergers, acquisitions, and high leverage. We must reemphasize strategic focus, strategic controls, and strategic leadership. U.S. firms, and others throughout the world, can gain stronger and more sustained competitive advantage by doing so. It is our fervent hope that this book facilitates those efforts.

Notes

1. Merck & Co., Inc. 1991. *Annual Report*. Rahway, New Jersey.

2. Markides, C. C. 1992. Consequences of corporate refocusing: Ex ante evidence. *Academy of Management Journal* 35:398–412.

3. Chandler, A. 1962. *Strategy and Structure: Chapters in the History of American Industrial Enterprise*, Cambridge, Mass.: MIT Press.

4. Williamson, O. E. 1975. *Markets and Hierarchies: Analysis and Antitrust Implications*. New York: Free Press.

5. Jensen, M. C. 1986. Agency costs of free cash flow, corporate finance and takeovers. *American Economic Review* 76:323–29; Fama, E. F., & Jensen, M. C. 1983. Separation of ownership and control. *Journal of Law and Economics* 26:301–25.

6. Ciscel, D. H., & Carroll, T. M. 1980. The determinants of executive salaries: An econometric survey. *Review of Economics and Statistics* 62:7–13; Tosi, H., & Gomez-Mejia, L. 1989. The decoupling of CEO pay and performance: An agency theory perspective. *Administrative Science Quarterly* 35:169–89.

7. Therrien, L., Hager, B., Zinn, L., & Landler, M. 1991. From chuck wagon to trail of Marlboro country. *Business Week*, April 15:60–66.

8. Merck. *Annual Report*.

9. Hoskisson, R. E., & Hitt, M. A. 1988. Strategic control systems and relative R&D investment in large multiproduct firms. *Strategic Management Journal* 9:605–21; Baysinger, B. D., & Hoskisson, R. E. 1989. Diversification strategy

and R&D intensity in large multiproduct firms. *Academy of Management Journal* 32:310–32.

10. Hitt, M. A., Hoskisson, R. E., & Ireland, R. D. 1990. Acquisitive growth and commitment to innovation in M-form firms. *Strategic Management Journal* (Special Issue) 11:29–47; Hall, B. H. 1990. The impact of corporate restructuring on industrial research and development. *Brookings Papers on Economic Activity* 3:85–135.

11. Hitt, M. A., Hoskisson, R. E., Ireland, R. D., & Harrison, J. D. 1991. Effects of acquisitions on R&D inputs and outputs. *Academy of Management Journal* 34:693–706.

12. Power, C. 1992. The queasy feeling at Bristol-Myers. *Business Week*, August 10:44–47.

13. Merck. *Annual Report*.

14. Bremmer, B., & Schiller, Z. 1991. Three who bucked the urge to merge—and prospered. *Business Week*, October 14:94.

15. Walsh, J. P., & Kosnik, R. D. 1993. Corporate raiders and their disciplinary role in the market for corporate control. *Academy of Management Journal* 36:671–700.

16. *Business Week*. 1993. Executive pay: The party ain't over yet. April 26:57.

17. Gomez-Mejia, L., & Balkin, D. 1992. *Compensation, organizational strategy, and firm performance.* Cincinnati, Ohio: Southwestern.

18. Jensen, M. C. 1989. Eclipse of the public corporation. *Harvard Business Review* 67(5):61–74.

19. Rappaport, A. 1990. The staying power of the public corporation. *Harvard Business Review* 68(1):96–104.

20. Hoskisson, R. E., & Johnson, R. A. 1992. Corporate restructuring and strategic change: The effect on diversification and R&D intensity. *Strategic Management Journal* 13:625–34.

21. Hitt et al., Acquisitive growth; Hoskisson & Johnson, Corporate restructuring.

22. Nelson, R. R. 1989. Research on productivity growth and productivity differences: Dead ends and new departures. *Journal of Economic Literature* 19:1029–64.

23. Kobrin, S. J. 1991. An empirical analysis of the determinants of global integration. *Strategic Management Journal* (Special Issue) 12:17–37.

24. Lee, W. B., & Cooperman, E. S. 1989. Conglomerates in the 1980s: A performance appraisal. *Financial Management* 18(2):45–54; Williams, J. R., Paez, B. L., & Sanders, L. 1988. Conglomerates revisited. *Strategic Management Journal* 9:403–14.

25. Hill, C. W. L., Hitt, M. A., & Hoskisson, R. E. 1992. Cooperative versus competitive structures in related and unrelated diversified firms. *Organization Science* 3:501–21.

26. Gupta, A. K. 1987. SBU strategies, corporate-SBU relations, and SBU effectiveness in strategy implementation. *Academy of Management Journal* 30:477–500.

27. Hitt, M. A., & Keats, B. W. 1992. Strategic leadership and restructuring: A reciprocal interdependence. In R. L. Phillips & J. G. Hunt, eds., *Strategic Leadership: A Multiorganization Level Perspective*, New York: Quorum, pp. 45–61.

28. Hitt, M. A., Hoskisson, R. E., & Nixon, R. D. 1993. A mid-range the-

ory of interfunctional integration, its antecedents and outcomes. *Journal of Engineering and Technology Management,* 10:161–85.

29. Porter, M. A. 1992. Capital disadvantage! America's failing capital investment system. *Harvard Business Review* 70(5):65–82.

30. Hoskisson, R. E., Johnson, R. A., & Moesel, D. D. 1993. Corporate restructuring intensity: Effects of governance, strategy and performance. Paper presented at the Strategic Management Society meetings, Chicago.

Indexes

Name Index

Organizations Index

Subject Index